Tom & Pat Crawford
Aug 5, 1977

Tom & Pat Crawford

THE COMPLETE BOOK OF HOME CRAFTS

THE COMPLETE BOOK OF HOM

CRAFTS

Edited by Pamela Westland

A Studio Book

The Viking Press · New York

Designed by John Munday

ACKNOWLEDGMENTS

We are grateful to Gemrocks Limited,
Brunswick Centre, Bloomsbury,
London WC1, England, for very kindly
lending from their extensive stock the
great majority of the mountings, stones
and equipment shown in the chapter
Take a Handful of Pebbles.
We also wish to acknowledge the work
on the individual chapters which was
contributed by Marcus Alexander,
Paula Critchley, Audrey Vincente Dean,
Eileen Geipel, Valerie Janitch, Mary
Kehoe, Anna North, Avril Rodway,
David and Margaret Sorrell and
K. Whitbourne.
Thanks are due to Lucy Forrest,
Rebecca Gregory, Susannah Critchley
and Lucy Davidson for permission to
reproduce their work.

Photographs by
Studio Lorenzini
Line drawings by
Alan Newman/Gus Clarke/Gita Hahn

Contents

Introduction

Learning a home craft is a satisfying and creative way of filling family leisure time. In this book, there are sixteen different crafts, many of which are taught in schools but have tremendous potential for development as a family pastime, when sharing a hobby makes it all the more fun. There are crafts to appeal to all members, whether they have any particular skills or not. Those who might describe themselves as being useful with a needle will enjoy the chapters called TAKE A NEEDLE AND THREAD and TAKE A FEW BITS AND PIECES. In the first of these sections, there are designs ranging from collage to soft toys, all of which can be made, as the designer says, on a rainy Sunday afternoon when the shops are closed. In other words, they are all made from bits and pieces in the workbox, scraps of fabric, trimmings, buttons and so on. The next section shows how to use a needle and thread as an artist does a sketchbook; how to see the design possibilities in everyday life, in a greengrocer's window, on a walk along a country lane, and in the garden.

Most children go through a phase when they have a craze for papercraft. In the chapter called TAKE A PIECE OF PAPER, the whole family can practice a number of techniques – cutting, tearing, folding, bending – to make sculpted figures, pictures and a toy theatre. In much the same way, TAKE A ROLL OF FOIL shows how to make Christmas decorations, cover storage jars, design a candlestick, lamp base, even a jewel box, using kitchen foil.

Few of us are born artists, but to enjoy the chapter TAKE A POT OF PAINT you don't have to be. Again, it teaches the techniques and the use of the different materials; rather than "how to draw" and "how to paint". Younger children will not need teaching how to paint with their fingers or with straws. These skills seem to come almost naturally. But following on from there, once a feeling for the materials has been gained, there are designs for lino cutting, marbling and block printing. TAKE A TIN OF DYE brings out the fabric designer in us, beginning with simple knotted patterns and encouraging confidence to try pretty sunbursts, stripes, checks and other geometric shapes.

Nature lovers will find several sections of special interest. The chapters called TAKE A HANDFUL OF PEBBLES and TAKE A HANDFUL OF SHELLS recognize the living beauty of natural objects. The first gives instructions for tumbling and polishing stones to make jewelry of all kinds, and to decorate vases, boxes and so on. The shell ideas vary from planting a garden in a large specimen shell to making miniature toy animals, from covering a picture frame to filling a storage jar as a pretty bathroom ornament.

The chapter called TAKE A BUNDLE OF RUSHES evokes a feeling of the country and of the past. The designs range from the familiar mats, place mats and baskets to pictures of exceptional charm. The art of both drying and pressing flowers is covered under the heading TAKE A BUNCH OF FLOWERS and there are decorative ideas dating from Victorian times onwards. Macramé is the subject of the chapter TAKE A BALL OF STRING, with designs for a swinging waistcoat and a large circular floor rug, sturdy belts to wear with jeans and a sampler wallhanging. And because beads and macramé have such an affinity, the chapter which follows is TAKE A PACKET OF BEADS. There you will find instructions for using beads decoratively in all kinds of ways – appliqué, weaving, embroidery – and for making beads from felt, pasta and paper. Those who reject any craft that requires attention to minute detail might take like ducks to water to the section TAKE A PILE OF NEWSPAPERS. The papier-mâché designs are bold and simple statements: crude masks for children to make and wear, a centerpiece for a children's party, lampshades, a fruit bowl and other decorative (but not fussy) items for the home. Similarly, TAKE A PACKET OF PLASTER gives designs for plaques, pictures, figures and other decorations, some of which can be made literally with a trowel.

Self-hardening modeling clay, a material familiar to school-children, is the material used throughout the chapter TAKE A BALL OF CLAY. Here we show how it can be molded or rolled out into a slab and used to make decorative figures, lidded pots, animals and an amusing nursery lamp. Simple carpentry with the minimum of tools is taught in the section TAKE A PIECE OF WOOD, some of the designs being the kind of work that older school-children might begin, others those that young homemakers will want to make together.

In each of the sixteen chapters of family craft and leisure, there are simple stage-by-stage illustrations so you can see at a glance how to make the designs shown in color throughout the book.

TAKE A BALL OF STRING

Macramé

Macramé, the art of creative and decorative knotting, is a craft which, in other forms, is familiar to people in all walks of life. Sailors hundreds of years ago passed the time on board ship by knotting rope to make things such as fenders, bell ropes and covers, spray screens and rowlocks. Other more delicate items which they made, like covers for sea chests, fringes and tablecloths, they sold around the world at every port.

But the navy cannot claim to be the first service to use macramé, for an Assyrian frieze, in the British Museum, dating from about 850 B.C., shows a military tunic, heavily fringed and with intricate detail; it is reasonable to suppose that the craft originated in the Middle East.

Fishermen have their own knots; so do herdsmen, hunters, gardeners, butchers and ware-housemen who tie up packages.

The encouraging thing about macramé is that there is no mystique or secret about the knots used. A housewife tying a knot in a length of thread will tie an overhand knot, though she might not call it that, and has the foundation of macramé fringing; and every schoolboy tying a square knot has mastered the flat knot, which forms the fabric of the deck chair cover, waistcoat and some of the belts in this book.

Those who like to work in fine materials, as the Victorians did to create their fringes, antimacassars, mantelpiece covers and lamp shades, can use cotton or linen thread or, progressively thicker, package string, dishcloth or mop cotton. Others who feel more confident with thicker, coarser material—people who might describe themselves as "all thumbs"—will be happier with butcher's string, rug wool, jute, cable end, garden twine, sisal, piping cord, even clothesline. You really can please yourself—see the belt pattern made up in seine twine and again in jute for the contrasting effects you can achieve. Any firm, not too elastic yarn is suitable for macramé work, but natural materials are better than synthetics, which tend to slip in use.

Another big plus about macramé—you do not need any special tools. Anna North, who designed all the macramé articles, started her interest in the craft one rainy afternoon with just a cushion, a clothespin and ball of package string. Even now, she uses nothing more complicated than a huge piece of corrugated cardboard to set out the design for a garment; an office clipboard to secure a belt, and a piece of foam sheeting to pin out a tablemat.

Other helpful items are long dressmaking and glass-headed pins, T pins, crochet hook, knitting needle, blunt, large-eyed wool needle, ruler or tape measure and scissors.

Color is such a personal thing that it is impossible to say do and don't. In macramé, the knots themselves create patterns and rhythms that make added color generally superfluous.

Like a Country Kitchen When Anna North does use color—for the handbag, vest and two of the belts—she sometimes makes her own dyes, using goldenrod, onion skins, tea or coffee, but usually uses multipurpose dyes in natural looking, subtle shades like olive green, desert dust or orchid. On her kitchen stove, Mrs. North keeps huge pots, like stockpots in an old country kitchen, but hers contain dyes for all the things she makes for demonstration. The first dyeing of a batch produces the maximum intensity. Used again, the dye is diluted but tones perfectly; yet again, it is paler still: a belt made of three dyeing stages of string is one of the most pleasing color effects you could ever see.

Beads and macramé are made for each other: in belts, wall-hangings, jewelry, curtains, garment fringes. Anna North makes beads from garden clay fired in a kitchen stove, or uses wooden ones from the toy store. There are pages of other ideas for making and using beads in Chapter 2.

The First Steps

The holding cord Take a piece of cord—the holding cord—about 18 inches long. Wrap each end of the cord around itself in an overhand knot and pull the ends through the loops, as shown in detail below. Pin through these knots (Diagram 1), so that the cord is taut across the working surface—a piece of board, padded with toweling or velvet, or a cork tile.

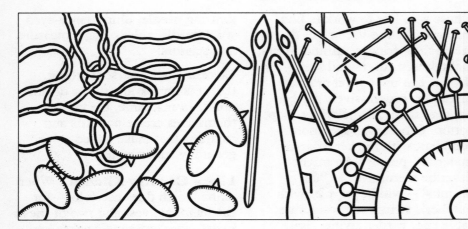

Overhand Knot
Lark's-head knot
To set on threads for practice, choose a medium weight cord and cut 8 lengths each 48 inches long. Take one thread, double it, and insert loop end under holding cord from top to bottom. Bring the 2 loose ends down over the holding cord and through the loop. Pull them to tighten loop. This knot, shown in Diagram 2, is the lark's-head knot. Mount the remaining threads in the same way.

If your work would be better with the "purl" knot of the lark's-head at the back of the design, mount the cords with a reverse lark's-head knot. This simply means that you start with the loop above, instead of below, the holding cord, and loop as described.

Far right: a clipboard used to hold the mounting cord securely.

The half hitch knot, shown in the photograph, top right, is worked with 2 cords, or multiples

of 2. When it is worked twice, it is called the double half hitch (DHH). The half hitch knot can be worked from the left or from the right. To tie it from the left, the right-hand cord—known as the knot-bearing cord—should be held taut. The left-hand cord is brought in front of it, then taken up and under it, the free end being brought through the loop formed.

To work from right to left, the left-hand cord becomes the

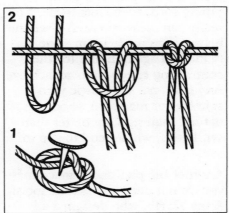

knot-bearing cord and is held taut. The right-hand cord is then looped over it and pulled tight.

To make a chain, shown far right: If half hitches are worked alternately from left and right, a chain is formed; it is useful for heavy fringes or to give a firm edge to a belt or wall hanging. The chain can be worked with single cords or, for a bulkier effect, with double cords.

As with all macramé knotting, it is

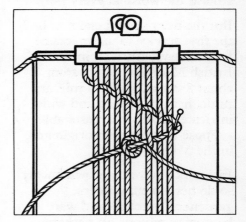

important to prevent the working cords from twisting and giving an uneven fabric. Stroke the cords gently downward as you work.

This chain is the basis of the fabric making the top yoke of the waistcoat shown in this chapter. In that case, the half hitch knots are worked across 2 cords, out to the sides to bring in two more, and and back. Worked loosely, a netted effect is achieved, although the fabric is firm and strong.

Jute garden twine dyed brick red and matching wooden counting beads make a swinging waistcoat that's right in line with today's easy fashion

Horizontal double half hitch cording, (*see photograph below*) following Diagram 1 below right imagine that the cords are numbered 1–8, left to right. Pin cord 1 taut over the others.

Make a half hitch knot with cord 2. Tighten. Continuing with cord 2, make the second half of the half hitch and tighten. The double half hitch you have knotted should be able to slide back and forth on cord 1.

needed, work additional knot-bearers in, weaving ends into the back.

Diagonal double half hitch, worked right to left (see Diagram 5). Follow the directions for the left-to-right diagonal working, but instead use the last strand (in this case, cord 8) as the first knot-bearer, pinning it securely diagonally across the vertical cords to be knotted.

Then start working double half hitches with cords 7, 6 and so on.

To make the pattern cross over at the center (*see photograph below*) one knot-bearer becomes a working cord for just one knot, then each knot-bearer carries on diagonally.

This pattern figures in the belts, pendant and wall hanging that follow.

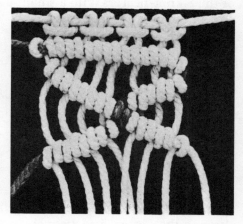
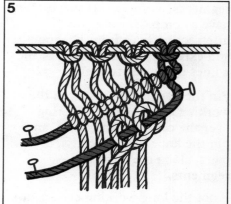

Continue along the line, half hitching with cord 3, cord 4 and so on. To work a second row, pin cord 1 taut across the vertical cords, parallel to the first row, as shown below. Now work double half hitches back, starting with the last cord and finishing with cord 2.

Diagonal double half hitch, worked left to right. *Diagrams right.* The principle is the same as that for the horizontal double half hitch, except that the knot-bearing cord, cord 1, is pinned diagonally down and across the vertical cords instead of straight across them (Diagram 2). Using cord 2, work a double half hitch over cord 1 and tighten (Diagram 3). Work with each successive cord. For a second diagonal row in the same direction, use cord 2 and pin it across the work parallel to cord 1. Using this as a knot-bearer, proceed as before, knotting first with cord 3 (Diagram 4). If more diagonal rows are

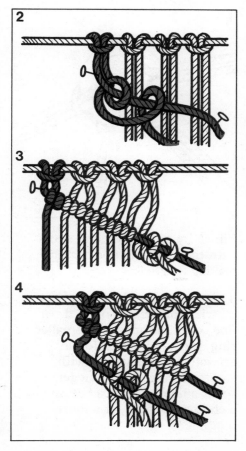

From a macramé deckchair 'canvas' to a fringed crochet rug, there's very little that can't be made attractively from a ball of string

To Make a Circular Mat

Working in the round is a good way to begin macramé, for it is simple to do and the work progresses quickly. The mat illustrated measures about 10 inches across and is made of natural jute.

You will need: 8 lengths of cord 30 inches long and 1 length 24 yards long.

With lark's-head knots, set each of the 8 knot-bearers onto a small circular ring—such as a curtain ring—Diagram 1.

A circular pattern of this kind relies for its effect on a neat finish, and so it is important to pin it out carefully before starting. Use a piece of foam rubber padding, or cardboard padded with toweling, as a working base.

Mark out a piece of plain paper with a circle, 10 inches in diameter. Divide the circle, through the center, into 8 equal segments, as shown. If you do not have a compass, trace the intersecting lines from Diagram 2, and extend them until each of the 4 lines measures 10 inches.

Pin the paper in position on the working board, center the ring over the center of the circle, and pin the knot-bearing cords, in pairs, along the 8 marked segments.

Knot the long working cord neatly over any knot-bearing cord and start with a double half hitch knot over the next knot-bearing cord. Proceed all around, leaving the working cord to "float," forming a loose spider web pattern.

After 12 rounds have been completed, bring adjacent knot-bearers to the center of each section, as shown in the photograph. Pin them in place, and continue working over them for a further 6 rounds. Knot the working cord in neatly.

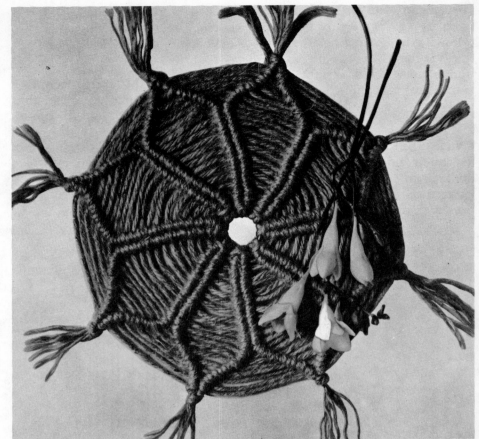

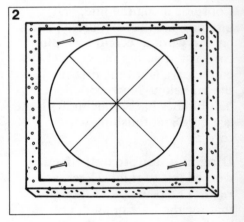

Finish by tying overhand knots with each pair of knot-bearers, making 8 tassels.

This pattern can be carried out in a variety of weights of cord. In fine cotton or linen on a smaller ring, it could be used for an attractive pendant, and with stouter cord and on a bigger scale, a floor mat for a bathroom, a children's room, or a foyer.

To Make a Sash Tie Belt

The made-for-each-other look of this belt is achieved by dyeing the jute garden twine saxon blue, and decorating it with homemade pottery beads painted the same color. Wooden beads would be equally effective. The twine was dyed in the skein with a multipurpose dye, simmered for 20 minutes.

You will need: 12 strands of twine each 4½ yards long for a belt with waist measurement 24 inches, plus ties. Use a clipboard if you have one, or pin the cords to cardboard, and proceed as follows.

Find the center of each strand and place under clip or pin. This belt is started from the center, and so the cords are not knotted to a cord bearer. Shorten ends to about 18 inches long, using the "butterfly" knot (Diagrams 1 and 2). Think of the cords as being numbered 1 to 12, left to right.

Using cord 7 as leader, work diagonal double half hitch (DDHH) to the left, beginning with cord 6. Work 3 half hitches (HH) with the last cord—1—to allow for curve.

Using cord 8 as the knot-bearer, work DDHH to the left again, next to the first row and ending with cord 1. Do not knot with the knot-bearer.

The 2 leaders are now at the left, thus *altering the numbering* of the cords. Using what is now cord 8 as leader, DDHH to the right with cords 9–12, working 3 half hitches with cord 12.

Using cord 7 as leader, DDHH to right again, inside previous row, with cords 9–12. You have completed the top half of one motif. Now thread a bead on to the 2 center cords.

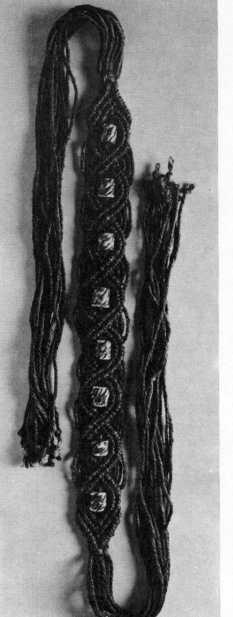

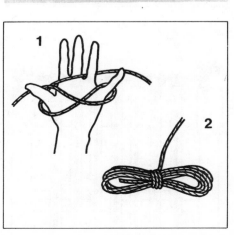

Using what is now cord 2—the inside leader—work DDHH to the right with cords 3–6. Using cord 1 as leader, DDHH to right with cords 3–6. Tie 3 HH with the first cord, to fill out the curve.

The 2 left-hand leaders will now be at the center of the work. Using cord 11 as leader, DDHH to the left with cords 5–10. This means knotting with the 2 left-hand leaders as well, achieving the crossover effect between motifs.

Using cord 12 as leader, work DDHH to the left again, next to the previous row with what are now cords 6–11. Work 3 HH with cord 11, to complete motif. Continue in the same way to make 4 more motifs, using the same leaders throughout.

Now turn belt around and work in the same way toward the other end.

To finish: Using cord 1 as leader, work 1 DDHH to right with cord 2. Add this cord to cord 1 and using both as leaders, work DDHH with cord 3. Add this to cords 1 and 2 and using all 3 as leaders, work DDHH with cord 4. Do the same with cords 5 and 6. Now work the same cording on the right side, using cord 12 as leader, then 11 and 12 together, and so on until all cords are at center. The cord gets thicker toward the middle.

Taking 2 cords from left and 2 from right, tie a square knot around all the others to finish.

Trim fringe to same length—about 27 inches—and tie an overhand knot at the end of each cord.

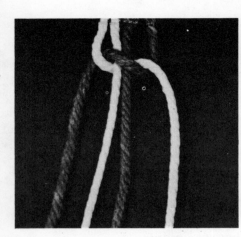
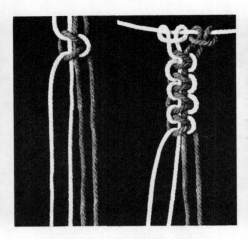

To tie half knots and square knots

The half knot (above) can be tied in either direction—left or right cord over the filler cords. The half knot is easily recognized as the first half of a square knot, or reef knot (center, above).

To practice half knots, set 2 cords (which, doubled, give you 4 strands) on a holding cord with lark's-head knots. Using the center 2 as filler cords, knot with numbers 1 and 4.

To do this, place cord 1 under cords 2 and 3, the knot bearers. Place cord 4 under the end of cord 1, over cords 3 and 2, through the loop and out under cord 1. Tighten.

The position of the hand, steadying cords 2 and 3, the filler cords, and holding cord 1, is shown clearly in Diagram 1.

The square knot, *above and right,* is 2 half knots, making a square knot.

It makes attractive braids and is useful for handles and other trimmings. The alternate square knot pattern, shown on the right, makes a close fabric. To practice, set 8 cords on a holding cord—16 working ends. Work from left to right.

1st row: Work square knots, using 4 cords for each. 2nd row: Leave first 2 unworked; continue across

row, working square knots with 4 cords for each. Leave final 2 unworked. Repeat these 2 rows, keeping regular loops. Double rows of square knots (lower half of photograph) produce a firmer fabric.

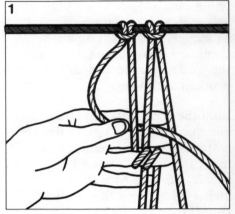

Below: ways of securing work to a chest or chair.

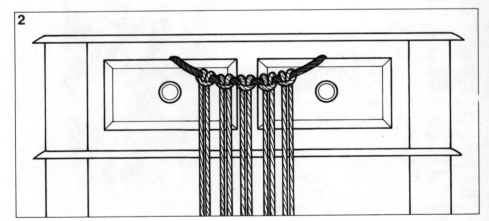

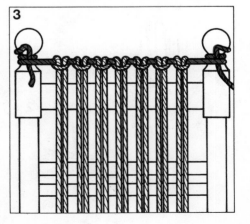

The alternate square knot
pattern, shown on the opposite
page, makes a strong, firm fabric,
suitable for many uses around the
house. Here it gives a smooth,
durable cover for a deck chair.
The extravagant fringe adds a
decorative finishing touch.

Materials: the chair in the
photograph used a 3 lb. ball of
6-ply garden twine—jute—
bought from a hardware store.
Any thick, strong string would do.

Cut 32 strands, each 9 yards long.
Find the center of each cord and
mount on front bar of deck chair
with lark's-head knot. Wind the
cords around bar of chair twice, so
that they are very close together
and do not leave any gaps. It is
important that the cords fill the
bar, as they tend to stretch and
grow thinner when the chair is in
use, and the "fabric" narrows. If
your chair frame will hold more
cords, set-on as many as possible,
making sure that the number of
working cords is divisible by 4 for
the square knot pattern.

To work, turn the chair upside
down, with the working cords
hanging down and the chair
frame making a firm working area.
Tie "butterfly knots" to shorten
cords to a reasonable working
length, and release more cord as
you need it. As the work proceeds,
you can either set the chair on a
low table or simply wind the
knotted fabric around and around
the bar until a comfortable
working height is reached.

To work the pattern: 1st row:
Work square knots with each set of
4 cords all the way across.

2nd row: As 1st row. It is
important to pull the center cords
of knots up firmly to prevent the
fabric from sagging.

3rd row: With cords 1 and 2, work
chain of half hitches. Work
square knots across rest of row

with 4 cords, and end with half
hitch chain of last 2 cords.

4th row: As 3rd.

Continue with this pattern until
you have enough fabric to reach
the back rail. On the chair in the
photograph, this measurement
was 38 inches.

When the correct length has been
reached, wind all cord around the
back rail twice, firmly, to fill the
space.

Knot a fringe, using overhand
knots, in any way you like. A
detail of the one we used is shown
in the photograph left.
Alternating groups of overhand
knots, with at least 2–3 inches
between them, were used.

Avoid finishing with a skimpy
fringe. If you have insufficient
length of cord left, attach extra
cords. Otherwise it will just look
as if you had not taken care to
sew in the ends properly and will
ruin the finished appearance of
your work. This chair is finished
with a fine flourish!

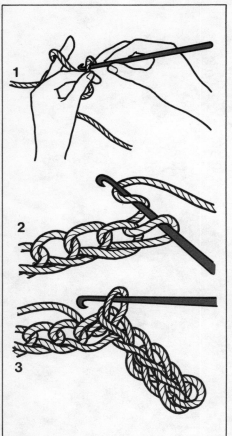

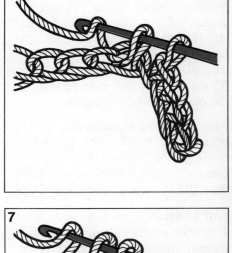

Instant Crochet

To work a Slip Loop and Chain   Follow the diagrams above to see how to hold the crochet hook and yarn. Make a slip loop and put it onto the hook, holding the base of the loop between thumb and first finger of left hand and taking yarn over 1st and 2nd fingers and under 3rd and 4th fingers (Diagram 1). Lift yarn with second finger and lay back of hook against strand. Pick up strand with hook and draw through loop on hook. This makes 1 chain (Diagram 2).

To make a slip stitch, insert hook into next chain, under both top loops, and pick up strand; draw it through foundation chain, and through loop on hook (Diagram 3). Work along foundation chain.

To work a Double Crochet Stitch   Diagram 4 shows a foundation chain already worked, as described in the first column. To work double crochet, insert hook into 2nd foundation chain, under both top loops. The first chain counts for the first double crochet and must be worked into at end of each return row.

Pick up yarn with head of hook, draw it through work, making 2 loops on hook (Diagram 5). Pick up yarn as above and draw it through the 2 loops on hook.

Work 1 double crochet into each chain.

To work a Triple Crochet Stitch   Pick up the strand held in left hand, bringing yarn over hook, then insert hook into 4th foundation chain, under both top loops. The first 3 chains count for the first triple crochet and must be worked into at end of each return row.

Pick up yarn with hook and draw it through work, making 3 loops on hook (Diagram 6).

With yarn over hook, draw it through first 2 loops, then with yarn over hook again, draw it through last 2 loops (Diagram 7).

Work 1 triple crochet into each chain.

A Mat to Last Forever

The materials you have been using for macramé are equally suitable for crochet and in this rug we combine both techniques. The rug is quick and easy to crochet, if you follow the simple directions on the opposite page, and then you will be ready to finish it off with a long, decorative macramé fringe. Just one word of warning: this rug has proved very popular with some cats we know, for claw practice!

You will need: 6 lb. of 5-ply jute garden twine; a coarse crochet hook (one suitable for rugmaking would be ideal).

Tension: 5 triple to 3 inches in width, 4 triple rounds to 5¼ inches in depth.

Measurement: Diameter excluding fringe, 37 inches.

Abbreviations: Ch., chain; d.c., double crochet; tr., triple; foll., following; rep., repeat; sl.st., slip stitch; cont., continue; rem., remain(ing); beg., beginning. Instructions given in parentheses must be worked as stated after 2nd parenthesis.

To make the rug: Make 12 ch. and join into a ring with a sl.st. Working through back loop only, con. in d.c. as follows:

1st round: Make 1 ch. for first dc., then work 1 d.c. into same place as ch. came from, (2 d.c. into next d.c.) to end of round; join last d.c. to the 1 ch. at beg. of round with a sl.st.—24 d.c.

2nd round: 1 ch. for first d.c., 2 d.c. into next d.c., (1 d.c. into next d.c., 2 d.c. into foll. d.c.) to end; join with a sl.st.

3rd round: 1 ch. for first d.c., 1 d.c. into next d.c., 2 d.c. into foll. d.c., (1 d.c. into each of next 2 d.c., 2 d.c. into foll. d.c.) to end; join with a sl.st.

4th round: 1 ch. for first d.c., 1 d.c. into each of next 2 d.c., 2 d.c. into foll. d.c., (1 d.c. into each of next 3 d.c., 2 d.c. into foll. d.c.) to end; join with a sl.st.— 60 d.c. Now working through both loops, cont. in tr. as follows:

1st tr. round: Make 3 ch. for first tr., then work 1 tr., into each of next 3 d.c., 2 tr. into foll. d.c., (1 tr. into each of next 4 d.c., 2 tr. into foll. d.c.) to end; join last tr. to top of the 3 ch. at beg. of round with a sl.st.

2nd round: 3 ch. for first tr., then work 1 tr. into each of next 4 tr., 2 tr. into foll. tr., (1 tr. into each of next 5 tr., 2 tr. into foll. tr.) to end; join with a sl.st.

3rd round: 3 ch. for first tr., 1 tr. into each of next 5 tr., 2 tr. into foll. tr., (1 tr. into each of next 6 tr., 2 tr. into foll. tr.) to end; join with a sl.st.—96 tr.

Cont. in this way, for a further 7 rounds, increasing 12 tr. as before in each of these rounds, by working, before the increase group, 1 more tr. than that on the preceding round.

On completing the final round— 10th tr. round—there will be 180 tr. in round; fasten off.

Fringe: Cut two lengths of twine, each 28 inches long, and with the aid of the crochet hook, draw them through a tr. of last round of crochet and fold double—4 working ends each 14 inches long. Tie with an overhand knot close to crochet. Mount and tie double twine in every tr. of last round of crochet.

Alternating position, tie a 2nd line of overhand knots, approximately 2 inches below, then a 3rd line about 2 inches below the 2nd. Neatly trim edge of fringe.

To Make a Buckle Belt

The texture and appearance of a belt can vary enormously, depending on the type of cord you decide to use. The one shown in the photograph on the left was made of fine seine twine and is delicate enough to wear in the evenings. The one on the opposite page was made from 5-ply jute garden twine, in tan color, and is sturdy enough to pair happily with jeans and a tie-dye shirt.

Look around for interesting buckles to give individuality to your belts—we chose a plain steel one and a pierced brass one, as decorative as an antique buckle.

You will need: Buckle with 2-inch bar, ball of 5-ply jute garden twine. (A smaller, 1½-inch buckle is needed for the seine twine design.)

To work: Cut 6 strands each 24 feet long. This gives a belt 36 inches long. For a different measurement, cut the strands a generous 8 times the length required.

Mount each cord on the bar of the buckle with lark's-head knot (see Diagram 1 opposite). You now have 12 cords. Imagine them numbered 1–12 from left to right. Shorten cords to a manageable length by winding butterfly fashion and securing with a rubber band.

1st row: Using cord 1 as leader lay it across other cords and double half hitch (DHH) over it with them. This gives a firm foundation for knotting.

*2nd row: Work 3 square knots across, pulling center cords gently to make a firm knot.

3rd row: With cords 1 and 2 work 1 half hitch (half of the double half hitch, in other words), then work 2 square knots using cords 3, 4, 5 and 6 for one and cords 7, 8, 9 and 10 for the next.

Finish the row with a HH using cords 11 and 12.*

Repeat the above pattern of alternating square knots (enclosed within stars *), for about 8 to 10 inches. Adjust the length of belt here, if necessary, so that the next pattern which measures about 10 inches, is centered at the back of the belt.

Back pattern: Using cord 12 as leader, lay it across the others and knot a row of DHH over it, as next to the buckle.

Step 1: Taking cords 1 and 2, make a chain of 3 HH. Repeat with cords 11 and 12. These chains make a firm edge.

**Step 2: Using 6 and 7 as leaders, lay them diagonally toward edges of belt and work DHH over them with 5 cords on each side. This forms the top half of the diamond.

Step 3: Gather the 6 center cords together and work 1 square knot over them with cords 3 and 10, making a decorative center, as shown in detail in the photograph on the opposite page. If you prefer, a large bead can be threaded onto the center cord, in place of the square knot.

Step 4: Using same leaders, bring them diagonally back to the middle and DHH over them. Lay left leader over right leader and DHH over left with right.

This completes one diamond and starts the next.

Step 5: Make a chain of 7 HH with cords 1 and 2 and with cords 11 and 12.**

Repeat the above pattern (enclosed within double stars **) 5 times, using same leaders throughout.

Finish pattern with 3 HH chain on either side and a straight cord across, as at the beginning, using 12 as leader.

Now return to first pattern

(enclosed within single stars ★) with alternating square knots, and continue until belt measures waist measurement plus 5 inches, ending with a row of 2 square knots. Omit HH either side.

Next, work 1 square knot with center 4 cords.

Using cords 1 and 12 as leaders, work 3 rows of cording diagonally toward the center. This gives a firm finish.

Complete the belt by weaving ends back on underside with a large tapestry needle, loosening stitches with the point of a knitting needle to make it easier.

You will find that the prong of a buckle goes through the alternating square knot easily, so no special holes are necessary.

Diagram 1 shows how to set threads onto the bar of a belt buckle. As usual, the lark's-head knot is used, and the threads pulled tightly and spaced out evenly.

The detail photograph on the right shows how a square knot is worked in the center of a diamond made by diagonal double half hitches. Cords 3 and 10 are used to work the square knot over the center 6 cords, numbers 4–9.

If preferred, a bead can be threaded onto one of the center cords and, if it is not large enough to stay in the center, can be secured with an overhand knot.

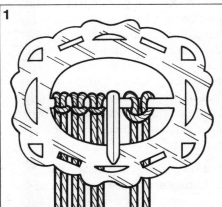

To Make a Pendant and Chain

A variation on the "string of beads" theme for jewelry, with a personality all its own—a pendant and chain made from fine package string and a handful of small beads.

The string was dyed old gold, after the work was completed because, with this less absorbent, slightly shiny twine, the ends would tend to show the natural color when they were cut.

You will need: two cords 2 yards long, and two cords 6 yards long. Seven cords 3 feet long, one 2 feet long.

To make the chain: With the shorter cords in the middle, secure all 4 cords to a foam rubber pad or clipboard, about 27 inches from one end. Shorten the long ends by making a "butterfly knot" as described previously. The 2 center cords are the core, and do not need shortening.

Work in half knots, as described below, until chain measures 26 inches. You can make it shorter or longer if you like, but make sure that it is long enough to go over the head. The half knot will twist as you work. You can see the effect in detail in the photograph on the right. Turn the work over and over as it spirals.

To make the pendant: When you have completed the desired length of chain, pin it in a horse-shoe shape on the working surface. Lay a 2-foot-long holding cord across both ends. Cut 7 cords 3 feet long and tie one half hitch in the middle of each. This forms the decorative picot top for the pendant.

Pin picots in place above the holding cord, between ends of chain, and work a row of DHH cording, knotting with holding cord and cords from the chain as well as the 14 from the picots. You should then have 24 working cords.

Using 1 cord in each group of 4 as a knot-bearer, and following the photograph, work in diamond pattern, placing a bead or square knot in the center of each diamond. The principle of the diamind pattern is explained in the directions for making the buckle belt.

Work three rows of three diamonds, then one of 2 and bring the pendant to a point at the bottom.

Finish by knotting all the ends into a tassel, as described on the opposite page.

Half knot sennit or spiraling sennit   To practice, attach 2 cords to a holding cord with lark's-head knots. Imagine the 4 working ends numbered 1 to 4,

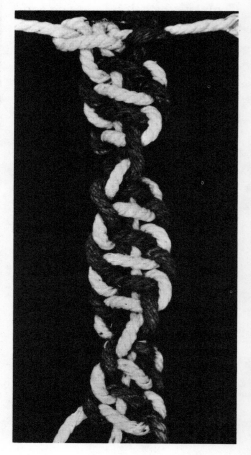

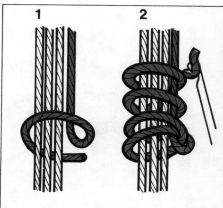

left to right. Cords 2 and 3 become knot-bearers.

Place cord 1 under the holding cords and over cord 4. Place cord 4 over the holding cords and up through the loop, under cord 1.

Place cord 4 under cords 2 and 3 and over cord 1. Place cord 1 over the holding cords and up through the loop, under cord 4.

Do not attempt to straighten the half-knots as they twist: let them find their own direction.

An essential part of the design of the pendant shown on the opposite page is the neat and decisive tassel which finishes it.

To make this, wrap one end around all the others (Diagram 1, below, left), working toward the top. Thread the "working" end on a large-eyed needle or loop it through a crochet hook (Diagram 2). Insert it under the encircling cord, as shown in Diagram 3. Pull the needle or hook through the loops and tighten (Diagram 4).

The photograph shows a vest made in dyed jute garden twine. A feature of this garment is the heavy knotted fringe, made with overhand knots, and the "abacus" wooden counting beads which decorate the front and the ties. General instructions for making macramé garments are given on the following page.

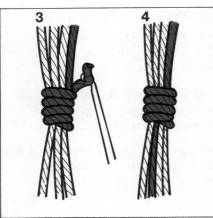

To Make Garments

You can adapt any paper dressmaking pattern to macramé. Choose a pattern one size smaller than you normally take, and cut off the seam allowance. Pin it out on a large working surface, such as a piece of corrugated cardboard. To give you guidelines as you work you can, if you like, mark the pattern into one-inch squares.

Pin a length of cord along the shoulder and neck line, and attach working cords to it with lark's-head knots. Outline the armholes with more knot-bearing cords, pinning them securely to the pattern.

The vest in our photograph was made up, at the top, of a series of half hitch chains. The "scalloped" yoke effect of the back (see photograph on previous page) was made by pinning a holding cord to the required shape, in position, with the working cords secured to it with double half hitches. Then new working cords were attached to the holding cord, in the usual way. The main pattern is square knots, worked loosely to give the effect of netting. If a garment is to be lined, all the seams can be sewn by machine over the knotting.

When extra working cords are needed, for instance when shaping an armhole, they can be added into the design as shown in the diagrams.

On the right, Diagram 1, a cord is slipped in between a half hitch knot on a chain—the outside chain of a garment.

Diagram 2 shows the insertion of a further working cord into a square knot chain.

To begin the handbag shown on the opposite page, attach threads, along the bar of the handbag frame, as shown in Diagram 3. They are secured with the usual lark's-head knots.

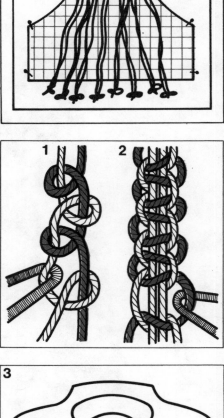

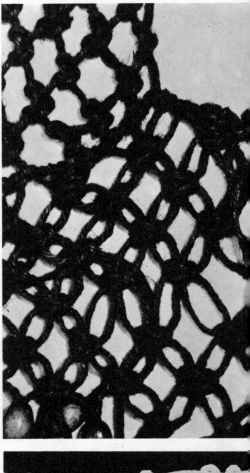

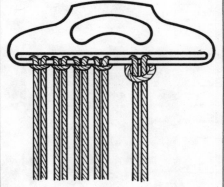

Photograph : The vertical double half hitch. There are many knot-bearers and only one working cord which, consequently, has to be very long. The working cord makes a DHH around each vertical cord in turn, passing behind the cord each time. At the end of a row, it works 2 DHH on the last cord, and proceeds back in the opposite direction.

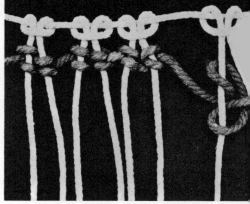

To Make a Handbag on a Frame

This handbag is 10 inches wide and 14 inches long.

You will need: a medium-weight package string, dyed Sherwood green.

Cut 24 cords each 3 yards long and mount them to the handbag frame. For this pattern, cords must be in groups of 6 or 8. In this design, the "leaves" are made with 12 cords, 6 on each side. Extra 3-yard strands are added as leaders in the rows of cording.

First, 2 rows of horizontal DHH are worked. Then the leaf pattern as shown below.

A further row of horizontal DHH separates the leaf pattern from the main "fabric" of the handbag, alternating square knots, using the cords in multiples of 4.

After 6 rows of alternating square knots, work 3 rows of vertical DHH. The long working cord was added and tied in to the end of the work.

A further 3 rows of alternating square knots complete the design.

Work the reverse side in exactly the same way.

To make up the bag, cut 2 cords about 54 inches long and lace front and back together, starting at the top of the bag so that the lacing cord becomes part of the fringe.

Bringing the lower edges together, join by tying overhand knots close to work, using 2 cords from the front and 2 from the back. Finish the fringe with an overhand knot at the end of each cord.

To make the handle, cut 2 cords about 5 yards long—the length, of course, will depend on individual requirements. This one was 32 inches.

Fold each cord 1 yard from end and, pushing cords together, mount on end of one bar. Work handle with square knots, using shorter cords as core and longer ends to tie knots. Thread ends with a large-eyed blunt needle into work on either side and other end of bag.

Draw around the outline of the handbag to cut a lining to fit.

To make the "Leaf" Pattern

Imagine the cords numbered 1–12, left to right.

Using cord 1 as knot-bearer, diagonal DHH over it with cords 2, 3, 4, 5, 6. Using 12 as knot-bearer, Diagonal DHH over it with cords 11, 10, 9, 8, 7.

Using cord 2 as knot-bearer, diagonal DHH over it with cords 3, 4, 5, 6, 1.

Using cord 11 as knot-bearer, diagonal DHH over it with cords 10, 9, 8, 7, 12.

Join the two "leaves" by half hitching over the right-hand knot-bearer with the left-hand knot-bearer.

Now renumber cords 1–12, left to right.

Using cord 6 as knot-bearer, diagonal DHH to the left with cords 5, 4, 3, 2, 1.

Using cord 7 as knot-bearer, diagonal DHH to right with cords 8, 9, 10, 11, 12.

Using cord 5 as knot-bearer, diagonal DHH to left with cords 4, 3, 2, 1 and 6.

Using cord 8, diagonal DHH with 9, 10, 11, 12 and 7, completing the leaf pattern.

As you work this pattern, you will find it necessary to curve the knot-bearers, to make the leaf shape.

To Make a Sampler Wallhanging

Macramé wall-hangings can be, and often are, samplers of the various knots. Just as the alphabet, number and prayer samplers of the eighteenth and nineteenth centuries were an exercise in embroidery stitches, so in macramé samplers can be an exercise in pattern and texture. The one illustrated is made in three sections. The two outside sennits or braids, attached separately to the holding rod, are square knot braids with a "button" at the top (see method below). Below the pottery bead, a row of half knot braid twists into the final flurry of a generous tassel.

The main part of the hanging is, again, a series of square knot braids and "buttons" of different sizes. A row of horizontal DHH breaks up the design and "changes the pace" into rows of twisting half hitch braids outlining alternating square knots.

Floating cords contained by the diagonal knotted cords have pottery beads held by overhand knots at random.

Two rows of horizontal DHH follow, then a fringe effect with double rows of overhand knots, above another row of HDHH.

Below that, at the sides, a row of half-hitch chain worked with two cords together; floating cords given interest with overhand knots; 2 rows of DDHH outlined by diagonals of square knots.

Finally, there are 2 rows of horizontal DHH; pottery beads secured by overhand knots in floating cords; 2 more rows of HDHH, and a fringe made of 6 cords knotted together.

Making a Square Knot "Button"

You can give your work a further dimension by making a "button"

in a chain of square knots. The wall hanging above shows clearly how effective they can be.

This decorative loop requires 5 or 6 knots out of the square knots you are forming. To make it, you simply pick up the filler cords and pass them through the center of the work 5 or 6 knots above. Pull tightly until a ring is formed, and continue knotting as before, below it. The next square knot will hold the "button" securely in place.

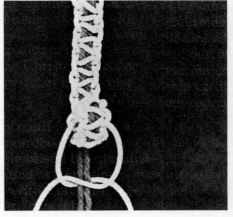

TAKE A PACKET OF BEADS

Beadwork can take many forms; beads can be sewn or glued to ground materials; they can be woven to form a solid or open "fabric," or used together with embroidery. It is also possible to make many exciting beads yourself and children especially enjoy doing this. In this section we shall be dealing with beads in all these different ways.

Any bead project needs a certain amount of preliminary planning.

round pearls, with loops of tiny silver beads in between each petal, the whole flower head surrounded by an outer ring of round, iridescent crystal sequins. You can see the graphic effect of this in Diagram 1.

For the richest effect, beads should be massed together. By themselves they are often small and insignificant, but sewn in clusters with intermingling colors and textures they convey a fairy-tale

(Diagram 3) to fill flower petal shapes prettily.

Finished arrangements may be cut out and mounted to make attractive jewelry; bracelets, belts and chokers are a few suggestions.

The beads may be sewn over a background of gold lace applied to satin or velvet (Diagram 4). This type of embroidery is called "Viennese."

The buttons you make yourself,

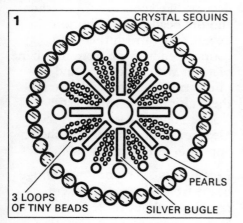

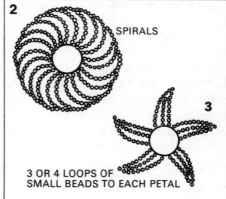

When sewing beads to material, keep the number of colors contrasted with the ground fabric down to two or three; each color may however be represented by more than one texture.

It is important to maintain variety and interest in your work by contrasting the shapes and sizes of the beads and sequins you use. For instance, you could compose a flower design from petals made of long silver bugle beads and

effect. Try placing one or more beads on top of a large sequin, or bring your needle up through the material, thread on several round beads and stab down to leave a raised loop. Arrange the loops haphazardly, clustered thickly together surrounded by flatter sequins or embroidery stitches, or sew them in spirals around a central important solitaire (Diagram 2). Use graduated loops

from pieces of material over metal discs with snap-on backs, which you can buy from notions stores, are also successful—and far more individual—when embroidered with beads.

Basic techniques
As with most crafts, there are a few basic points about beadwork technique which make all the difference to the finished appearance of the work.

It is not advisable to try to stitch beads onto material held in the hand, with the possible exception of felt, which has sufficient "body" to enable it to remain resistant to puckering. With the fabric held taut in a frame the beads can be more accurately positioned.

You will find it helpful to pass the thread lightly through beeswax or candle wax before use, to preserve it and prevent undue tangling.

Having threaded the needle through the beads, pass them along the thread and lay them on the ground fabric; then pass the needle through it again so that no thread shows; take care not to buckle the string of beads by taking too short a stitch. Single beads are best attached by a backstitch.

When the work is finished, it can be stretched and flattened if necessary by tacking it down with pushpins on top of sheets of lightly dampened blotting paper. Be careful, as sequins will buckle if they come in contact with water. Let the work dry naturally.

The threads at the back may be strengthened by brushing them very lightly with rubber cement; or you can paste a piece of tissue paper over them.

Bead embroidery should in most cases be dry cleaned. Very often, however, you may be making something purely ornamental, such as a Christmas decoration, which will not need cleaning. Here it is much quicker to stick the beads in place, using Elmer's glue or Duco cement, rather than sew them. Sequin, sequin-shapes and flat-backed rhinestones can all be applied in this way. So can large round beads, though it is often more reassuring to secure them with a stitch.

Hold the sequin in one hand with tweezers, and the container of glue in the other. Apply a dab of glue and set the decoration in place accurately with the tweezers. Sometimes, according to what you are making, it is possible to thread the beads on dressmaker's pins and push the pins, with a light dab of glue, into the surface.

Bead arrangements are often most attractive when combined with hand or machine embroidery. Be prepared to work a few samples on an extra scrap of material

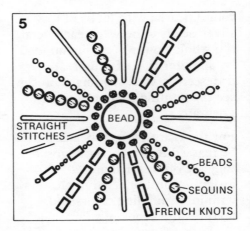

before you embark on the main piece. Try out several arrangements. The embroidery itself can be very simple, just straight stitches, woolen French knots to resemble tiny beads of a different texture, or chain and stem stitches which may encircle arrangements, emphasizing them decoratively (Diagram 5).

Free machine embroidery, either with zigzag or running stitch, is attractive where a light and delicate effect is the aim. This should usually be worked before the beads are applied. You can get a number of ideas from a book of jewelry designs, which can be so easily adapted for beadwork.

In your search for beads, don't rely only on the craft stores. There is no need to buy all the beads you use. Ask your friends and relatives if they have any to spare, for a wonderful source of odd beads.

Make a Packet of Beads

Purely for fun, you may try making your own beads. The skirt of the doll shown later in this section is decorated by beads made from rolled-up strips of felt.

Paper beads   You can make them in the same way from paper, any colored paper, even magazine pictures. Cut the paper strip 9 inches long and $\frac{1}{2}$ to 1-inch wide; taper the sides to a pointed triangle. Roll most of the strip of paper onto a fine knitting needle, tightly and evenly, then dab the remaining 2 inches or so with glue before you complete the rolling. Hold the work until the glue dries. Cylindrical beads are made from 9-inch strips of paper or felt with straight sides.

When you have made enough paper beads for a necklace or bracelet, paint them if you like, either plain colors or with simple designs like spots or stripes, then slip the beads onto a knitting needle and varnish them. Of course, beads made from magazine pictures will be colorful and interesting to begin with. String them alternately with plastic or wooden ones for variety. A few ideas for arrangements are shown opposite, in Diagrams 6a–f.

Felt beads   You can make huge beads from pieces of felt; cut rectangles about three times as long as they are wide. Sew the short ends together and run gathering threads around the top and bottom edges. Draw up one gathering thread and insert stuffing, then draw up the other. You may want to enclose a small lead weight to make the bead hang better. Leave the beads plain or embroider them, or even apply tiny wooden beads at random for a decoration of contrasting texture.

Clay beads   It is fun to make round beads from modeling clay,

Beads to make – from strips of felt – and others to buy decorate this colorful jewelry or work-tidy doll

Greetings for Christmas and New Year of 1971 Greetings from Audrey Heseltine for Christmas and New Year 1971 Greetings from Audrey Heseltine for Christmas

Greetings

from

Audrey Herson

6(a)

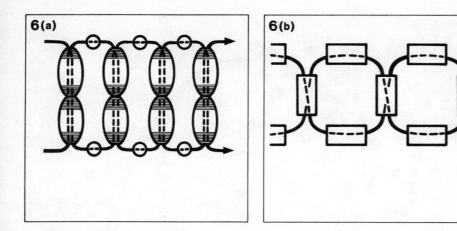

6(b)

6(c)

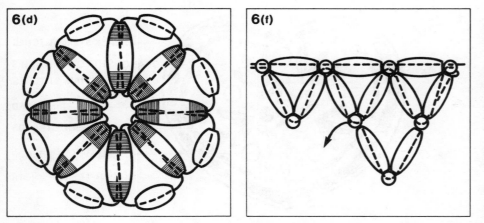

the kind which sets hard without firing. Form tubular beads by rolling sausages of the clay and then piercing them before they get hard, or roll balls for round beads. When set, they can be painted and varnished to resemble ceramics. For another kind of bead, roll out the clay into sheets and cut out small rectangles, then imprint them with a button or similar object. Pierce two holes at the top and leave them to dry.

7

CLAY BEADS

6(d)

6(f)

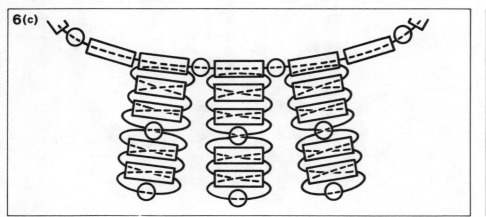

Alternate them with small round beads threaded as shown in Diagram 7.

Beads from oddments
Children love to make "grocery" beads, stringing pieces of short, thick macaroni on strong thread. Use powder paint to paint the macaroni and leave the beads in a warm place to dry.

Other attractive necklaces for children can be made from short lengths of colored drinking straws alternated with painted macaroni shells or stars, or acorns pierced, threaded and varnished. Melon seeds, just as they come from the fruit, can be threaded on a string and left to dry. It is easier to pierce them from side to side than through the pointed ends.

Beech nut husks, painted inside with powder paints, make pretty floral shapes to gather together for a brooch. Set a shiny wooden bead in the center of each.

6(e)

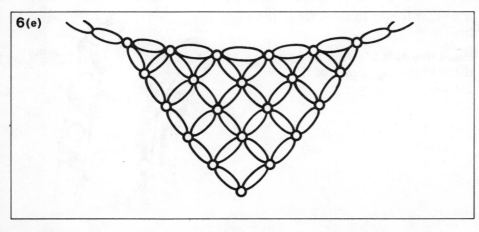

Shiny, glittery, flamboyant, festive – beads evoke the spirit of Christmas and make joyous decorations and greeting cards to keep for ever

Heart-Shaped Locket

This pretty trinket for a teenager is quick and easy to make from odds and ends.

You will need: 9-inch square of felt in mauve; embroidery wool in pink, purple, black, orange; absorbent cotton for stuffing; approximately 60 black half inch wooden beads; 5 purple and 1 pink bead in same size; 1 lead curtain weight (optional).

To make the locket   Trace the outline of the heart (Diagram 1) onto the felt and work around it in chain stitch, using purple wool. Work a line of black stem stitch inside this. In the center of the heart sew 1 pink bead surrounded by a ring of 5 black ones. Encircle them with 10 French knots in pink. Using orange, work 5 groups of 3 straight stitches each, placing a group between every other French knot. Sew a purple bead in between every group of orange stitches.

After completing the embroidery, cut out the heart around the outer line of purple chain stitches. Cut an identical size piece for the back of the locket and with wrong sides facing, sew the two together, leaving an opening for stuffing with absorbent cotton. Insert a small lead weight to make the locket hang better. Close opening.

Beginning at the top center, couch a double strand of pink wool around the sides of the locket over the stitched seam (Diagram 2). Place each couching stitch ½-inch apart and pull up the wool in a small loop between each. Sew black beads over the couching.

To make the necklace   Cut and sew sufficient ¼-inch strips of felt to make 2 lengths of 30 inches each. Wind this with a strand of pink and a strand of orange wool used together (Diagram 3). Press work, then sew a black bead between each twist. Stick or sew

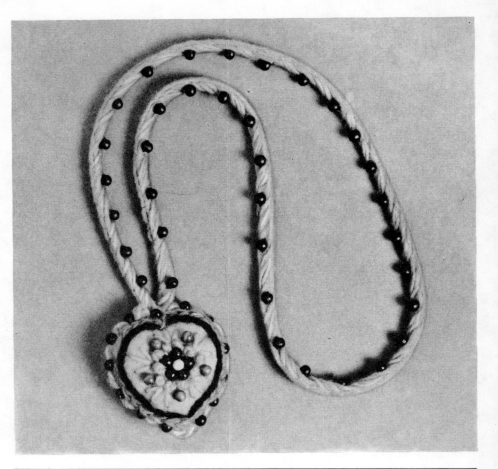

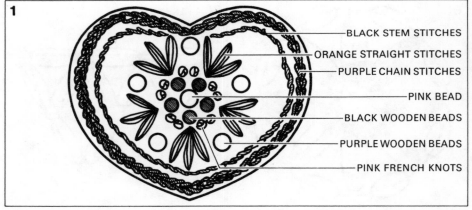

1

BLACK STEM STITCHES
ORANGE STRAIGHT STITCHES
PURPLE CHAIN STITCHES
PINK BEAD
BLACK WOODEN BEADS
PURPLE WOODEN BEADS
PINK FRENCH KNOTS

the other length to the back of the first strip.

Place the ends together and sew them to the top center of the locket.

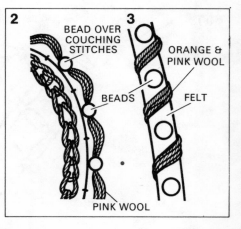

2
BEAD OVER COUCHING STITCHES
BEADS
PINK WOOL

3
ORANGE & PINK WOOL
FELT

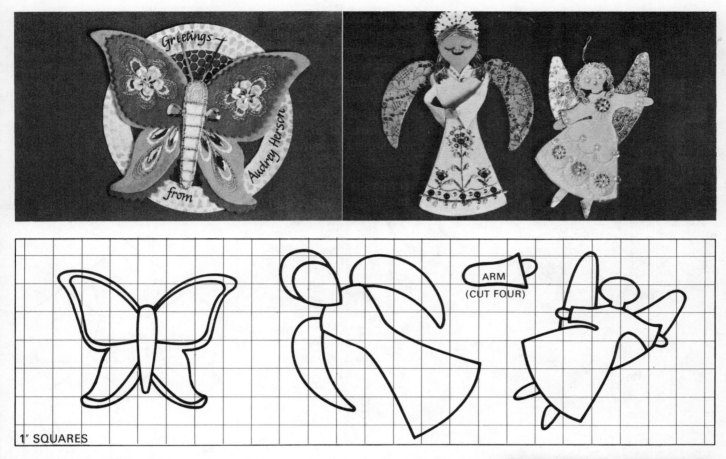

1" SQUARES

Christmas Cards and Decorations

The glitter and sparkle of beads are well suited to the excitement of Christmas, and these ornaments and decorations have been designed to enter into the spirit of things. The greeting cards are so pretty, and show such thoughtfulness, that they will surely count as presents!

To make the flat decorations

Draw 1-inch squares onto a piece of paper, or use graph paper, and copy the outlines of the butterfly and two Christmas fairies from the diagrams above. Cut out the outlines in stiff paper.

Using scraps of felt for the wings of the butterflies, the bodies of the fairies, and their faces, and, following the photographs carefully, work the embroidery by hand or machine. You can make the decorations more intricate or simpler, as you choose. Sew beads

and sequins in place or stick them down with clear glue.

Cut out the pieces of felt to correspond with the paper shapes, and stick them on. Cover the fairies' wings with scraps of lace, use tiny pieces of golden thread or narrow trimming for the hair, and embroider the features, or use beads.

Cut the arms and hands for the larger fairy from pieces of felt, double; stitch together and stitch firmly to felt body.

Attach thin golden cord for hanging to the Christmas tree, or over the fireplace, as in the color photograph.

The butterfly motif is stuck to a circle of thin cardboard such as oaktag or 1 ply bristol board and, if it is to be used as a greeting, the message written on with felt-tip pen or India ink.

The snowflake motif is embroidered on fine material and decorated with beads. It is then cut out, allowing plenty of margin, and stuck to a circle of thin cardboard, with an appropriate greeting.

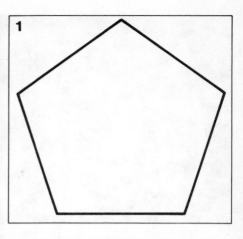

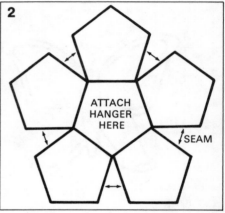

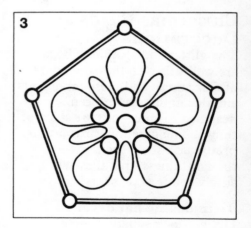

The pink Christmas tree This is made from a semicircle of felt, stiffened with iron-on interfacing. A circle 8 inches in diameter will make two trees.

When the embroidery is complete, cut the circle in half, and sew the straight edges together. Add beads and sequins and a star cut from white felt, for each tree.

The trunk is a sharpened length of dowel stuck into a circle of plywood. The trunk is covered with narrow strips of white felt, bound around and around, and the plywood base painted white, and trimmed with a scrap of braid.

The tree can be trimmed with sequins and golden beads to your heart's content, to glitter as brightly as candle flames.

The "patchwork" ball This is made of 12 pentagons cut from thin cardboard. Trace the shape from Diagram 1. Cut 12 exactly the same size. Cover the shapes with different colored fabrics. Join 5 pentagons around the sides of one central one (Diagram 2) and sew them together up the sides to form a cup shape. Repeat with the other 6 pentagons. Attach a hanger to one central pentagon and a tassel made of golden beads threaded on short lengths of strong thread to the other. Decorate each pentagon with felt shapes glued on and sequins and beads which are threaded on pins and stuck through the cardboard (Diagram 3).

Sew all the pentagons together, cover the seams with thin golden cord glued in place, and secured at each corner with a bead threaded on a pin.

The angel   To make the angel, cut a piece of thin cardboard 5 inches long and 4 inches high to make a cylinder 1½ inches in diameter. Cut a piece of brown felt 5 by 4 inches and decorate it with embroidery, sequins or braid down the center of the shorter dimension. Wrap the felt around the cylinder and sew down the center back. Cover the felt at the top and bottom, and add 2 lengths of braid to trim.

Cut a piece of thin cardboard for the wings and halo, following Diagram 1. Cut the shape again in white felt. Cut an inner circle in brown felt for the halo, and trim the edges with pinking shears. Cut a smaller wing shape in peach felt and sew to the white felt shape. Paste the inner halo to the white felt, and paste the complete wing-and-halo shape to the cardboard. Decorate the wings with sequins and beads.

Paste the wings behind the body cylinder. Cover half a styrofoam or paper ball, about 1¾ inches in diameter, with fine golden material for the head and add two sequin shapes for the demure eyelashes, and a single sequin for the mouth (Diagram 2). Paste the head in front of the halo and surround it with about 4½ inches of golden Christmas tree garland.

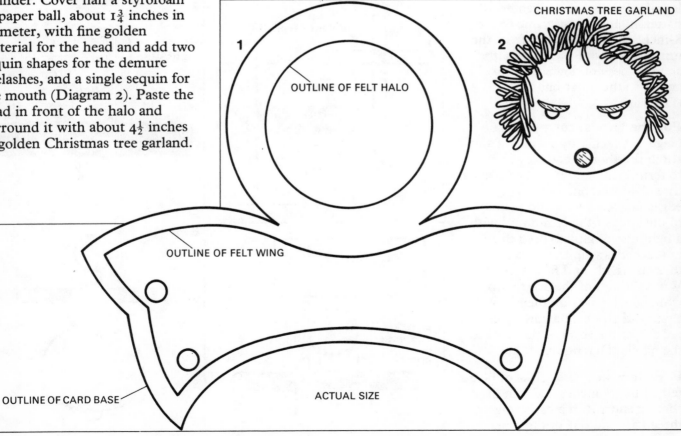

1   OUTLINE OF FELT HALO

2   CHRISTMAS TREE GARLAND

OUTLINE OF FELT WING

OUTLINE OF CARD BASE

ACTUAL SIZE

Bejeweled and Beaded Doll

You can make this doll to hold rings and pendants, as she does here, or sewing aids. Or she need not work at all. She could just be a bright and beautiful and lazy doll.

You will need: 2 pieces of wooden dowel, $\frac{3}{8}$-inch diameter, 8 inches and 6 inches long; 3-inch circle of plywood, $\frac{1}{2}$-inch thick; 9-inch squares of felt in mustard, forest green; 12-inch square of felt in red; small pieces of felt in light beige and white; length of thick white wool; Kapok or polyester fiber stuffing; approximately $\frac{1}{2}$ oz. golden beads, medium size.

To make the doll: Drill a hole in the center of the circular piece of wood to fit one end of the 8-inch length of dowel, which may be tapered with a knife if necessary. Cover the circular piece top and bottom with red felt. Shave off part of the 6-inch length of dowel at the center to flatten it, and do the same to the 8-inch length, $2\frac{1}{2}$ inches from the untapered end. Paste and tie the shorter piece of dowel at right angles to the other one (Diagram 1).

For the hands, cut 2 pieces of beige felt each 1 by $1\frac{1}{2}$ inches and stitch the shorter ends together to form cylinders. Run a gathering thread around one of the longer edges on each piece, slip them on to the ends of the arm dowel with a light dab of glue to hold them in place, draw up the gathering threads tightly and fasten them off. Wind the rest of the arms with white wool, covering them closely. Paste and stitch a narrow piece of red felt at the seam of the wool to the hands (Diagram 2).

For the head, cut a piece of beige felt $2\frac{1}{2}$ by $5\frac{1}{2}$ inches and join the shorter ends. Run a gathering thread around one of the other

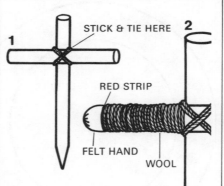

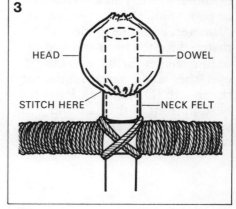

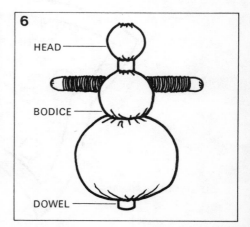

ends and draw up tightly. Slip it onto the end of the dowel and stuff firmly. Gather up the other end and fasten off the thread. Cut a strip of beige felt 1 by 6 inches for the neck and roll around the dowel under the head. Sew the ends together and stitch to the lower edge of the head (Diagram 3).

For the bodice, cut a piece of mustard felt $2\frac{1}{2}$ by $5\frac{1}{2}$ inches. At a distance of $1\frac{1}{2}$ inches from each shorter edge, cut a $\frac{3}{4}$-inch vertical slit $\frac{1}{2}$-inch down from the top edge (Diagram 4). Slip these slits over the arms (Diagram 5) and stitch the shorter edges up the center back. Gather and stuff as for the head. Sew bodice to neck.

The skirt is a piece of red felt 5 by 9 inches. Sew the shorter edges together. Gather one long edge and slip the skirt onto the dowel below the bodice. Stuff and finish as for the head. There should now be about $\frac{1}{2}$-inch of dowel projecting from the lower gathered edge of the skirt. Stick this firmly into the center of the wooden base (Diagram 6).

Making the felt beads You need 8 red and 8 green felt beads. For each one, cut a strip of felt 9 by 1 inches. Taper each long side so that ends meet in a point. Fold over wide end $\frac{1}{2}$-inch. Holding fold down, dab glue lightly along center of strip to narrow end. Roll strip lightly from wide end to narrow end. Sew red and green beads alternately around lower edge of skirt, with a small golden bead in the center of each. Cut a strip of mustard felt $\frac{1}{2}$ by 11 inches; pink the edges if possible. Paste around skirt above felt beads; sew golden beads along center of strip (Diagram 7).

Paste a few loops of white wool at the top of the bodice to suggest a portion of blouse, and paste a

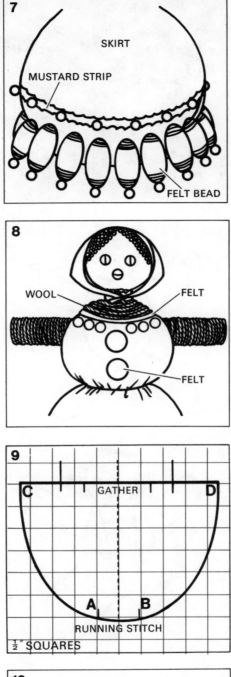

7 SKIRT
MUSTARD STRIP
FELT BEAD

8 WOOL   FELT
FELT

9 C   GATHER   D
A   B
RUNNING STITCH
$\frac{1}{2}$" SQUARES

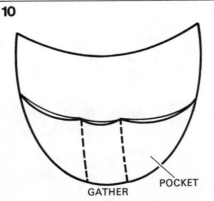

10 GATHER   POCKET
GATHER

narrow strip of green felt to edge it. Stitch golden beads around the green strip. Roll 2 narrow strips of green for buttons and paste to the bodice with a golden bead sewn in the center of each. Attach a thread to the center of the doll's forehead and string 3 or 4 lengths of golden beads to either side of the head for hair. Cut a triangle of red felt, $7\frac{1}{2}$ inches along one long edge and 5 inches along each of the other two; paste down lightly to cover the rest of the head and catch the ends together under the chin. Cut two $\frac{1}{4}$-inch-diameter circles of green felt for eyes and one of red for the mouth. Paste and stitch to the face (Diagram 8).

Cut the apron, following Diagram 9, from mustard felt. For the pocket cut a piece of mustard felt 5 by $1\frac{5}{8}$ inches; gather up the center $2\frac{1}{2}$ inches along one long edge to $1\frac{1}{2}$ inches and sew this gathered portion to the part A to B of the apron. Pin the upper corners of the pocket to outside edges on the apron and curve lower corners to fit. Sew in place. Cut a white apron slightly larger around the curved edge C to D; pink edge if possible. Place under the mustard piece. Running-stitch two vertical divisions in center of pocket to fit embroidery scissors, or small pendants (Diagram 10). Gather up the straight edges of the mustard and white pieces together and draw up to 2 inches long. Place around doll's waist and add a narrow strip of white for waistband.

Salt Pastry Nursery Frieze

You could play a partical joke on a favorite uncle with this salt pastry because it looks good enough to eat, but is as tough as iron. It is the ideal medium for children who want to mix and knead and shape and bake, and admire their handiwork practically forever.

To make the dough you will need: The proportion of 4 cups of plain flour to 1 cup of salt; $1\frac{1}{2}$ cups water.

For the trimmings you will need: Curtain rings; buttons; glass beads; paints; matte varnish; cord. Each figure is about 5 inches high and the flower decorations are about $2\frac{1}{2}$ inches in diameter.

To make the dough: Mix the flour and salt together and carefully add about $1\frac{1}{2}$ cups of water, until dough is pliable but not too soft to hold its shape. Knead it well.

Make all the figures on pieces of aluminum foil so that they can be put directly into the oven.

To make girl figures, start with a ball of dough flattened to about 2 inches in diameter. Add a pear-shaped piece for the body. Moisten the dough with water when joining pieces. Roll a length of dough into a sausage, cut off 2 pieces for curving arms and 2 for legs; join them to the body. (Diagram 1 shows the basic figure.)

Add small strips for the hair and twirl them to suggest curly locks. Press on tiny knobs for nose, cheeks and beads. Indent eyes and mouth (Diagram 2).

Flatten a piece of dough to about $\frac{1}{8}$-inch thick, cut a strip 1 by 5 inches and add it to the body for a frilly skirt. Other strips form frills and bands. Press one or two

buttons into the dough. Edges can be indented with fork prongs, matchstick or any round object. Press a hole in each hand for a cord to pass through (Diagram 3). Make three girl figures.

To make the boy figures, begin in the same way, but add pieces of dough for shirt, collar and tie, straight strips for hair and flat strips to resemble short trousers (Diagram 4).

To make the flowers joining the dancing children, see the illustration, Diagram 5. For these, cut discs of dough, each about ¼-inch thick, with an egg cup, and decorate in various ways with curled strips, petals, beads, curtain rings and buttons. Press 2 holes in each flower for the cord.

To bake the dough: Bake all dough in the oven at 325°F. Test for hardness at joints with fork prongs. If the dough is at all soft return pieces to the oven. Browning adds to their appearance. Figures take about 1½ to 2 hours, flowers less.

To decorate the shapes: Partly paint each piece with poster paint, then varnish back and front with matte varnish. String cord in and out of each piece to hang the finished work in a garland. In a dry atmosphere, the figures will keep indefinitely.

You can use this salt pastry to make beads. Try rolling some from the trimmings, pushing a hole through with a knitting needle and baking them with the figures. Of course, they will not take so long to harden.

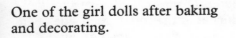

One of the girl dolls after baking and decorating.

Indian-Style Beaded Bag

Soft as the finest gloves, bright as Oriental brass, this bag is the ideal accessory for a plain dress or outfit, with anything from a suit to a long evening dress.

You will need: Chamois leather. Look around for 2 medium-sized pieces each to give an area about 12 by 17 inches; approximately 500 each coral and black faceted beads in plastic; 300 each golden and white, all size $\frac{1}{6}$-inch diameter; rubber cement. The bag is $7\frac{1}{2}$ by $9\frac{1}{2}$ inches, excluding handle, and beaded on one side only.

To make the bag: Do not cut the leather until the work is finished. Work beading as much as possible in a frame. Lightly draw a rectangle on the skin, $7\frac{1}{2}$ by $9\frac{1}{2}$ inches; allow plenty of margin so that the work can easily be enclosed in the frame.

Begin with the center motif. Mark a dot in the center of the rectangle, $4\frac{1}{4}$ inches from lower edge. Lightly indicate 8 equidistant lines radiating from it, each about $1\frac{1}{2}$ inches long, for guidance only (Diagram 1).

To bead the central motif, begin by sewing one black bead on the center dot. Bring needle up slightly to the side of it, string on 6 golden beads and thread through the first golden bead again. Couch beads around center black bead, taking a stitch between each. Surround the golden beads with a ring of 8 white beads, then with another ring of 16, white and red alternately. Continue to follow Diagram 2. When 6 rings have been completed, work each red, black and white ray by stringing 3 beads for each row and adding subsequent rows horizontally, placing a couching stitch between each bead.

For the golden rays, string 7

golden and 1 black bead and lay them along the ray. Go back and take a couching stitch between each bead. Single beads are secured with a backstitch.

To work borders, start in center of lower edge; begin at ruled line. Bring up needle, string 4 black beads and one golden one, lay beads vertically up toward center of work and push needle through to back. Take needle up again on ruled line, a little to one side of

first row, string 3 black beads and 1 red; lay by side of first row. Repeat, stringing 2 black beads, 2 red and 1 golden in next row, then 1 black, 3 red, then 4 red. Half a triangle has now been worked. Continue in this way to corner. At this point follow Diagram 3. Work up to top corner of bag.

For the back, cut another piece of chamois the same size as the front. To line the bag, cut two

pieces of chamois $\frac{1}{4}$-inch smaller all round than the outside pieces. Apply rubber cement to wrong side of one lining piece and carefully apply it to the wrong side of one of the outer bag pieces. Repeat with the other lining piece. With wrong sides of front and back pieces together, sew sides and lower edges together with close buttonhole stitches about $\frac{1}{4}$-inch long (Diagram 4). Leave about $1\frac{1}{2}$ inches at the top of each side open. Turn in about $\frac{1}{8}$-inch of outer

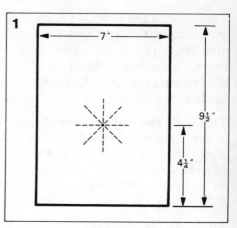

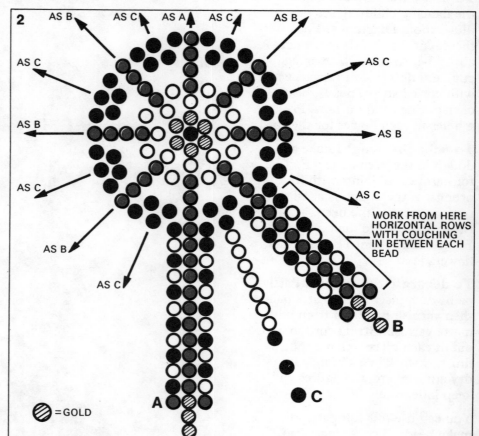

WORK FROM HERE HORIZONTAL ROWS WITH COUCHING IN BETWEEN EACH BEAD

AS B   AS C   AS A   AS C   AS B
AS C   AS C
AS B   AS B
AS C   AS C
AS B
AS C

A   B   C

= GOLD

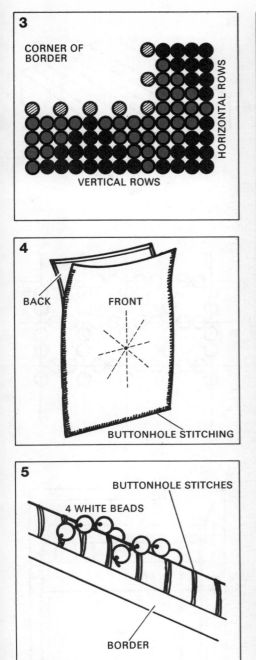

3

CORNER OF
BORDER

HORIZONTAL ROWS

VERTICAL ROWS

4

BACK   FRONT

BUTTONHOLE STITCHING

5

BUTTONHOLE STITCHES

4 WHITE BEADS

BORDER

layer around top and side openings, pasting the hem down with rubber cement.

Sew white beads on loops over side and bottom seams and around both sides of top opening edges. To form loops, attach thread at one side of seam, string 4 white beads and take a stitch diagonally over seam; bring needle out opposite the end of the loop, on other side of seam (Diagram 5).

For fringe at bottom, attach thread at one corner, string on 14 golden beads and one black. Push beads up to bottom of bag; take needle up around black bead and through all the golden ones. Secure thread with a backstitch and continue across bottom of bag (Diagram 6).

To make draw string, cut 2 strips of chamois each 1¼ by 23 inches. It will be necessary to join strips to get the length; make overlapping seams as smooth as possible. Apply rubber cement to the inside of each strip and fold in two lengthwise. Cut 6 vertical slits in top portion of bag, starting 1 inch from open side edges and 1¼ inches from top edge. Run draw strings in and out, starting and finishing from right side (Diagram 7). Even up strings and tie ends together in a knot.

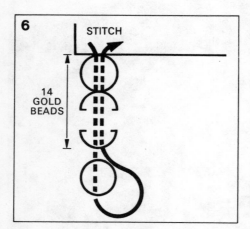

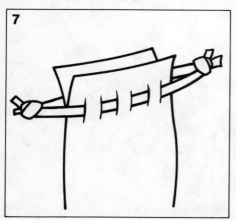

Weaving with Beads

Bead weaving, an ancient art, can be accomplished with the aid of a child's wool-weaving loom with a roller at one end. The notches for the threads will be too wide apart but weaving the beads will soon pull the threads together. It is also possible to make one's own loom by nailing a 3-inch piece of wood, notched to take threads, to each end of a long strip of wood. Add two nails at the center of the outside of one piece for securing the loose ends of the warp threads.

If you are unable to tackle any woodwork, a simple loom may be made by winding threads around a strong cardboard box with notches cut in it (Diagram 1). To weave a band longer than the box, knot the warp threads at the beginning and wind the ends around a small piece of wood or paper roll, securing the finished work with rubber bands.

For a lattice effect the warp threads may also be threaded with beads, so that the horizontal woof is woven at intervals between vertical rows of warp beads (Diagram 2).

As an example of bead weaving, we have chosen a tie, worked with a vertical diamond motif.

Beaded Tie

You will need: 1 50-yard spool of gray buttonholing thread; 2 oz. pink and 2 oz. dark blue, 1 oz. turquoise and ½ oz. silver-lined rocaille beads, all size ⅓ inch diameter; 1 clasp; beeswax or candle wax (optional).

In general, for this type of beadwork, calculate the length of each double warp thread like this: having chosen your design and decided on the length of your finished work, add 18 inches and then double the total.

The main part of the tie is 13 inches long.

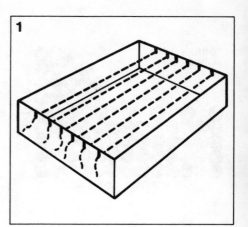

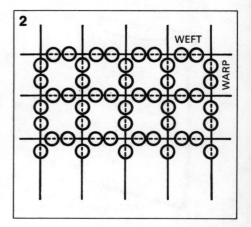

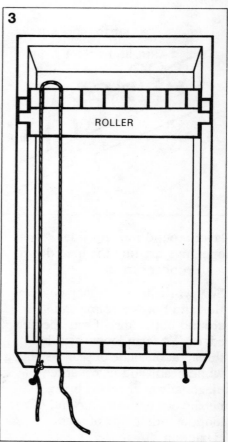

To make the tie Cut the warp threads. You will need 11 threads each 74 inches long. Place the end of one of the threads through one of the notches opposite the roller end of the loom, take it up to the corresponding notch at the other end and through the adjacent notch at the same end. Then bring it back through the next notch to the first one used. Even up the loose ends and wind them around the nearest nail (Diagram 3). Continue threading the rest of the warps in the same way; one more warp thread is used than there are beads in the design. If you are using a simplified type of loom without a roller, thread it up in exactly the same way. This process is called "spanning the loom."

For the pattern, follow the chart, Diagram 4.

Thread a fine needle with buttonhole thread and draw it lightly through the wax, if used. This is the woof thread. With the doubled ends of the warp threads nearest to you, count up to the tenth warp thread from the left-hand side and tie the loose end of your woof thread to it, about 8 inches away from the doubled ends of the warp threads. String 3 dark blue beads and slide them along the thread until they are underneath the spaces between the 10th and 13th threads. With your finger below the beads, push them through the spaces between the warp threads. Bring the needle up between threads 13 and 14 of the warp and push it through the beads in the opposite direction, this time above the warp threads (Diagram 5). Pull the woof to take up any slack and straighten the beads in a row. Weave all beads in the same way, having one more bead at each end of the row until the full 21 beads width is reached.

When a new thread needs to be

started, make a knot at the left-hand side and bring weaving thread back through several beads of the previous row, then cut it off (Diagram 6, point A). Thread your needle with a new waxed woof and bring it through a few beads of the last row, from point B, then make a knot at the left-hand side. Continue weaving.

When the work measures 13 inches, divide it in two and discontinue the center bead. Each half will consist of 2 blue beads, 6 pink and 2 more blue (Diagram 7). Continue in this way for 20 more rows, then leave off a bead at each side until only the 2 central ones remain. Remove the work from the loom, tie all the warp threads neatly together in pairs and darn the ends into the work to secure them, cutting off excess. Leave the 2 center warp threads over the 2 center beads at the top of each division (Diagram 8). Thread sufficient blue beads onto these warps to enable them to meet around the back of the neck, and add a clasp.

For the knot of the tie, cut 8 warp threads each 24 inches long and span the loom. Weave 24 rows of beads, each row consisting of 2 blue beads, 11 pink and 2 blue. Remove work from the loom and darn in warps; cut off excess. Sew the first and the last row together and stitch the knot around the top of the tie (Diagram 9).

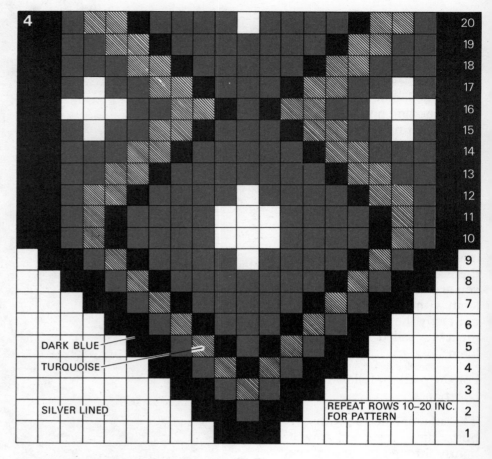

DARK BLUE

TURQUOISE

SILVER LINED

REPEAT ROWS 10–20 INC. FOR PATTERN

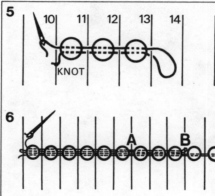

KNOT

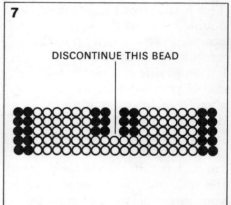

DISCONTINUE THIS BEAD

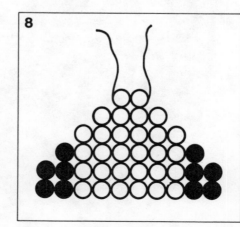

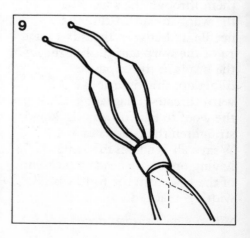

TAKE A HANDFUL OF SHELLS

Shells

Collecting shells on the seashore must be an almost universal holiday pastime for children—and for some adults, too. It is like a treasure hunt, but what happens to the treasures? As you will see from the designs in this section, quite ordinary cockles, limpets, whelks, and other common shells can be made into delightful ornaments, arrangements and groupings, making an everlasting scrapbook of holiday memories.

Most of the shells used here were collected on local English beaches by Paula Critchley, her family, friends and pupils—and a great number of them all on one wintry afternoon. Others, not available locally, were bought economically, as a selection of large and small shells, from a shell shop. Many arts and crafts stores and shell specialty shops, like others you may know of, offer a mail order service, and are invaluable for supplying the slightly more exotic shapes and colors that can make all the difference to a design.

If you feel inspired by the pictures, mirrors, animals and so on that you can make, and want to start a collection of shells, here's an idea of what to look for and how to recognize what you find.

Types of Shell

The second largest group in the animal kingdom are the mollusks (the insects are the largest). They are invertebrates, and usually have a fleshy mantle which extracts calcium from the water and from their food, to make their shells.

The tiniest group are called tooth shells, shaped like an open-ended tusk. There are 200 marine species. Chitons live in shallow water, and there are 600 different sorts. They look rather like wood lice, and have eight-plated shells of a regular shape; they are often found on rocks.

Bivalves are a large group of about 10,000 species; they have two valves joined by a hinge and include cockles, mussels, scallops, clams, oysters (all of which are edible) and ark shells, lucinidae and razor clam shells.

Gastropods are the largest group of all, with 80,000 species, mostly marine, but fresh-water and land ones, too. They have a single shell and are usually coiled. They include whelks, periwinkles, wentletraps, augers, tritons, conchs, abalones, limpets and cowries.

It is hard to believe that invertebrates can produce such incredible results—the intricate patterns of cones and top shells, the sculptural qualities of murex shells and tritons, the strange shapes of conchs and the delicate colors of so many.

Beachcombing

Stony beaches, except those with sandy areas, are not usually the best places to collect shells, as so many will, sadly, be broken. On sandy beaches, nearly all the shells are bivalves and can be collected as the tide goes out, and dug up from just below the surface of the sand. A good time to comb these beaches is when the extra-low spring tides occur, to find the more unusual shells that are not exposed at other seasons.

On rocky beaches, the very best time to collect mollusks is at spring tides, during the new and full moon, when the water goes out farthest. Look mainly for gastropods on rocks, in crevices, in rock pools, attached to seaweed and posts. (Mussels, which are bivalves, also attach themselves like this.) Follow the tide out, as the species will vary between high and low tide marks.

Muddy beaches, or those with a sand-mud mixture, are often good hunting grounds for razor clam shells, carpet shells and clams.

Estuaries, with their mixture of fresh and sea water, are not the best places in which to find marine mollusks, but there will still be plenty of rather limited varieties.

Diving for shells is great fun, but proper equipment and a thorough knowledge of safety rules are a must. Only for the lucky few!

Cleaning your shells

Shells with living invertebrates must be put into a pot of boiling water as soon as possible after collecting. Boil for a few minutes to kill them. To remove those invertebrates that do not come away in the water, use a small, sharp knife for bivalves and a bent pin for extracting the shellfish from gastropods.

All empty shells need cleaning in water; a small nailbrush or old toothbrush will get off any dirt. Some shells, like mussels, often need a lot of scrubbing.

Do not attempt to remove barnacles from shells—they are extremely interesting and add to the variety of your collection.

Some gastropods, the centers of their shells worn away by the sea, have a lovely spiral-staircase look—don't throw them away because they are broken. But discard any shells that are stained with rust or slime. Dry the shells on newspaper and secure bivalves that you want to keep closed with a rubber band.

Storing

Sort your shells into categories—the notes above will be helpful but you will probably need a reference book to identify the more unusual species—and then put them into shallow boxes with lids or in the drawers of a small cabinet.

Using your Shells

Selection and arrangement of shells depend largely on two things. First, having a large enough collection of shells from which to choose contrasts of texture, shape, size and color; and second, having the patience to find just the right shell, or shells, to suit your purpose.

Shells can be glued to most rigid or semirigid surfaces such as cardboard, wood, masonite (the rough side), canvas or other coarse, heavy fabrics mounted on a

rigid surface. They can be stuck to earthenware, pots, and boxes; made into pictures and mirrors, and planted with house plants.

An "allover" shell design can be mounted on a piece of masonite. The one shown above with other shell pictures are described fully further on in this section.

The technique of gluing or cementing shells—which will be explained in appropriate detail with each design—is not at all difficult when doing two-dimensional subjects, as there is a straight surface on which to work. When fixing shells onto others—to make the small animals shown later in this section, for instance—use only those shells which fit naturally together; don't try to force shells of totally disparate shapes—they will only fall off when glued and result in unnecessary disappointment.

One does see in stores designs

using shells painted in bright, primary colors and looking like anything but shells. We feel, however, that with their subtle colors and natural beauty, they should never be painted or have holes drilled in them. (Some shells have natural holes made by the sea: that's different!) The background colors against which shells look their best are those associated with their habitat: from light, sandy colors to deep brown, and pale sea blue to dark seaweed green. As you can see from the color photographs, shells, in all their natural beauty, are endlessly fascinating to look at—and to work with.

Revival of a Victorian craft – rows of shells delicately frame a mirror. Some are pretty enough just to be ornaments and one is a natural plant container

Fill a Jar with Shells

Shells are for looking at, and here is one of the simplest and prettiest ways to store a small collection. Any clear glass jar will do—it needn't even have a lid—just as long as the neck is wide enough for you to move the shells around.

No need to worry about "dust traps": the shells in this attractive bathroom ornament are there, fresh as sea-water, for keeps.

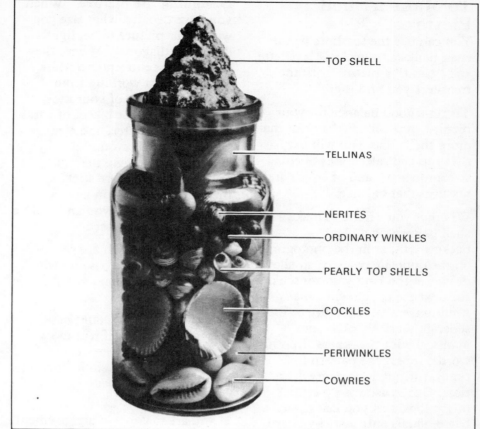

- TOP SHELL
- TELLINAS
- NERITES
- ORDINARY WINKLES
- PEARLY TOP SHELLS
- COCKLES
- PERIWINKLES
- COWRIES

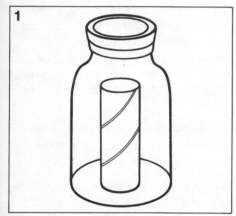

To stop the shells rattling around in the jar, and to enable you to place them in rounds rather than heaps, cut off a cardboard cylinder from a foil or plastic-bag roll. Lower this into the jar (Diagram 1) and center it so that it will press the shells evenly against the sides of the jar.

Lower the first layer of shells into the jar, between the cylinder and the glass. A thin-bladed kitchen knife is useful to place the shells and turn them over if they get into the wrong position. For the very small ones you can use tweezers. Continue filling the jars in layers of different colors and textures— or at random if you prefer—until the shells reach the top of the jar.

Instead of replacing the stopper, use a conical-shaped shell to close the lid of the jar. A top shell (as shown in the photograph), limpet, tun shell or frog shell (Diagram 2) would be suitable. A smaller,

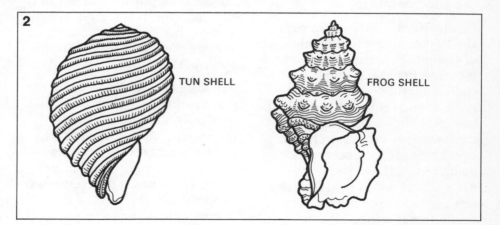

TUN SHELL   FROG SHELL

round shell of this kind, jammed into the top of the cardboard cylinder, would keep the arrangement firmly in place. The designer says she got this idea from a sandbottle. It always impressed her that it could safely be turned upside down, without a grain being misplaced!

Shells in all moods: Pinky-brown ones on a burlap ground make a formal picture; some fill a bathroom jar brimful and tiny ones make amusing animal figures

To Make a Shell Picture

You can use the seashore or the river banks as your artist's palette, and "paint" a picture with the treasures you find there.

To get a good balance for your picture, you will need a great many more shells than you will use, so that you can select ones of equal size and shape, and of colors and textures that balance.

Whether you decide to make a shell pattern on a plain background, as in the photograph on the opposite page, or an allover design of the kind you can see on the next page, you will usually need to treat your picture as four separate sections, each one identical with the others. In other words, repeat the pattern four times, turning it 90 degrees each time. Otherwise your picture might look as if you had tipped a bag of shells onto a sticky board and left them there!

Equipment   Other than your shells, you need only the minimum of equipment to make shell pictures. For the background, choose a rigid or semirigid surface, such as wood, masonite (use the rough side), strong cardboard, or canvas stretched over board. If the background is going to show, and you want to use a fabric, pick a rugged-looking one with a rough texture, such as coarse linen, slubbed rayon, burlap or heavy netting.

The only other things you will need are a heavy glue and a small stick to apply it; and pencil, paper, a ruler, compasses and T square to mark out your design.

If you have an old picture frame which you can use, so much the better. Design your picture, and cut the background to fit it. Otherwise, the simplest frame of a softwood such as pine is all you will need.

Designing the picture   When you have decided what size you want your picture to be, lightly draw two diagonals. Where they cross is the center point. Mark this, and start working from there. Select one of your most attractive shells or pieces of coral to use at the center, and arrange a few other shells around it (Diagram 1). Juggle the arrangements, before sticking them down, until you have a design that pleases you and will be easy to extend outward.

Oyster shells, which are relatively flat, are useful as a base on which to build up an "island" of shells in the middle.

Your arrangement could be sketched on paper if it is too complicated to remember. If the design is regular, a circle drawn in lightly with a compass will be helpful.

If you are making an arrangement of, say, cockleshells, where size is all important, it is a good idea to number the shells underneath and to mark the places they will occupy (Diagram 2).

Sticking the shells on: Use the glue sparingly, so that it does not ooze out on the background. Pour some into a bottle top and, using a matchstick or ice-cream stick, wind the glue onto it, like spaghetti around a fork (Diagram 3). Glue only the parts of the shell that will touch the background,

or the shells underneath, or you will have shiny, snaillike trails that are impossible to remove. Practice using just the right amount of glue for the size of the shell: too little, and the shell will wobble; too much and the mechanics of your art will be showing.

Ordinary cockleshells can be as interesting as any—it depends how you use them.

If you want to make them "stand up" in your arrangement, prop them up with other shells to keep their upright position while drying (Diagram 4). When the glue is set, remove the supporting shells and glue the next round or line.

Slippery shells don't stick very well to other slippery shells—at least, not unless you take care.

To stick, for example, auger shells inside a scallop shell, apply the glue to the augers where they will make contact and then tape them in position with Scotch tape until they are firmly fixed (Diagram 5).

Here is a star of shells, with all the glitter and romance of anything in the heavens. The design is mounted on canvas stretched and stuck on board. Notice how shiny and smooth, rounded and pointed shells are used in juxtaposition to add depth and interest. The center is built up of oyster shells and then, on top, a blaze of coral.

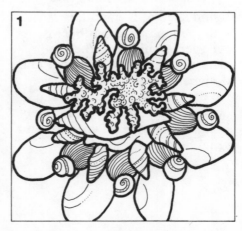

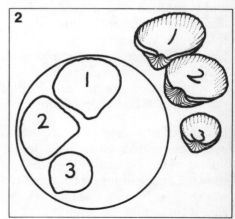

3

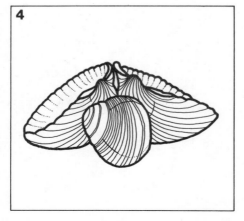

4

5

Shells All Over

If you look carefully at the photograph on the left, you will see that it is a ring-o'-ring of roses of cockleshells and smaller ones arranged to give an allover effect.

The background for this picture is a piece of masonite, used rough side out so that the shells have a better "grip."

The design was worked from the center outward, in rings. The central shell is a whelk, balanced on a periwinkle to give it height. It is then surrounded by tiny cockles and pink/orange Tellina shells, olive shells, periwinkles and tropical Tellinas.

See how interesting cockleshells look when they are arranged, as here, back to back. To do this, glue the first row near their base and prop them up from behind with other shells to keep them upright. Remove these shells and arrange the next row of cockles, facing in the opposite direction, propping them up in front with other shells until they, in turn, are dry.

Another design of this type is shown on the opening page of this section; again, the background is masonite. The color scheme for that one is quite different—mainly white and blue, with a little coral in the center and four black augers at the corners.

Pieces of coral can be tricky to stick on, as their branches do not offer a straight surface at all. Move the coral around until you find in which position the coral touches the background most. As coral is quite heavy, and needs a generous amount of glue, it is a good idea to "mask" the glued area, which might show, with other shells (Diagram 1).

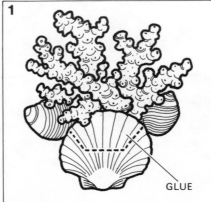

1

GLUE

A Sunburst Pattern on Two Levels

If you don't happen to have a piece of canvas board—and our designer was lucky enough to have one given her by a picture framer —it is a simple job to make one.

This picture was designed so that the "sun" was on the lower level, circles of shells glued to the masonite backing, and the "rays" on the mount, long shells reaching out to the four corners of the earth.

To make your own mount, it is simpler to glue a piece of coarse material over the whole area of the cardboard, tucking it over at the sides and gluing it at the back; the slightly frayed edges around the circle you will cut are all part of the design! If you cut the hole first, and then cover the cardboard with linen, you will find it a very exacting task to tuck the fabric evenly under the circle.

To cut the hole, find a saucer or plate the right size, place the cardboard on several sheets of newspaper to protect the table surface, and cut firmly with a sharp matte knife or X-acto. If you have the mount on a small table, you can walk all around it without having to move it.

The center of the picture, mounted on the back of masonite, was made of a limpet shell surrounded by little white shells of the Tellina group, encircled by yellow periwinkles, auger shells, cockles and rose-petal Tellinas. The radials are composed of small tropical club shells and yellow periwinkles. (The design could be adapted for the use of other shells if different varieties are more readily available.)

When both designs were complete, the linen-covered mount was glued to the masonite and left undisturbed until it was dry.

To make sure you get your design

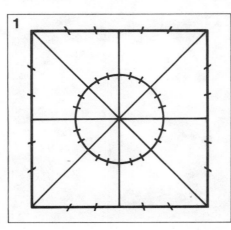

evenly spaced, measure it carefully first. On the canvas board, draw the horizontal and vertical "quarter" lines, then the diagonals. This gives you eight divisions. Putting your compass point at the center, draw a circle with the same radius as the plate you will use for a cutting guide. Divide each eighth into three, so that you have 24 "sunray" lines (Diagram 1). Stick your radial shells carefully over the lines you have made.

Decorating a Trinket Box

The Victorians used to love decorated boxes—and there's no reason why we shouldn't keep up the tradition. You can buy plain wooden boxes in craft stores, ready for any attractive finish you like to apply.

The one shown in the photograph was a chocolate box, with the wrapping removed.

Sticking shells to a vertical surface is practically impossible, so stand the box up first on one side and then the other, and stick the shells onto the horizontal face. The third and fourth sides present the problem of having to rest on the two sides already covered with shells. To keep the box from sliding around, and the shells from being damaged, stand the box on several thicknesses of towel or a cushion while working.

Think of your shell pattern rather as a tapestry. This one uses cockleshells (always the easiest to collect) as the background color, arranged in rows as neat as cross-stitches. The bold pattern in the center of the lid, and along the front, uses the more colorful and rough-textured shells, but uses them sparingly.

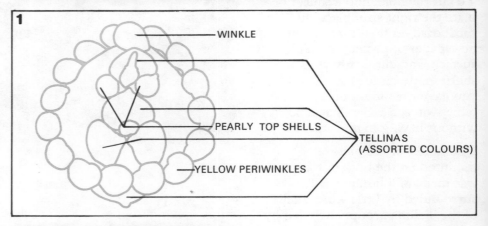

1   WINKLE

PEARLY TOP SHELLS

YELLOW PERIWINKLES

TELLINAS (ASSORTED COLOURS)

. . . and a Double Clam Shell

Would you believe it? This double clam shell is a trinket box, too: it holds two coral necklaces and a pearl bracelet.

Naturally, you would look for a well-marked shell in good condition. If it has come apart, glue it together again, holding the two parts together with a rubber band until the glue has hardened.

From your collection, sort out a number of yellow periwinkles of similar size and glue these around the outside of the shell top. At the hinge end, there is a dark winkle shell and in the center, Tellinas of varying colors and three pearly top shells. The "handle," underneath the top shell, is a pink Tellina.

The Most Fantastic Animals You Ever Saw!

Think of an animal and our designer can make it in shells. Not only that, she can make some you never even heard of!

Cat   She says that the inspiration for the "tortoise-shell cat in bed" design on this page came from a sundial shell which makes the cat's "body."

As you can see from the photographs here and on the following pages, all the toy animal designs.are amazingly simple, and very few features or extra materials have been added. The skill comes in seeing the possibilities in the shells in your collection and having the patience to find others to use with them.

The cat's bed, a large mussel, was chosen for the helpful flat surface it presented. First the paws, two Tellinas, were stuck in it, then,

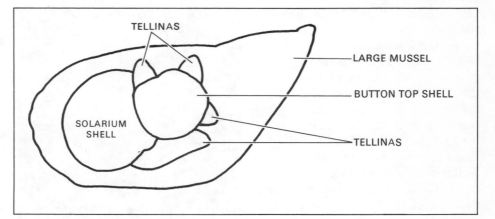

slightly overlapping the right paw, the solarium shell for the body. Two smaller Tellinas were glued to the buttontop (or similar umbonal) shell for the ears, and the head was balanced on smaller shells, now hidden, and stuck in place. Two small dabs with a green felt-tip pen are the only additional features this smug pussy needed!

More animal designs overleaf.

Bird   Not much chance of getting this one to eat out of your hand, judging by the expression! The clam shell forming the body was found with a hole in it—convenient for jamming in an auger shell for the beak. Small pearly top shells are stuck on for the eyes, and pieces of coral for lower feathers. The bird measures $2\frac{1}{2}$ inches from back to tip of beak.

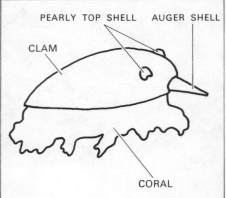

Owl   The top shell which forms the body of the owl has tiny shells and encrusted sand all over it—like feathers. With two eyes painted in with brown felt-tip pen, the cockleshell takes on all the appearance of an owl's head, complete with the formidable bird-of-prey beak. Small coral chips are used for the claws and Tellinas for the wings. Another small Tellina is stuck underneath the back of the top shell for balance.

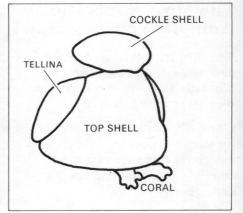

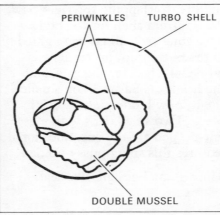

Woodland Insect   This, we are assured, is a purely imaginary creature inspired by the ridged, tubular shape of the Turbo shell which forms the body. This already seems to take on a slithering motion, and needed very little adornment. A double mussel was wedged into it, to make the head, and two periwinkles formed the eyes. Quite an unusual effect, with only four shells. The insect is $2\frac{1}{8}$ inches long.

Moth Shells have almost as many variations as the wings of butterflies and moths. Here is a case in point. The "leaf" is a flat oyster shell and the body a light-colored, spiraling auger. A periwinkle makes the head and the four wings are mussels, carefully chosen to pair into two large and two small ones. For the antennae, two short lengths of thin copper wire were glued to the inside of the periwinkle.

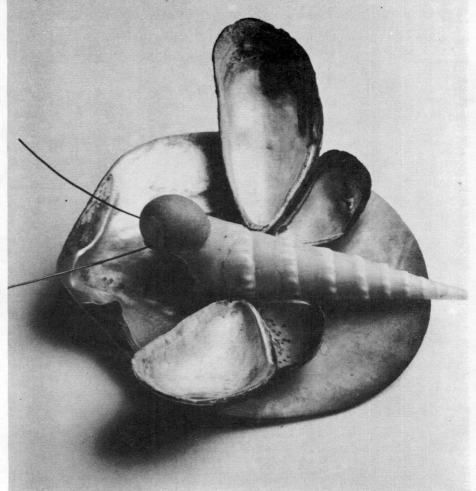

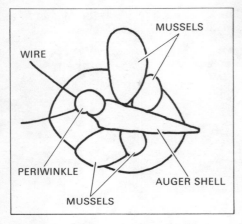

MUSSELS

WIRE

MUSSELS

PERIWINKLE

AUGER SHELL

Bear This is a shell collage, a bear going shopping, mounted on white cardboard. A well-ridged oyster shell makes the pear-shaped body and is stuck first to the card. The head is a limpet shell (with a perfect inquiring nose!) and the ears, miniature cockleshells. Tiny mussels are used for the front paws, a scallop for the shopping bag and boat shells for the hind paws! These are glued to the cardboard under the oyster shell.

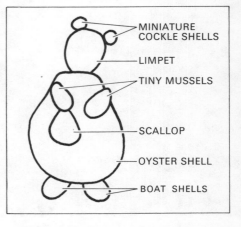

MINIATURE COCKLE SHELLS

LIMPET

TINY MUSSELS

SCALLOP

OYSTER SHELL

BOAT SHELLS

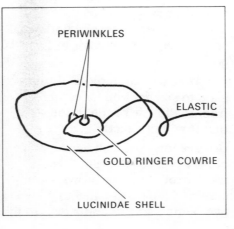

PERIWINKLES

ELASTIC

GOLD RINGER COWRIE

LUCINIDAE SHELL

Mouse He seems to be keeping a wary eye on the cat, two pages ago! The mouse is comfortably situated in a creamy Lucinidae shell. The body is a gold-ringer cowrie and the alert ears, tiny periwinkles. Since Paula Critchley could not find a shell long and thin enough to make the tail of a self-respecting mouse, she used a piece of fine white elastic. The mouse, the tinest of our collection, is $\frac{7}{8}$-inch long.

Through the Looking Glass

Shells make the prettiest frame for a mirror, and certainly not just for the bathroom. In the color photograph you can see how elegant this mirror is—truly as pretty as a picture.

Equipment You can use any picture frame, even an old one, as long as the sides are parallel and reasonably strong. Old paint should be sandpapered off first and the frame given one undercoat and one or two top coats of flat enamel paint.

A glazier will cut a piece of mirror glass to size for you. Measure from the inside of the frame so that it will fit exactly.

Besides this, you will need a piece of plywood cut the same size as the mirror; a roll of brown gummed tape, $1\frac{1}{2}$–2 inches wide; two picture screws and a drill to fix them into the frame, some picture wire, and heavy glue.

Place the frame face downward on a flat surface and lay the mirror in position. Spread glue fairly liberally over the back of the mirror and the vertical areas on the inside of the frame. Place the plywood on top of the mirror back, put a heavy weight, such as an iron or a pile of books, on top and leave several hours until the glue has hardened.

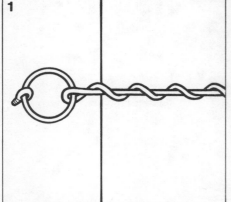

Two mirrors framed with a collage of shells

The mirror on the opposite page was designed from a collection of predominantly white shells, yellow periwinkles and coral colored augers.

On this page, the mirror is almost all sparkling white, accented by a "show piece" of coral.

Shell mirrors are suitable for any room in the house, but they do benefit from being set against a plain, or wood wall. Intricate wallpaper patterns would tend to draw attention away from the detail of the shell shapes.

To neaten the appearance of the back of the mirror, and to stop dust getting in, cover the opening between the plywood backing and the frame with strips of brown gummed tape. Hold these briefly under a tap, or wipe with a wet sponge and then stick in position.

Mark the positions for the screws on the back of the frame, about 1–1½ inches in from the sides and at a distance between one quarter and one third of the top-to-bottom measurement of the frame. Fix the screws firmly in position, and add picture wire or nylon picture cord. If using wire, cut a double length and twist the two extra lengths over the single wire to strengthen (see Diagram 1).

How Does Your Garden Grow?

Plants that are not too temperamental, like wandering jew, all varieties of ivy, spiderflower, cacti, and many more, can be successfully grown in shells. Choose a shell with a wide aperture and any length from about 6 inches to 2 feet (if you're lucky: that's the longest shell in the world, the Australian Trumpet Shell).

To plant the shell, first put a handful of small stones at the bottom, and shake them well so that they settle at the farthest end. This provides adequate drainage for the plant and stops it becoming waterlogged.

Release the plant from its original pot by squeezing the sides of the pot if it is plastic, and tapping the end if it is earthenware. Try to keep the soil surrounding the roots intact.

Hold the shell upright, and ease the plant into it, pushing the soil down firmly with your fingers. Water, with the shell again held upright, using a can with a long, thin spout.

The photograph on the left shows a spiky, mature spiderflower whose variegated light and dark green leaves contrast well with the creamy-coral coloring of the shell.

. . . with Silver Bells and Cockleshells

Well, cockleshells are admittedly rather small to hold even the tiniest flowers, but this Triton shell provides a sturdy container for the wandering jew.

Large shells can be planted with a variety of house plants; two or three of contrasting texture and color look most effective.

Water the plant sparingly. Little and often is a good rule, as the shell has no drainage holes.

A Shell Full of Flowers

The beauty of natural containers, such as sea shells, is complemented by the use of flowers, either fresh or dried. Even tiny shells found by the sea or river can hold nosegays of minute spring flowers, making the very most of the first snowdrops, aconites or violets. Fill the shell with white "Florapak" or a similar water-retentive material and keep well watered.

When arranging dried flowers, fill the shell with white Plasticine to within about 1 inch of the rim. This is a suitable holding material for all but the flimsiest stems because it adheres well to the container and gives good rigidity. You may have to make holes in the clay with a needle to take the less sturdy stems.

A Plateful of Shells

Seaside souvenir shops offer wall plaques set with shells, but they are rarely as pretty as these. If you have as yet only a small collection of shells, or the children are impatient to try to make something themselves, these designs, worked on old saucers and plates, are ideal.

The shells are pasted to the earthenware with spackling-type of plaster filler, which has a long drying time and therefore gives plenty of scope for rearrangement.

To cover a saucer of average size, or a small tea plate, you will need: 1 package of spackle; 1 tablespoon; an old spoon or knife for mixing; a vessel, such as an empty coffee jar; poster paints, powder paints or a tube of watercolors for coloring the spackle.

For each saucer, mix 8 level tablespoons of spackle with 4 tablespoons of water. Always use in this 2-to-1 proportion for shellwork. Mix to a thick, smooth paste with old knife or spoon. Then, using any of the types of paint mentioned, color the spackle as you like it.

The designs shown here were set in spackle filler colored charcoal gray with a heaped teaspoon of black poster paint.

Spread the filler onto the saucer or plate to a thickness of about $\frac{1}{8}$-inch. Don't overdo the filler base; if it is much thicker than this, the shells will sink in.

Level off the edges with a knife to give a smooth finish. Now begin to set your shells.

You can see from these two photographs that a rim of cockleshells around the edge is effective, whichever way up they are. Press the shells gently into the mixture; if you are too heavy-handed it will ooze up unattractively.

Fill in the center with a design of contrasting shells and tiny pieces of coral if you have any. Large shells, such as the whelk, need an extra dab of filler underneath to keep them held firmly in place.

If your design is likely to be complicated, work it out first on paper, drawing around your plate or saucer and arranging and rearranging the shells until you like the pattern.

Leave the plate in a horizontal position until the shells set thoroughly

TAKE A HANDFUL OF PEBBLES

You're sitting on the beach, idly running handfuls of pebbles through your fingers, an assortment of minerals thousands of years old, rich in interest and potential beauty, rolled together and smoothed by the incessant pounding of the sea. Or perhaps your attention has been called to a display of rough chunks of rock in a lapidary's window with samples of the same rocks cut and polished. Or you may have been given a piece of jewelry, a bracelet of glowing carnelians or a ring set with a delicate piece of pink rose quartz—something which has made you realize that semiprecious stones can be just as beautiful in the right setting as diamonds and rubies.

Whichever way your interest in pebbles begins, it is a subject which will continue to grow in fascination, whether you start to collect and polish your own specimens or buy ready-polished stones. It requires little imagination to see the very stuff of the earth we live on held in the hand, in the form of a piece of snowflake obsidian or a rich chunk of polished jasper—romance in the fullest sense of the word.

Perhaps the most rewarding way to begin is to make simple pieces of jewelry, using polished stones and ready-made settings. In this way, you will get to know the different types of stones; their quality when tumble-polished from rough specimens; how they can be cut and shaped to enhance their color and markings, and how to mount them to show them off to the best advantage. There are special lapidary stores (lapis: a stone—therefore, lapidary, one who cuts, polishes or engraves stones) which are absolute Aladdin's caves, their counters covered with bowls of assorted stones of all shapes and colors. If you live some way from a large town, you can send for specimens by mail, choosing from a catalogue giving you details and prices of what is available. These stores also supply settings made from base metal with a silver or gilt finish, or from silver, and all the other equipment you will need, such as adhesive, pliers, etc.

For the results you can achieve, it is not an expensive craft; ring settings and polished stones can cost less than a dollar. It is possible to make beautiful sets from matching stones as presents for friends, to sell at charity bazaars—but you will certainly want to keep many of your pieces yourself!

This chapter will tell you how to make various articles of jewelry, from bracelets to earrings, from cuff links to brooches; it will show the types of settings and fittings available and advise on the selection of stones to use. The techniques involved are basically simple; it is your taste and flair, your matching of setting and stone, which will produce a good or not-so-good piece. We have also included a section on working with polished pebble chips—a fascinating hobby which will lead you to look around the house and garden for objects to decorate.

Tumble-polishing
An interest in jewelry making often leads to the desire to tumble-polish stones for oneself; it is not too expensive to acquire a tumble-polish stones for oneself. The raw rock can be bought from the lapidary and here you can obtain advice on the sizes and types to start on.

Eventually, you will probably find that your interest in pebbles and minerals grows so much that you will want to collect your own specimens. Wherever you live, a beach, lake or river can provide you with water-worn pebbles; a good reference book will tell you what kind of stone to look for and how to identify them.

Generally speaking, you will not find pebbles of any great intrinsic value on American shores, although you may be lucky enough to pick up a piece of quartz or possibly jasper and jade. However, the subtle beauty, when polished, of amethyst, citrine or chalcedony, to name only a few common stones to be found, is as great in the author's eyes as the finest diamonds ever mined.

Simple Jewelry

In our color photograph you will see some of the effective jewelry it is possible for the amateur (even a beginner nine or ten years old) to make quite simply. Until you become more expert, it is advisable to work with the less expensive settings and stones, and you can make a really pretty ring or pendant very cheaply.

These are the things you will need:

Settings (or "findings") It is advisable to buy a selection of these, in both silver and gilt finish, then choose stones to fit them, both in form and color. In each section you will see some of the types of settings which are generally available, and of course you will be able to find many more. The simplest types of settings present a flat surface on which the stone can be stuck, but there are other types—for instance ring settings with claw fittings which have to be bent around the stones, or pendant settings which take a stone pierced to hold the wires.

Stones These can either be baroque stones—the rough stones tumble-polished to emerge in natural shapes with no completely flat sides or sharp corners; cabochon cut—that is cut with a rounded or curved top into oval, rectangular or other shapes, ground and polished; or faceted by hand, with small surfaces and sharp, straight lines where the facets meet, as for a diamond or other precious stone. The beginner will generally start by using baroque or cabochon stones.

Pliers A good pair of jeweler's pliers is a necessity for your work. Several types are available, some with flat pincers, others with round pincers and yet others with one flat and one rounded end. The latter kind, although more expensive, are very versatile as the round pincer can be used for opening jump rings, etc.

Adhesive The basic "stick one thing to another" substance you will need is epoxy resin. This is normally bought in the form of two tubes of different components —an adhesive and a hardener. You mix the two together as needed, being careful not to reverse the caps on the tubes when replacing and use the mixture to stick the stones to the mounts.

These adhesives are cold-setting, although placing in a warm position does help to speed up the process, and are extremely strong once completely set. Various brand names are available from lapidary stores.

Miscellaneous You will also need a variety of small aids, such as bottle tops and matchsticks for mixing and applying adhesive (as the adhesive sets hard after a short time, the things you mix on and with should be disposable); coffee stirrers for maneuvering small stones around; Plasticine or a dish of table salt in which to stick your jewels while the adhesive is setting, and an old cup on which to place rings to set; supply of tissues to wipe off surplus adhesive. Tweezers are also useful.

Three types of stone (Diagram 1): baroque, tumble-polished and with no flat sides; cabochon cut, which can have a rounded or curved top and be oval, rectangular or other shapes, ground and polished; and faceted by hand, with small surfaces and sharp, straight lines where the facets meet, as for a diamond.

You will need a good pair of jeweler's pliers. Diagram 2 shows three types: one with flat pincers, one with round pincers and another with one flat and one rounded end. This type, although more expensive, is very versatile as the round pincer can be used for opening jump rings and so on.

It is important to use the correct adhesive for your work; this is epoxy resin, bought in the form of two tubes, one an adhesive and one a hardener (Diagram 3). You mix the two together as needed.

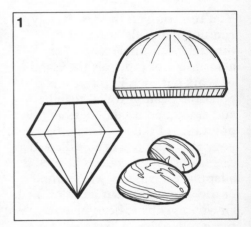

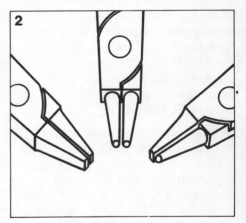

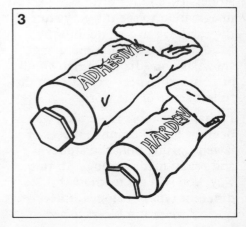

Pebble chippings have endless possibilities. They can be grouped to make decorative jewelry or used to cover vases, boxes or jars

Beautiful Bracelets

Encircle your wrists—or ankles!—with beautiful bracelets. The three types most rewarding for a beginner to make are shown on this page.

1. The type with flat "pads" on which the stones are stuck, the mounting being completely covered by the stone. Baroque stones can be used for this type of mounting, but generally speaking cabochon stones, matched in size and color, look best.

2. The type where the stone is stuck to the center of each mounting pad, but an edge of the pad shows all around the stone. In the case of the mounting illustrated, incised lines radiate out from the center of the mounting to form a pleasing pattern. The stones should be matched in size and shape, but an attractive effect can be achieved by grading the color. The finished bracelet shown in the photograph was graded as follows: dark green, light green, green and sand colored, sand colored and orange, pale orange, dark orange.

3. The third type of bracelet is the chain type where baroque stones roughly matched in size and color (or in contrasting colors) and mounted on pendant caps and jump rings are attached at intervals to the chain bracelet. Decide how many stones you want on your bracelet and lay them out roughly with the chain caps so that you can judge the finished effect.

In the case of 1 and 2, the stones are stuck with epoxy on the mountings and left flat to dry.

For 3, mount each stone on a cap, as described fully in the section dealing with pendants. Stick the stones in Plasticine while the epoxy sets, then fix on a jump ring, not pinching it closed at this stage. Lay the chain bracelet flat and carefully count out the chain

spacing between each pendant stone before passing the jump ring with pendant attached through and pinching closed.

You will also find wide, solid bracelet mountings in some stores, where a single stone or groups of stones are stuck on a shaped portion of the mounting.

1. A bracelet mounting with "flat" pads which are completely covered by the stones—in this case, amber-colored cabochon stones.

2. The decorative mounting pad is part of the design in this type. Round cabochon stones in colors graded from dark green to dark orange have been used.

3. A "charm" bracelet, where the baroque stones are matched for size and color and mounted on caps and jump rings, as pendants.

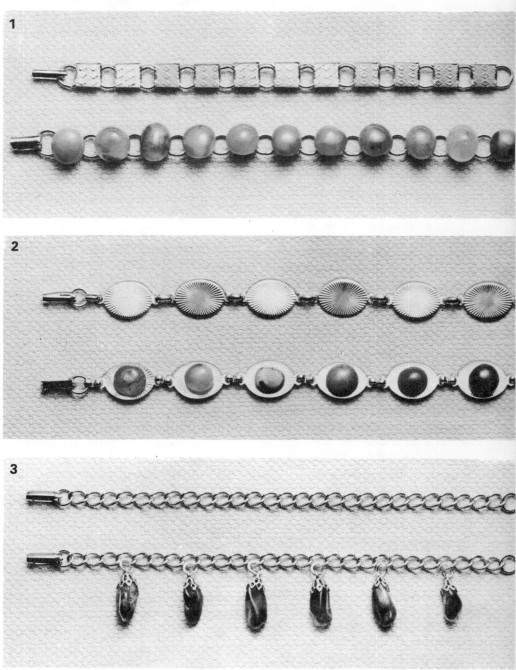

A handful of natural stones – treasures worth looking for on seashore walks or cheap to buy in specialist shops – and simple jewelry to make with them

Find Your (Semi-precious) Birthstone

Month	Stone	Color
Jan.	Red Jasper	Dark red
Feb.	Spinel	Purple
March	Aquamarine	Pale blue
April	Rock Crystal	Translucent
May	Chrysoprase	Bright green
June	Moonstone	Cream
July	Carnelian	Red
Aug.	Aventurine	Pale green
Sept.	Sodalite	Deep blue
Oct.	Abalone	Variegated
Nov.	Citrine	Yellow
Dec.	Amazonite	Sky blue

Popular Pendants

The simplest type of pendant for the beginner to make is the kind where a baroque stone with a suitably "pointed" corner is fixed to a pronged metal cap with an eyelet at the top. Then a small ring called a "jump ring" is put through the eyelet so that the pendant can be hung from a chain. This page shows some of the bell caps and jump rings available for making this kind of pendant, and some chains to hang them on. Don't always think of pendants as necklaces—they can be attached to bracelets, key rings, earrings and brooches, and two or more together make a most attractive set.

Since epoxy resins came into use for jewelry making, it has become much easier to make pendants. However tenuous and delicately filigreed the claw setting, the epoxy, once it has set, will hold the stone firmly in place.

However, it is not really practicable to expect a tiny bell cap to hold a large baroque stone satisfactorily; nor does it look balanced if you swamp a small stone by using too large a mounting. So be careful to match mount and stone carefully together—this is the "flair" we referred to earlier!

Select a stone   You will need to look carefully and critically through a heap of stones to find just the right one, or a matching set if you are making, say, a pendant and drop earrings. A particularly attractive stone may not lend itself to mounting on a bell cap, or it may have a badly flawed side which makes it unsuitable. When you have chosen a stone, work out which way you want the stone to face in the finished pendant, then select a suitable cap. You will have to visualize how the pendant will hang on its chain or mounting, so that you can plan how to fix the cap to the stone. For instance, if a jump ring is to go through it, the eyelet must face you when the cap is mounted on the stone, so that the pendant will hang on its chain with the correct face showing.

When the cap fits . . .   When you have worked out how the cap should go with reference to the other fittings and the stone itself, press it down tightly until the point of the stone touches the metal under the eyelet, and press the prongs or points of the cap down to fit the shape of the stone. If the metal is stiff, use the pliers to bend the prongs out (Diagram 1).

Using a coffee stirrer, place a little epoxy on the top of the stone where the cap is to go (Diagram 2) and a tiny dab inside the cap itself. Press the cap on the stone in the correct position and leave to set, pushing it lightly into Plasticine or salt (Diagram 3).

When quite set, pass a jump ring of suitable size through the eyelet, and nip the ends of the ring together with pliers to close it.

Specially shaped mountings
Another pendant which is not difficult to make is where a shaped mounting has a single stone or group of stones, of complementary shape and color, stuck onto it. The two copper mountings shown

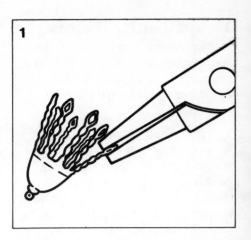

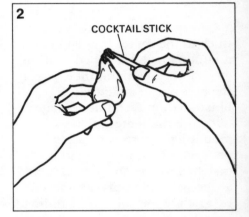

COCKTAIL STICK

are decorated with cabochon stones, chosen so that the mounting and stone shape enhance one another. This type of mounting is pierced at the top to take a jump ring for hanging.

Heart shapes   It is sometimes possible to buy shaped stones for pendant making, such as the heart-shaped one in the photograph. This particular example had holes pierced at each side of the top projection to take

Three different types of mounting for pendants: left to right, a decorative bell cap holding a piece of crystal, translucent and delicate; a heart-shaped piece of amber, secured through two holes pierced in the projection, and a chunk of rose quartz held by a tulip-petal-type cap.

Chunkier stones make sporty-looking pendants, ideal to wear with leisure clothes.

Shaped mountings in copper, in the shapes of a star and a Maltese cross, can be bought ready for decorating with stones. Both have been used as a background for cabochon stones, flat on the underside and curved on top.

the mounting, as shown. These mountings must be opened with pliers in order to fix each prong into the hole in the stone, then squeezed together to make the stone firm.

Sometimes the holes are drilled at an awkward angle, so you will have to spend some time adjusting the mount-wire to fit. The pendants can be hung on jump rings, as before.

A Ring for Every Finger

Of all jewelry, rings seem to have the greatest fascination for most people. Whether you wear a carefully chosen one for each outfit or a tremendous number together, if you are a "ring person" you can never have too many of them.

As you will see from the settings illustrated on this page, there is a great variety to choose from, ranging from the simple type with a flat surface on which to stick the stone, to the more complicated kind with a recessed place for a stone which must be a good fit. Usually, the settings are made so that they can be squeezed to fit the finger they are intended for, as you will see from the illustrations, so you need pay no attention to sizes when you buy your settings.

Flat settings   Taking the simplest flat setting first, look carefully through the bowls of stones to find one which will not only look attractive with the gilt or silver finish of your setting, but has also one flattish surface to stick on to it (or is cabochon cut). This means that you must pay attention to the other surface for color, attractive markings, lack of flaws and so on, as this is the one which will show. Try the stone on your finger to see that it will be a happy shape when made up into a ring.

To make the ring, mix your adhesive and apply a little to the flat surface of the stone to be stuck, or to the mount, and press them together. As the adhesive is not instant-setting, you can turn the stone until you get the best arrangement. Don't leave the ring to set, having put it down on its side. If you do this, the stone will certainly slide off the setting. You can either balance the ring on the edge of a cup (see illustration) with the stone uppermost and the two edges of the mount hanging over

the lip on each side, or stick the ends of the setting in Plasticine, with the jewel uppermost.

Leave the ring to set—it should be quite firm if left overnight, although the full strength of the adhesive and its resistance to heat and water are not completely developed for about three days. If you place the ring on a warm surface, such as a radiator, the full strength will develop in about a day. Extreme impatience to see the ring firm and finished? Then you can place it in the oven at 300°F, which will give complete setting in about half an hour. Be careful not to have the oven any hotter, or it will damage the surface of the setting.

Shaped settings   When you have made several rings with flat settings, you will want to try more elaborate forms. Shaped settings to take a stone of the right size are still simple to make and stick, but will involve more work in finding just the right stone. The setting in the illustration could have taken a cabochon or faceted stone, but in fact a baroque pebble was found which just fitted it.

Claw settings   A third, rather more difficult, setting is the claw setting. When you have selected your stone, bend the claws with the pliers so that when the stone is inserted, they will fit roughly around it. Place the stone in the setting and work the claws around

into position, then remove the stone and place adhesive on the mount. Replace the stone and squeeze the claws firmly into place with the pliers before leaving to set.

Whether you hanker for bright, modern jewelry or for the nostalgic shape of the past, there are ring settings to suit you. Right, you can see a selection of eleven types that are available in lapidary stores. The picture below shows a ring waiting for the adhesive to harden, balanced on the edge of a cup.

Below, left to right:
1. This ring has a flat green stone. 2. Ring with ornamental setting and baroque crystal stone. 3. Ring with baroque stone stuck on a flat surface. 4. A cabochon stone is fitted into the setting. 5. The large claws of this setting need careful bending with pliers over the stone.

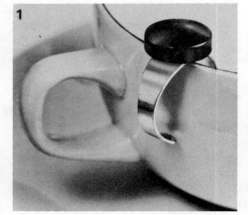

Jewelry for Men

Solve a difficult gift problem by making a handsome pair of cuff links or one of the other attractive and useful small gemstone pieces shown on this page.

Cuff links   Here are samples of different mountings suitable for cuff links. As you will see, some of them are suitable for use with baroque stones, matched in shape and color, while others are recessed to take the exact size of cabochon stones.

Choose stones which would be particularly appropriate for men—generally the more subtle colors of brown, green and purple would be better received than the pale pink of rose quartz!

The handsome brown striped tigereyes shown made up into cuff links are particularly suitable. The cabochon cut stone in the middle cuff link is a mottled dark purple.

Stick the stones firmly with epoxy in the usual way and make sure they are completely set before being used, as cuff links are subjected to a great deal of handling.

Tie clip   These small clips for holding the tie in position lend themselves to the mounting of a small baroque stone as in our photograph, and are inexpensive to make. The stone we show is a pale gray-white.

Key ring   Mount your baroque stone as if you were making a pendant, and attach to a key ring mount with a jump ring (see photograph).

Right, as personal as the key of your door, a key ring with a pendant, mounted on a cap and suspended on a jump ring.

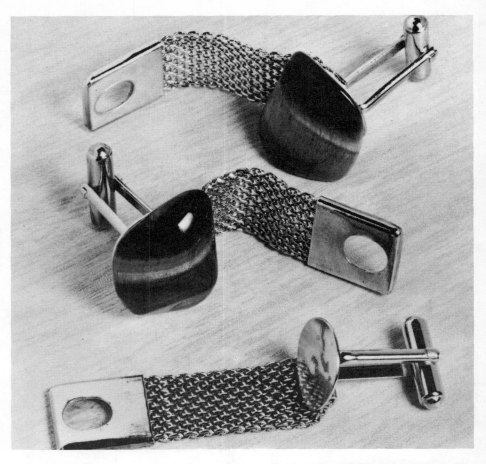

Top: a fine pair of cuff links set with tigereye baroque stones, shown on the right; they would be a most acceptable present. Below: three different cuff link mounts, showing the varying shapes available from lapidary stores. The oval one is set with a cabochon cut stone.

Above right, a tie clip: the small baroque stone is mounted on a flat disk covering a pin which pushes into a sheath.

Pretty Brooches

What could be more personal, as a birthday present or a Mother's Day gift, than a brooch you had made yourself? And nothing could be easier!

There are two main types of brooch suitable for the beginner to make. In the first type, the mounting does not show and is unimportant, except insofar as it holds the stone or stones on one side and the pin on the other.

In the second type, however, the mounting plays a more important part in the finished effect and is designed to form a visible and decorative setting to the stone or stones.

"Invisible" mountings The mountings come, as you can see, in various shapes and sizes to accommodate different stones, and they are suitable for any type of polish or cut. The large recessed mounting is particularly suitable for holding a mixture of small stones or chips.

As the variety is so enormous, we show just two examples (near right) of how to use these mounts. The flat mounting was used as a base for an unusual flat baroque stone, shaped roughly like a heart and a deep pink in color. It was a stone which needed no visible setting and was perfect for this type of treatment. The recessed mounting is filled with a mixture of pebble chips, made homogeneous by the enclosing shape.

Decorative mountings Here are two from a number of decorative mounts available. The leaf spray shown in the photograph, far right, has room in the center of a tiny flower shape for a small stone to complete the design. The other, bow-shaped brooch with its little eyelet is designed to hang a drop or pendant, and we show this in

place, a pretty, translucent smoky pink baroque stone. Our model seems happy with it!

Of course, you will find other types of brooch mounting in the stores and can experiment with the kind you prefer. You might even be lucky enough to pick up an old brooch at a rummage sale, and have some ideas for decorating it with stones of your own choosing.

Sets of Jewelry

When you have had some practice in making some of the separate items suggested on the previous pages, you may like to try your hand at making sets of jewelry— perhaps a matching ring, pendant and bracelet, or a pair of earrings with a brooch in similar stones or pebble chips.

It may seem obvious, but make sure before you begin that your mountings or findings for the set are all either silver or gilt finish, or you will immediately spoil the effect.

It will probably take you a little time to sort through piles of stones to find ones which match, but the satisfaction when you do is well worth the trouble. Sets from baroque stones will work out cheaper, of course, than those made from cabochon or faceted stones.

An attractive effect can be created by searching for stones which are similar in shape but different in color—this random effect comes as an amusing surprise—after all, everyone expects sets to *match*, don't they?

Earrings for All Ears

Pretty for parties, fun to catch a glimpse of under a long, swinging hairstyle, flattering to every face . . . there is a good variety of earring mounts available to give you scope for making earrings to suit you and your friends. The photograph on the far right shows six types, to fit ears that are pierced as well as those which are not.

Both types of mounting are made to take a pendant stone or one which is stuck on flat, and you will see both types illustrated, near right.

Obviously one of the most important things in the making of earrings is to match the stones well, both in color and shape, or

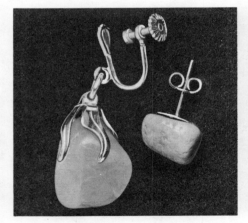

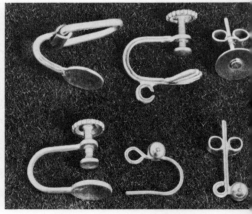

you will present a curiously lopsided picture when you are wearing them! Also, if making rings for pierced ears, do not choose stones which are too heavy, or they will be uncomfortable to wear.

As with cuff links, earring stones should be firmly mounted and hard-set before being used, as they are subject to a certain amount of strain in handling when they are put on and taken off.

Take a Handful of Pebble Chips . . .

We have already touched on pebble chips or the use of small pebbles when discussing brooches, and, in fact, working with chips is one of the most fascinating and entertaining branches of pebble-craft. In most lapidary stores it is possible to buy bags of assorted chips at a very nominal cost. All the items illustrated on these pages with the exception of the large lamp base were made from a pound of chippings, and there were some left over for use on future projects.

The interest in this craft lies in the fact that, apart from decorating objects specially bought for the purpose, one's eye begins to roam round the house and garden and one finds something—a jar, a piece of slate, an old box—which immediately suggests itself as a good subject for pebble work. For instance, the little vase started life as a small jar filled with peppercorns, and the pencil holder once contained a well-known brand of marmalade!

You need no special tools beyond the ones you use for jewelry making and you can use the same adhesives as well.

The advantage of having a bag of stones of mixed colors is that these, as well as the objects you are using as bases, will help to suggest a subject to you. For instance, the purple amethyst chips were just the color of wild asters (see the slate collage overleaf), and the fin-shaped piece of pebble edged with an orange border immediately registered as the perfect fish fin (see the fish in a box, right).

The first stage is to empty your chips onto a large piece of white paper and sort them into different stones and colors. This makes it far easier to find exactly what you want for any design, rather than sorting through the heap of mixed stones each time. It is rather the same as sorting out all the edge pieces from a jigsaw puzzle before starting work on it! When it is time to put the stones away for the night, simply scoop each heap of chippings into a separate jar.

From small beginnings
Begin with some simple object first, one you can work on flat, and graduate from there to more difficult projects.

It is best to lay out your design first of all, without sticking anything down, so that you can see roughly how it is going to work out and whether it will look better as an outline or filled in. When it is to your satisfaction, stick down the outline first, if it is going to be a filled-in pattern, lifting each stone separately, dabbing with epoxy and pressing in place. When this has been done, you can go on to fill in the center, fitting the stones as far as possible so that one dovetails into another. Allow to set.

Life becomes rather more difficult if you are working a design on an upright object, such as a jar or vase, as the epoxy resin is rather slippery until it is beginning to set, and the stones slide down, pulled by their own weight.

In these cases, we have found by trial and error, it is better to use an adhesive which rapidly becomes tacky so that the stone will stick firmly (it is usually necessary to put adhesive on both the stone and the surface you intend to stick it on) or to wait some time until the epoxy is beginning to set before sticking the stone. A heat lamp directed toward the epoxyed area will produce a tacky surface more rapidly and facilitate drying. Alternatively, you can build up your design a layer at a time, not sticking on a new layer until the one below is firmly stuck and will hold the chippings above.

This simple pottery jar was bought in a local craft store with a butterfly shape already decorating the lid, under the glaze. The spots on the wings, the shape of the body and head and the border suggested a simple way of enhancing the design using pebble chips. We sorted out a long and a round piece of black obsidian for the body and head, four pieces of turquoise, two rather larger

than the others, and a group of amethyst chips for the border. The decorated jar is now pretty enough for a dressing-table ornament.

Pretty for a child's room, the fish above was "framed" in a wooden box which once held liqueur chocolates. As the bottom of the box was rather marked with stickiness, we cut a white cardboard to fit. The fish theme was suggested by the perfect triangular fin, and we worked from there, using an assortment of dark stones. Three pointed stones to use as ventral and tail fins, then another piece for the nose.

As before, the stones were laid out to form the pattern and the outline stuck down before filling in the body. The fish needed an eye, so we stuck a piece of moss agate on top of the basic body stones. The design was completed by adding "seaweed" of green aven-

turine. Slate chip pendant. The basic bit of slate happened to be just the right shape to mount a handsomely marked pebble. The jump ring was carefully stuck to the top of the slate with epoxy and left on a bed of salt to set.

Yesterday it was full of peppercorns, today it is encrusted with jewels! This small empty spice jar is just the right size for a tiny posy or single flower, and the one in our picture was covered in an assortment of blue/green stones. As we wanted the stones to be particularly strongly stuck, we used epoxy, adding a line of stones as the previous one was stuck, whenever we had adhesive mixed and were working on something

else. So this is not a job to do in a hurry for quicker-than-instant effect. We encountered a slight problem at the top, which was shaped to take a screw-on lid. However, we pressed on a band of Plasticine the same color as the stones around the recessed part and stuck stones into this to come to the same level as the rest of the vase.

The craft store also supplied the wooden box used for the next form of decoration. The boxes come in different sizes and can be painted or varnished, or simply left plain before being worked on. They are useful for holding anything from jewelry to cigarettes. The design illustrates the effectiveness of a geometric pattern using blocks of different colored stones, the blocks being divided by a "line" of dark stones.

Experiment with dividing in different ways—into triangular or uniform shapes for instance—before you complete your design. Stick down stones forming the dividing lines first, then fill in the separate blocks closely as shown.

Above: Pencil holder for a child born under Leo had humble beginnings—it arose from a marmalade jar and a selection of chips. The design was worked out "on the flat" and transferred to the jar using tacky epoxy. Copy the idea with any sign of the zodiac for a really personal present.

A natural background for a natural object—the piece of slate was found first of all and we decided to work out a flower design on it. The lovely purple of amethyst chips suggested a wild aster, so we made an artless pattern with these, aventurine and carnelian. The finished effect seemed rather dull, with a blank at the top right-hand corner, so a "sun" of carnelians came into being to complete the picture.

Above: Lamp base, made from an old cider jar, took some time to make as each layer of stones was built up on top of the previous one to prevent slipping. A large object like this is, of course, expensive to cover, but when finished it is a handsome and worthwhile possession to keep, and as precious as any treasure you will find at the bottom of the sea.

Tumbling

If you grow really enthusiastic about jewelry making and other pebble work, the stage will probably come when you will want to "tumble"—that is, grind and polish—your own pebbles from the raw state. Not only is it cheaper to do this than to buy the stones singly if you are going to use them in quantity, but there is a great fascination in the idea of watching your stones go through the processes which turn them from chunks of raw rock into, eventually, finished pieces of jewelry.

An amateur can start tumbling pebbles in quite a small way, using a tumbler costing around twenty dollars, and you can buy mixed loads of raw rock from most lapidary stores, or send for them by mail. When you are starting out, you will not be quite sure of sizes and types of stone to buy, and here you can ask advice in the shop, or when writing to order.

Generally speaking, the stones in any one load should be about one inch in diameter or smaller, with one or two larger stones among them. One important thing to remember is that you should not polish hard and soft stones together—as the stones all get the same treatment, the soft ones will naturally, in the course of tumbling, be worn away. Before you become expert enough to know which are "hard" and which "soft" ones—by reading a specialized book on the subject—take the word of the expert in the shop.

So far we have talked about tumbling and the load of stones, but what exactly does the process consist of? In principle, it is roughly the same as the treatment rocks receive at the hands of the sea and rivers, but in a more intense form. The stones are rotated in a sealed "drum" on a special machine, together with water and carborundum grits, to wear off the roughness and smooth them down to a usable form. Various authorities recommend different methods of polishing— different sizes of grits and lengths of time for each stage—but we will give you a rough idea of the process as set out by the suppliers of the machines shown on these pages.

Stage 1   Fill the barrel with stones, shaking to settle them down. It should be filled $\frac{2}{3}$–$\frac{3}{4}$ full and not less, as the tumbling action is not effective if the barrel is underfilled. Then add water to come just over the top of the stones and one heaped tablespoon of carborundum grit for a $1\frac{1}{2}$ lb. capacity barrel. This grit should be a coarse grade—size 80 being most suitable (buy it from the lapidary store where you found your tumbler). Run the machine day and night for several days and examine a sample of the stones occasionally. This stage rounds the stones—if using beach-worn pebbles it will obviously take a shorter time than with jagged chunks of rock. Ten days' running and the addition of carborundum grit may be necessary for the latter, though seven days would be about average. When they seem sufficiently smooth, go on to the next stage.

Stage 2   Next clean the barrel and stones thoroughly, but on *no account* pour the waste matter down the sink—it could harden and block the plumbing permanently. Replace the stones with the same proportions of water and grit, but this time a finer grade—500. Allow at least seven days' running for this stage and do not add fresh grit as it would re-roughen the stones. Each day's running gives a smoother finish as the grit breaks down.

Stage 3   Clean barrel and stones *very* thoroughly and examine to make sure they are completely smooth, discarding any which are cracked or jagged. Not a speck of grit should be left on the barrel or stones. You could in fact buy an extra barrel which was kept only for the polishing stage. Repeat Stage 1, but use cerium oxide instead of grit and a very small amount of powdered wallpaper paste (about $\frac{1}{2}$ teaspoon) as this thickens the mixture and quiets the running of the machine. The resulting shining pebbles should be all ready for you to work on.

This gives a very general picture of what is involved in the tumbling process and of course more detailed instructions and hints will be given when you buy a tumbler. As the tumbling noise can sometimes become irritating when you are within earshot—and the author's husband certainly finds it so!—it is advisable to leave the

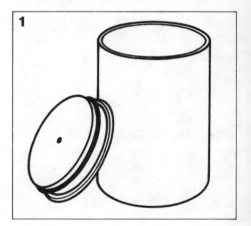

machine running in a spare room or garage if possible. The kitchen is definitely not the best choice.

The color picture shows a typical heap of tumbled stones; at the back you can see some of the rough chunks of rock which can be bought ready for polishing— together with samples of the jewelry and chipping work we have been discussing.

"Romance in the fullest sense of the word"—that's how we described the natural beauty of the stones you can find once you begin to be aware of the world of our native shores. See, in the first photographs, three uncut pieces of rock, just as they were picked up. They are of a size to be held comfortably in the hand—not too large to go into the tumbler, not too small either. In the second photograph, you see them after

they have been tumbled for several days, in water and carborundum grit. They are now rounder and smoother, but still have a dull surface.

The third photograph shows the stones after polishing in the tumbler, using cerium oxide instead of grit. They are now revealed in all their beauty, ready, as baroque stones, to take their place on a pendant, perhaps, or just to be left in a bowl, handled and admired.

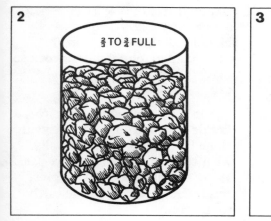

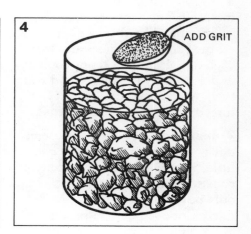

The sketches above show the tumbler barrel (Diagram 1). In Diagram 2, the container is $\frac{2}{3}$–$\frac{3}{4}$ full of stones of almost equal size and similar types. In Diagram 3 the stones are just covered with water, and in Diagram 4, a spoonful of grit is being added to the water.

Collecting Your Own Pebbles

The final step, working backward from jewelry making through tumbling stones bought from the lapidary, is collecting the specimens for yourself; if you become a real pebble enthusiast, this is what you will soon want to do. It is not really within the scope of this chapter to tell you in detail what to look for and how your specimens will polish—what you find will depend on your district and on the country you live in. However, a little information on rocks and minerals in general will help you to start.

Basically, there are three types of rock, and every pebble you find on the seashore or chunk of rough hammer-broken stone from the lapidary store must belong to one of the three.

Igneous rocks
These were formed aeons ago in intense heat by molten materials solidifying. The rocks either erupted from volcanoes and then cooled (volcanic rocks) or cooled under the earth's surface and were then, over the course of time, forced upward (plutonic rocks).

Volcanic rock, because it cooled down quickly and therefore had little time to crystallize thoroughly, consists of tiny crystals which can only be seen through a microscope. The main product of volcanic action is basalt, a very hard and compact rock which does not easily break down into pebbles.

Plutonic rock, as it cooled much more slowly, formed coarse-grained crystals. Granite is the most common of these rocks and it occurs all over the earth's surface. The components are generally silica, feldspar and mica, and they vary a great deal in color. Other varieties of plutonic rock are colerite and gabbro, but they are much less common than granite.

Sedimentary rocks
As the name implies, these were formed from sediment laid down in layer upon layer in salt or fresh water, the main sources being fragments of broken matter washed down by rain, and small organic remains. Over the years, the pressure from above consolidated the matter below into rock. Sedimentary rocks make up the largest of the three classes of rock and fall into the following groups:

Limestones   Much limestone was formed by the depositing of tiny particles of sea creatures' skeletons such as corals, sea urchins, shells, etc., which in the course of time became compressed. You will find in chalk (a very common kind of limestone) many complete fossils of the small creatures themselves. However, if the limestone has undergone crystallization it is not possible to see these.

Sandstones and grits   These rocks in fact consist wholly of sand grains. Nearly all the grains are quartz, but other minerals are contained too. The stone varies in hardness and color. Grits are coarse-grained sandstones, with angular grains.

Shales and slates   These were formed from clay, compressed and solidified, and they consist of thin layers, each of which marks the thickening of the clay bed.

Flints and cherts   These occur in chalk and are not crystalline. No one knows quite how they came to be there, and they are not sedimentary rocks in the strictest sense of the word. Geologists think the liquid rock flowed into the limestone at some stage and solidified in pockets.

Metamorphic rocks
Metamorphic rocks are rocks which have undergone a change of form and originally were either igneous or sedimentary. Tremendous heat or pressure or a combination of both brought about the change by crushing and melting the rocks so that they absorbed new minerals and gradually cooled and recrystallized into a different form. Gneiss, schist and marble are all metamorphic rocks.

This very sketchy outline will, we hope, be filled in by your own reading and research so that you will learn to recognize various types of rock and pebbles for yourself—not always easy, for the categories often have ill-defined boundaries.

If you set out seriously to be a collector you will need first of all a geological map of the district you intend to cover so that you can see the formation of local rock; a knife to scrape and scratch the specimens to test for hardness and take off some of the "skin" acquired from sea or river action; a magnifying glass; and a small hammer with which to break off small corners of pebbles or rock so that you can examine a clear exposed face.

In this way, you will be able to decide which group of rocks your stone belongs to and eventually what the stone is. And, as we said at the beginning of this chapter, this is the very stuff of the earth we live on.

TAKE A BUNCH OF FLOWERS

Using Pressed Flowers

Take a bunch of flowers and, if you want to enjoy them for longer than they will usually last, press them to preserve their color and beauty practically forever. You can use every kind of flower and leaf to make lovely pictures and collages, and to decorate lamps and shades, tableware, even jewelry.

How to press flowers and leaves: Any time from the beginning of spring is the time to harvest flowers for pressing, so start looking along the roadsides, in the fields and in your garden. Choose a dry day, and gather the blooms when the early morning dew has dried off and the flowers are fully open. However fresh and pretty the flowers might look after a shower, with pearllike raindrops balancing on the petals, do not be tempted to pick them. You would be making extra work for yourself, trying to dry out all that excess moisture, and it would almost certainly result in disappointment. Don't forget that some flowers close their petals as evening approaches. You will need to pick them before that.

When you go out to gather your flowers, take a jar or bucket of water with you, so that you can keep the flowers fresh. There is a lot of difference between flowers dried when they were at their best, and those that have wilted of their own accord.

To prepare the flowers, snip off the stalk of each bloom or, in the case of long spikes, such as delphinium and larkspur, each individual flower. Flowers with hard, thick middles cannot be pressed successfully. Pick off the petals one by one and press them separately. Always press material as soon after picking as possible. Because this is so important, it is best to work backward: decide when you have time to press the flowers, then go out and pick them.

Although children in bursts of enthusiasm often successfully press flowers between sheets of newspaper, this is not generally recommended, because the newsprint so readily comes off on the petals and gives them a smudged appearance.

Blotting paper is best. It is less expensive if bought by the package twenty sheets at a time.

Arrange the flowers and leaves between sheets of blotting paper, taking care that petals are all flat (Diagram 1 overleaf), and then lay them between the pages of a large book or layers of a special flower press (Diagram 2). Thick flowers and leaves may need to be pressed in double sheets of blotting paper to absorb all the moisture.

Very fine leaves and most grasses, on the other hand, can be successfully pressed between layers of face tissues, which of course are less expensive than blotting

paper. These, too, should be inserted between the pages of a book. If you weight the book with something moderately heavy, like a brick or an iron, the flowers will dry slightly quicker. But you must be careful not to choose something too heavy and squash them completely (Diagram 3).

Since the object of the exercise is to dry the flowers as quickly as possible and to retain as much as you can of their natural color, avoid leaving them in a damp room. This means, especially, that you should not banish them to the cellar, a shed or the back of the garage. If you do you might be greeted with mildew-bespeckled petals instead of the bouquet you hope for. A warm, sunny place, such as a windowsill, is ideal.

The more delicate flowers will take about four weeks to dry and press completely, the thicker ones at least six weeks. This can seem a tantalizingly long time, especially since it is absolutely imperative that you do not try to check on progress. The slightest disturbance to the flowers at this stage could ruin your efforts so far.

When the time comes to start arranging your pressed and dried materials into pictures, you will need some stems, to give a completely natural effect, so pick and dry these at the same time as your flowers. Clover, daisy and primrose stems are supple and

useful for this, and so are buttercup and clematis montana.

Don't shun anything in the garden —there is practically no leaf or flower lacking in possibilities. Raspberry leaves, for instance, have a beautiful color and texture and dry well for use in pictures and collages. The reverse side is silvery gray.

You will also want a selection of silver leaves, such as cineraria, which look so delicate and almost translucent in the dried state.

What Flowers Shall I Press?

While it is true to say that practically any flower or fern, leaf or stalk is useful, only experience —or the list below!—can tell you the different characteristics and properties which each one has. Here are some ideas to guide you on what materials to press at first, and what to use them for when you have. Here is a brief list of different flowers and their treatment.

Anthemis (camomile)   Holds its color well, whether you choose the pale yellow or deeper golden variety. Pick when it has been open for 3–4 days, even if not all the florets are fully opened. Press stems separately. Needs a very heavy weight.

Auricula (primrose)   Pick the mauve or white varieties. Pull the flowers from the stalks, and separate from stamens and calyx.

Broom   All varieties of this spiky, graceful plant dry a very dark color, so use them in designs where you need the black or dark brown contrast, or are seeking a monotone effect.

Buttercup   In this case, press flower and stalks together, trying to achieve a soft, natural curve in the stalks. The color will last for several years. The flowers make pretty splashes of color where a "sunburst" effect is wanted, and the small, side leaves are useful for portraying hands in collage work.

Celandine (poppy family)   The harvest of many a country walk, celandine needs pressing very soon after picking, as it is quick to wilt. The flowers are at their best against a dark background, or set on a dark leaf. The flowers bleach to almost white within a year.

Real enthusiasts could take blotting paper and book on that country walk, and press the flowers on the spot.

Clematis   The variety Nelly Moser turns a pale brown, while Jackmanii is the color of blue-black ink. Press some of as many colors as you can find, using only the petals, and sometimes using the reverse sides in your design. Many of them develop an interesting stripe or textured effect on the reverse.

Clover   The white clover will soften to a pale beige, and the mauve color will mellow to a heathery brown after a time. The circular shape is useful in designs for simulating heads. Press together with the stalk, making it curve, and use a heavy weight.

Cosmos   The simple shape of this flower makes it adaptable for a number of designs. It is good for color retention, with even the deeper mauve keeping its color for at least five years.

Daffodil   Look at the shape of a daffodil trumpet upside down—it is perfect, in a dried flower picture, for a skirt. For the best results, slice each trumpet in half. You will retain the shape and lose some of the bulk.

Daisy   In the designs that follow, you will see that the daisy has lent itself to many another flower, as an extra-pretty center. Press it with the stalk intact, for you will certainly want to use some complete.

Delphinium   Don't believe what you hear about all blue flowers fading fast—this one doesn't. Separate the florets from the stalks and press each one separately. You might want to press some petals individually, as the depth of color is so good to have.

Capture the everlasting beauty of pressed flowers in picture collages, simple shapes like the butterfly or applied decoration to household objects

Goldenrod   Press each flower stalk separately. It will deepen to a rich golden brown.

Heather   Snip away the stalks and press only the flowers. The purple varieties keep their color well. The white goes creamy after a time.

Honeysuckle   This repays the time you will spend in picking off each individual blossom and pressing it separately. You can use the graceful petals wherever you want a gentle curve; when dried, they lend themselves well to "Oriental" type designs. You can, of course, reassemble the florets to make a full flower again.

Hydrangea   Pick the flower heads when they are at different stages—some green, some pale and some deeper pink, and press the florets separately.

Marigold   These flowers, which tend to lose the strength of their color after a year or so, are best used one on top of the other in a design, for extra color effect. It might be necessary to change the blotting paper after about a month, as the flowers hold a great deal of moisture and take longer than most to dry.

Pansy   The yellow ones retain their color, and the mauve and blue ones quickly copy it—they turn yellow, too. However, the petals are a very pretty shape and you might consider them worth drying in any case.

Roses   There is nothing quite like the smell when you open the book at the page where you have pressed the rose petals—it is your own special potpourri. You will have to accept the fact that rose petals when dried are not pink, or yellow, or white—they are cream or brown, depending on the depth of the original color.

Tulip   Tulip petals are large, and you will need to allow them plenty of space in your blotting paper book. The colors will certainly fade, but it doesn't matter, if you achieve something like expensive watered silk.

Vetch   The flowers keep their stripy color well, and are pretty for feathery outlines.

Wild Chervil   If you are making a large picture, you can use the frondy heads of this flower complete. Otherwise, separate the florets and use them like little stars; they are particularly effective in groups.

Zinnia   Flowers like this, with hard middles, need pressing petal by petal. Pull them off gently without tearing and make sure that they do not overlap on the blotting paper.

What Leaves Shall I Press?

You will certainly want to press various leaves to add to your designs.

Ash   They dry black and so are useful for dramatic effect, especially when overlaid with pale flowers or petals.

Beech   Dry when young in early spring and they will turn a pale green. Later in the season they will give you the autumnal color you might expect.

Blackberry   Wait until they are turning deep red. When dried, the color will be deeper still.

Cineraria   You will certainly want to press some of these silver leaves to high light your work.

Clematis Montana   The leaves and stalks dry black, and give the effect of an artist's line in charcoal. Dry as many as you can, as you will be surprised how many you need in arrangements.

Honeysuckle   The leaves dry a very dark brown, darker than any autumn leaf, and so they give strength and weight to flower pictures.

Ivy   There's nothing to compare with the shape of an ivy leaf. Somehow it is especially pretty in pictures, greetings cards and so on with a nostalgic, Victorian feeling.

Japanese Maple   The leaves change season by season and you will want to pick some at every stage, and to use some on the paler, reverse side. They are good for butterfly wings.

Oak   Again, pick some of the young leaves in early spring, and some in autumn. You will find that you use them in quite different ways.

Prunus   The trees grown for the ornamental quality of the blossom in spring are also rewarding material for pressing. The leaves vary from deep cyclamen to the darkest plum color.

Raspberry   As already mentioned, the raspberry leaf is particularly worthwhile for the silvery color to be found on the under side of the leaf. Pick some of varying sizes so that you have plenty of selection.

Obviously, this list cannot be complete, and every enthusiast who has become aware of the garden, field and roadside as a source of raw material for pressing will want to experiment. To give your flowers and leaves the best chance of pleasing you, lay them very carefully on the blotting paper, making sure that no two overlap. Label each page with a full description of the materials there, and save yourself hours of frantic searching for the very petal or frond to use in the designs on the following pages.

Dried flowers arranged in a glass make a perfect present for a friend in town – they will never need watering, dusting or rearranging

Flower-Decked Table Accessories

You can practice simple pressed flower arrangements by decorating a set of place mats, coasters, and napkin rings. These are pretty, thoughtful presents for children to make and give.

You will need: Thin cardboard (the sizes are given under the heading for each item); newspaper; wallpaper paste (powder); a piece of self-adhesive transparent plastic covering slightly larger than the cardboard; brushes for paint and paste; bowl; spoon; fabric adhesive; pressed flowers, leaves and stalks; paint.

To make the napkin rings:

Pour three cupfuls of water into a bowl. Sprinkle 3 level teaspoonfuls of wallpaper paste into the water. Stir well and let stand for 15 minutes.

Cut a piece of cardboard 1½ inches wide and 7 inches long for each napkin ring you wish to make. Curl, then glue the cardboard to form a circle.

Tear the newspaper into narrow strips and brush them with paste. Wind them around the circle to strengthen it. You will need three layers. Smooth the outside surface with fingertips to make it level and free from air bubbles. Paint any color you choose (ours were pink) and let dry.

Make an arrangement of pressed flowers and leaves for each napkin ring. Keep the designs in the same scale, but vary colors or the actual flowers you use. Then each member of the family will be able to recognize his napkin easily. You will find that flowers like pansies, violas and buttercups are suitable. Glue the flowers in place on the rings with a light application of the fabric adhesive in the centers only.

Cut a piece of the transparent adhesive plastic 3½ inches wide and 7 inches long for each napkin ring. Remove the backing sheet and smooth the plastic around the ring, overlapping it neatly at the back. Make ½-inch-wide snips all around the excess strip of the plastic covering, then fold each piece over and inside the ring.

To make the coasters: For each coaster, cut a 3-inch square piece of cardboard (or any other shape you wish instead).

Tear newspaper into narrow strips, as described above, brush with paste and cover the cardboard with two layers of newspaper, wrapping over the edge. Stand the mat on a piece of plastic sheet, place another piece on top, and then weight it with a heavy book or a brick so that the mat dries completely flat. When the paste has dried, paint each mat, being careful to cover the whole surface evenly, and allow to dry.

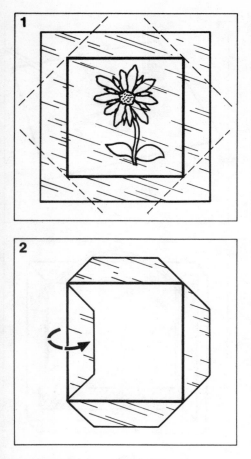

Again, glue a simple design of flowers and leaves onto each mat—these can all be the same if you wish.

Cut a 5-inch square of the plastic covering for each mat, remove backing and smooth over the front of each mat. Cut off the corners, as shown in Diagram 2, and fold the excess over the edges to the back. Smooth to give a neat finish and press down.

To make the place mats: Each of our place mats measures 7 by 9 inches. You could make yours smaller, or could add some larger ones for vegetable dishes, following these general instructions.

Cut two pieces of cardboard each 7 by 9 inches and glue firmly together.

Tear the newspaper into strips, brush with paste and cover mat with two layers of newspaper, wrapping over the edges. Stand

mat on a piece of plastic sheet, cover with another piece, and weight as before, so that it dries without buckling at the corners.

Paint each mat and leave to dry.

Glue an arrangement of flowers on each one, perhaps choosing larger flowers in the colors you have arranged on the napkin rings and coasters. Decide whether to position your design in the center of the mat or in one corner. Remember, if you bring the flowers out to the corners, your design will be appreciated even when there is a plate standing on the mat.

Cut a piece of plastic covering 10 by 12 inches, remove the backing and smooth the material onto the front of the mat. Again, cut the corners and wrap the overlap neatly onto the reverse side, pressing it down firmly. On the large place mat, petals from a daisy and a marigold are

re-formed into the flower shapes. Contrast in color and texture is provided by the pressed poppy and spray of shepherd's purse.

Child's Pendant and Matching Bracelet

The children will enjoy making and wearing this bright jewelry.

On the bracelet, a small daisy makes the center of a flower of marigold petals, and on the pendant, a stem of fuchsia is topped by a flower made of goatsbeard.

You will need: Thin cardboard (used cereal boxes would do); newspaper; wallpaper paste; fabric adhesive; paint; self-adhesive transparent plastic covering; paintbrush; length of cord long enough to go easily over head.

To make the pendant: Cut two 3-inch squares of the cardboard and glue them firmly together. Paint both sides of the cardboard a pale color and leave under a weight to dry.

Try out an arrangement of a dried flower and a spray of leaves, or a small posy of dried flowers, and, when you have a pattern that pleases you, glue the flowers to the pendant with fabric adhesive, using the handle of a paintbrush to paint spots of glue.

Cut a 5-inch square of the clear plastic, remove backing and smooth over the front of the pendant, being careful not to disturb the pressed flowers.

Cut off the corners of the plastic as shown in Diagram 1, fold each side over to the back and stick down neatly (Diagram 2).

Glue the two ends of the cord to the back of the pendant, checking first that it hangs at the right level (Diagram 3).

To make the bracelet: Sprinkle one level teaspoonful of the wallpaper paste into one teacupful of water. Stir well and let stand for 15 minutes.

Cut a piece of cardboard 1 inch wide and 10 inches long. Curl and glue into a circle to fit over the wrist. Tear newspaper into narrow strips, soak the strips in paste, then wind around the bracelet to strengthen, covering the cardboard with three layers. (Diagram 4).

Smooth to remove any bumps and air bubbles, then leave to dry.

Paint in a color to match the pendant (ours was pale yellow) and let dry again.

Make an arrangement of dried flowers or petals and leaves and glue to the bracelet.

Cut a length of clear self-adhesive plastic 2½ inches wide and 10

inches long, remove backing, then wind around bracelet, overlapping the edges at the back.

Make 1-inch snips around the excess plastic, then fold over each piece on to the inside. Press firmly to obtain a neat finish.

Pressed-Flower Pictures

Perhaps one of the prettiest ways to preserve a collection of pressed flowers is to mount and frame them. You can make a design of a nosegay of bright summer flowers, or use separate petals, leaves and smaller blooms to achieve any design you please—fantastic birds, butterflies at least as colorful as any you have ever seen, fish with intricate patterns for the scales, or an abstract, decorative collage.

In this summer nosegay, the designer has blended buttercups and a pansy, fuchsia and bindweed, with petals from poppy, marigold, clematis and daisy.

Buttercups and rose petals brighten the wing-tips of this otherwise autumnal butterfly.

It is usually best to choose a plain paper or fabric for the background, so that all the emphasis is on the flowers themselves. See how effective the brown wrapping paper background is for the small butterfly picture on this page. It is a perfect complement to the autumnal colors of the four leaves that form the wings. Notice, too, how easy it is to mix and mingle the seasons; spring buttercups provide the high lights.

You will need: A picture frame with glass. If you do not have an old one waiting to be used again, look for simple ones, like those photographed here, in the five-and-ten. They are cheap to buy and perfect for this type of

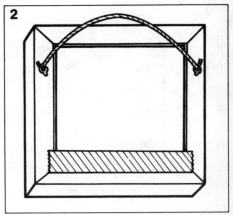

work. Material for the background. This can be felt, cotton, silk, velvet or any other smooth fabric, or use plain papers. Other requirements are fabric adhesive, a paintbrush, pressed flowers and leaves.

To make a picture Cut the background material to the right size for the frame. If it is fabric and the frame is not to have a mount, you will need to cut it slightly larger and turn in the edges neatly all around. Stick them at the back.

On this background material, begin by arranging a few flowers and leaves in the kind of design you want. For the butterfly, choose leaves of equal size and similar colors, match buttercups and petals for size and rearrange them until you have the effect you like. To move the petals and small flowers about without damaging them, push them with the tip of a paintbrush (Diagram 1).

Then, using the adhesive sparingly, stick the leaves and flowers in layers until the design is complete.

Insert the picture into the frame, making sure that the glass presses tightly against the flowers.

Seal the open edge of the frame with a gummed paper strip to prevent moisture or dust getting into the picture (Diagram 2).

When making a "nosegay" picture using a number of flowers, don't be tempted to put in too many. Too much overlapping in an arrangement of this kind looks crowded and detracts from the beauty of the individual flowers.

Table Lamp and Shade

We see summer flowers at their best on a bright, sunny day, with the light catching them at different angles and shining through the petals. It is not surprising, therefore, that pressed flowers make a most attractive decoration for a lamp and shade. You can see the effect in the color photograph.

You will need: 1 dark green wine bottle; a standard light bulb fixture; a plain drum lamp shade; clear varnish; soft varnish brush; self-adhesive transparent plastic; fabric adhesive; artist's small paintbrush.

To make the lamp: The bottle in the photograph was decorated with buttercups, daisies, a viola with a daisy center, and small fronds of fern, keeping to a mainly yellow-green color scheme.

Paint one side of the bottle with a thin layer of clear varnish and arrange the flowers in position. Leave undisturbed for about half an hour while varnish dries. Cover the flowers with another layer of varnish, leave to dry and, if necessary, repeat with a further layer (Diagram 1).

To make a shade: Arrange the design for the shade on a piece of paper and then glue each flower and leaf to the shade, applying fabric adhesive sparingly with the handle of a paintbrush.

Cut a piece of self-adhesive plastic large enough to cover the shade, and allowing a generous overlap. Remove part of the backing and begin covering the shade, starting at the back so that the overlap does not show (Diagram 2).

Trim off the excess at each side with a sharp pair of scissors.

Insert fixture into the top of the bottle, add shade, bulb and plug.

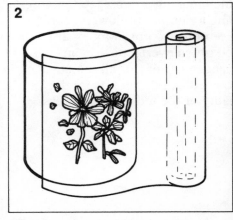

Using Dried Flowers

The materials used require little or no special treatment—though, of course, you could achieve colorful effects with other flowers, if you dried them, according to type, in containers filled with household borax, in granular or crystal preparations, or in a warm, airy place.

Satinpod seed cases, despised as weeds by some proud gardeners, dry on the plant. You simply have to rub each head between your fingers, remove the two brown, papery covers, release the seeds onto the garden for next year's crop, and use the shining sprays.

Helichrysum, or strawflowers, too, dry on the plant, though they benefit from a period hanging upside down in bunches in the attic or some other dry and dark place. They are very easy to grow, and range from the palest cream to deep, regal plum color.

Statice, known as an everlasting flower, produces sprays of minutely soft, papery trumpet shapes and is very delicate and pretty. Most florists sell it now.

Starflowers are sold in bunches dyed to practically any color of the rainbow. You will see it used in our designs with the tiny flower heads massed together in a cone, stuck into a plain candle, and in little bunches in a bell jar arrangement. It is one of the most versatile and useful of all—and is especially pretty, alternated with cloves, stuck in an orange to make a decorative, aromatic pomander.

Grasses, oats, barley and wheat can be used in their natural, sun-drenched color, or can be bought dyed. If you have the opportunity to pick your own, wait until just before the natural harvest time. If you pick them when they are green, they will be far from everlasting.

A "Candle" for Thanksgiving

The arrangement in the photograph is based on a curved teak candlestick 4 inches high by $1\frac{3}{4}$ inches wide.

The main part of the arrangement is an assortment of dried grass and seed pods, gathered on a country walk. If you cannot gather your own, you can buy packages or bunches of barley heads, oats and grasses, and bunches of dried helichrysum, in many large stores.

You will need: A candlestick (see above); a barley head; assorted dried bleached grass seed pods as available; including oats, if possible; 5–6 helichrysum heads in golden brown (or pinkish mauve); a straight rod about 4 inches long (this can be a thin stick, a broken knitting needle, etc.); white plasticine; pins.

To make: Roll some plasticine into a ball and then push into the hole for the candle, add more, if necessary, to fill the hole with a small mound above. Push the rod right down to the base of the candle hole, then turn the candlestick to be sure that the rod is absolutely straight. Now use more plasticine to build up the base around the top of the hole, and then mold it around the rod, tapering slightly toward the top. Recheck that the rod is straight!

Cut the barley stalk about 4 inches below the head, then push it down into the top of the plasticine so that the overall height, from the top of the candlestick is about 9–10 inches (not including the whiskers!). Now begin to surround the barley with delicate grass-heads, cutting them about 6 inches long and pushing down into the top of the plasticine. Continue to circle the plasticine with an assortment of grass seed pods, growing heavier and protruding at a wider angle as you

progress downward—see the illustration. Add the oats at the widest point about two-thirds of the way down (our arrangement was 6–7 inches wide at this stage).

Fill in with some more delicate heads, as illustrated, and finally encircle the top of the candlestick closely with helichrysum heads: fix these with a pin stuck through the center of the flower, the head pushed right down so that it is buried and not visible.

Flower Cone

Choose your own color scheme to suit a room. Ours was pinkish mauve helichrysums (sometimes called strawflowers), separated by bright green starflowers. The twist pattern at the top is made up of pink and violet starflowers. You can buy this from florists.

You will need: A $7\frac{1}{2}$-inch high by 3-inch diameter cone; about 18 pink (or golden brown) helichrysum heads; about 200 starflowers each in violet pink and green (or yellow/gold/green or natural/brown/green); about 50 yellow starflowers; dried grass seed heads; pins.

To make the cone: Fix the larger helichrysums around the base of the cone with pins (pushed into the "furry" center, so that the head of the pin is hidden), the petals almost touching and level with the lower edge (Diagram 1). Then fix the smaller helichrysums to form a second row above, each head set between the two below, as illustrated, petals almost touching the lower row.

Now cut the stems of some yellow starflowers about $\frac{1}{2}$-inch from the head, and push them into the cone to form the centers of a third row of flowers between the second, and directly above the first (you will find it easier to handle these tiny, papery flowers if you use a pair of tweezers). Circle these closely with as many starflower heads as necessary to form a "flower" of the right size, alternately pink and violet. When this row is finished, repeat with a fourth circle of "flowers," slightly smaller than the previous row, and positioned as before. Continue in this way to the top of the cone—which should be about seven or eight starflower circles—the "flowers" diminishing in size until the top circle is formed only of alternate single pink and violet starflower heads.

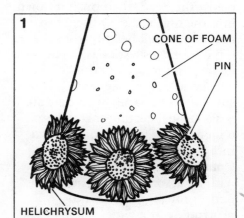

Finish with a yellow starflower right on top.

Stick grass seed pods at right-angles to the cone all around the base between the helichrysums, as illustrated. This helps to balance the cone the same way that roots support a tree.

Then divide the helichrysums and the "flower" circles with green starflower heads, so that each is separated from those around it, and all of the cone is covered.

A Centerpiece

The dramatic effect of the satinpod and fir cone arrangement is emphasized by vivid lime green flower heads contrasting sharply with the natural tones of the bleached satinpod and dark fir cones and bark. We used a pale cream candle, but you could match this to your choice of colored flower-heads instead.

You will need: A piece of cork bark about 12 inches long by approximately 4 inches at the widest point; 4 or 5 small fir cones; 4 or 5 dried flower-heads in lime green, bright green, burnt orange, gold or red; satinpod, preserved leaves, dried grasses, etc., as available; a 6–7-inch candle; white plasticine; fine wire; pins.

To make the arrangement: Take a piece of white plasticine the size of a golf ball. Push the base of the candle into the center, so that it is buried at least an inch—this will automatically flatten the base—then mold the plasticine up so that it holds the candle firmly.

Take another piece of plasticine the size of a walnut—then roll into a "sausage" and press down firmly to grip the bark over the area where you want your cascading foliage to be (Diagram 1). Secure with pins, then add more plasticine wherever necessary to build up and surround the base of the candle.

Decide positions of cones: twist a short length of wire around the stalk, so that the ends form two prongs (Diagram 2)—push these and then the base of the cone firmly down so that they are embedded in the plasticine. Use larger cones near the base of the candle, smaller on the cascade.

Push short stalks of satinpod leaves, etc., into the plasticine to form an attractive and

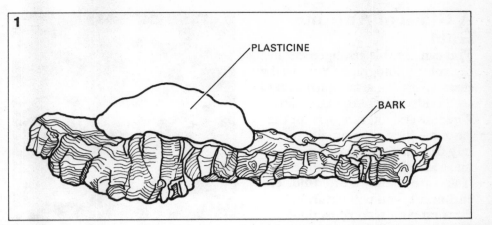

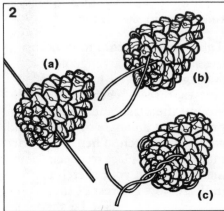

natural-looking arrangement, as illustrated, keeping it fairly low—especially at the end of the "cascade." Position all foliage at an angle to the base of the candle, so that it will not be too close to the flame.

A Glass of Autumn Gold

You can see this arrangement in the color photograph. You need a clear, sparkling glass, a handful of seed pods, and a little trimming. The flowers you can grow in the garden—they are annuals—or buy from a florist. Just a few make an effective splash of color. If you are already a dried-flower enthusiast, you will naturally draw on your own collection, adapting the design according to what you have. These could include lavender, statice, poppy heads, Chinese lanterns, skeletonized leaves, heather, cones, nuts and so on.

You will need: Six brown and yellow helichrysum heads (strawflowers); 1 gold or bleached head of barley or wheat; 12 small, bleached heads of oats; 6 Phalaris colored in brown and/or gold; 20 starflowers in each of the following colors—yellow, deep gold and brownish-green; assorted dried natural grass seed heads; a large brandy snifter; dark green plasticine; silica gel crystals (obtainable from druggists); Saran wrap; gold braid to trim; clear adhesive.

To make the arrangement: Roll a strip of plasticine the size and shape of a golf ball, then flatten the base slightly. Surround with the helichrysum heads, as illustrated, fixing them securely with a pin right through the flower (push the head of the pin down into the center, so that it will not be visible).

Trim the barley (or wheat) of the longest "whiskers," cut the stalk about an inch below the head, and then push into the center top of the plasticine. Now push a fine steel knitting needle—or similar object right down in the plasticine ball, close to the barley. This will enable you to lift and turn the arrangement without disturbing it.

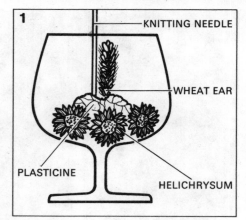

Lift it now, and lower gently into the glass (Diagram 1).

Check that the helichrysum heads are positioned correctly, and that the ear of barley is central, and not higher than the rim of the glass. Take out, make any necessary alterations, then recheck. While it is inside the glass, study the position in relation to the shape of the bowl, noting the area where the greatest width is required— and how the design needs to narrow. It is a good idea to jot this down in sketch form.

Take out, and begin to build up the shape of the arrangement by adding the heavier heads and grasses, three of each kind, evenly around the plasticine, so that they protrude at an angle to correspond with your sketch. Then lower once more into the glass to check (now make notes on your sketch to indicate how the rest of the arrangement needs to be shaped).

Now, cutting short lengths from first the oats, and then the more delicate grass heads, push them into the plasticine (holding the stems with tweezers) so that they fill out the upper two-thirds of the design, as illustrated. Check these for height and width by holding the arrangement in front of the glass, to avoid damage by repeatedly taking it in and out past the narrow rim: you can see from the illustration that the most delicate grasses extend beyond the width of the bowl, so that they are held by the sides, curving gently upward. When you are satisfied, add the bleached heads and the starflowers, to complete the middle and lower half of the design, cutting them to length (none should exceed $1\frac{1}{2}$ inches) and inserting with tweezers. You may find it helpful to make a hole first, with a needle or a pin, if the stalks are delicate. Add a few more fronds of grass, if necessary.

When the arrangement is finished, wash the glass in soapy water, then dry and polish it very thoroughly (especially inside). Tip a level teaspoonful of silica gel crystals into the base, and then very carefully lower the arrangement into the glass. Ease out the knitting needle, and use it to push any awkwardly positioned pieces in the right direction.

Cut a circle of Saran wrap $\frac{1}{4}$-inch larger than the top of the glass. Snip the excess all the way around, to form tiny tabs. Smear a little clear glue around the rim of the glass, then place the wrap over the top (making sure the under-side is free of dust or other particles), and stick the tabs around the outer rim, very gently pulling the wrap so that it is smooth.

Stick the trimming around the rim, slightly overlapping the edge.

Miniature Victoriana

Again, the arrangement consists of no more than an assortment of dried, bleached grass seed heads, with whatever else you have.

You will need: One large and one small cheap glass tumbler from a five-and-ten. Ours were 4 inches and 3 inches high respectively, and $2\frac{1}{2}$ and $2\frac{1}{4}$ inches across the base. The flowers and seed heads of your choice. For example 3 pale colored helichrysums

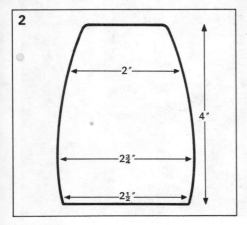

(strawflowers) for each glass; oats, dyed light and dark blue; approximately 60 starflowers for each glass, dyed in bright and in dark green; assorted dried grass heads; satinpod (optional); dark green plasticine, silica gel (obtainable from druggists); stiff white cardboard; colored paper or felt; narrow velvet ribbon or braid; clear glue and Scotch magic transparent tape.

To make each arrangement:

Turn the tumbler upside down on the cardboard and draw around the rim; cut this circle for the base.

Roll a walnut-sized ball of plasticine and flatten the base slightly; stick firmly to center of cardboard, securing further with a central pin, driven up through the cardboard. Fix the helichrysum heads against the plasticine, close to the cardboard, push a pin right through the flower, to hold it securely, burying the head in "furry" center.

Measuring the satinpod against the tumbler, push one or two short stalks into the plasticine (if this is omitted, use grasses instead). Now place the tumbler gently over the arrangement, to check the height, width and positioning. Remove the tumbler and make any necessary alterations—then recheck: study carefully in relation to the shape of the tumbler, noting where the balance of foliage is required. Sketch the measurements as in Diagram 2.

Add tiny stalks of colored oats, cutting them a little shorter than the satinpod: then begin to fill out the shape of the arrangement, inserting each stem with tweezers (you may find it helpful to make a hole first, with a needle or pin). Add the heavier grass heads first, then the starflowers, and finally the more delicate fronds of grass. Cut the starflower stems in varying lengths, to occupy the lower two-thirds of the

arrangement, pressing some right against the plasticine to fill any gaps. Check for height and width by holding in front of the tumbler.

When you have completed the arrangement to your satisfaction, wash the glass in soapy water, then dry and polish it thoroughly. Smear the cardboard base around the plasticine, with glue, then sprinkle some silica gel crystals over so that they stick.

Very carefully lower the tumbler over the arrangement: then turn it upside down, so that the base card rests on the rim of the glass. Stick transparent tape around the rim, to cover about $\frac{1}{4}$-inch of the glass, the remainder overlapping; snip this into tiny tabs, then stick firmly down all around edge of cardboard. Cut a circle of felt or paper the same size, and stick over base to neaten.

Finally, stick velvet or braid around rim to cover the tape.

Apothecary Jar

Here's another alternative, a glass-lidded storage jar from a five-and-ten. As before, a piece of cardboard is cut slightly smaller than the base—it has to go in the narrower neck—and a piece of plasticine pressed onto it. The arrangement is begun with the tallest grasses, as curving and frondy as you can find. Because you will not want to keep pushing your arrangement into the jar, it is best to make a sketch, drawing around the outside of the jar with a pencil, and then checking the height and width of the flowers and grasses against that as you add them. When you are satisfied that they are in the right scale and look balanced and attractive, push a knitting needle through the plasticine and carefully lower the arrangement into the neck. Tie a ribbon bow around the stopper if you like.

Flower Basket

Transform a simple cane fruit basket into a container for a permanent flower display—and see how pretty it looks against a plain, textured wall. Coverings like grass cloth or burlap are particularly suitable backgrounds for this kind of decoration.

You will need: A shallow, round wicker fruit or bread basket measuring about 9 inches in diameter; 2 styrofoam balls, one $2\frac{1}{2}$ inches in diameter and the other $3\frac{1}{2}$ inches; fine string; about 18 helichrysum heads; satinpods; grass seed heads, as available; pins; wire to hang.

To make the flower basket:
Cut the styrofoam balls in half, using a sharp knife; put one half of each aside for the Oriental Wall Hanging. Now cut a slice $\frac{1}{2}$-inch thick off the flat face of the larger ball, leaving the smaller as it is. Fix ties through each, as described for

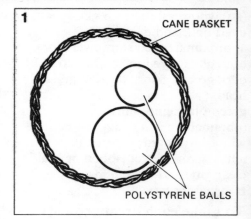

wall hanging, but in reverse, so that the ends extend from the rounded side: tie inside basket in the position shown in Diagram 1.

Cover the flat faces of the balls closely with helichrysum heads, overlapping the edges: finally, add satinpods, grasses, etc., as illustrated.

Fix a loop of wire at the back to hang.

Flowers and Candles Go Together—
especially at Christmas

The beautifully decorated candles sold in the shops are so expensive, that we have included some simple ideas for decorating them yourself.

Top row, left to right:
1. A piece of bark makes a holder for a plain gold candle. If you can, scoop out a hollow with a penknife, line it with plasticine and push the candle firmly into it. Decorate with a single helichrysum flower, pushed tight against the candle and secured with a glass-headed pin.

2. A plain white household candle is spiraled with an ivy-leaf decal. The base is a plain dark green metal candle stand (an old saucer would do) with a walnut-sized piece of plasticine pushed into the middle to hold the candle. For a final touch, and carrying out the clinging motif of the transfer, a circlet of variegated ivy leaves. These will dry slowly indoors— but then the candle won't last forever, either!

3. This is one of the prettiest candle ideas around. Start with a plain pink pillar candle, a short, chubby one, and pierce a pattern of holes on it with a fine sewing needle. Press a starflower head into each hole, using tweezers to handle the flowers. The candle stands on a plain saucer.

4. No flowers this time—simply a dark glass holding an ordinary nightlight. Only it's not quite so ordinary now—we painted the outside a matte black.

5. A delicate Dutch design, a decal again, decorated another household candle. If you wish to add a circle of dried pink flowers, to echo the color scheme, so much the better.

Center row, left to right:
6. The base of the tall, golden candle is buried in a mound of

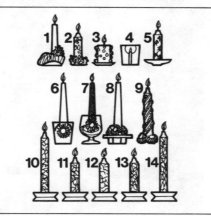

plasticine which is disguised by a circle of yellow helichrysum flower-heads pressed in with pins.

7. The same treatment for a dark green candle, secured with plasticine into the base of a brandy glass. One of these for each guest at the dinner table would, surely, be just as acceptable as a liqueur!

8. A cheap glass candleholder, the cheapest we could find, is given a lift by a bright pink candle and a

cluster of matching flowers. Any container you use will look pretty, this way.

9. A deep red barley candy twist candle has a spiral of starflower heads. Each one is stuck in a hole made with a fine needle. In this case the base was a piece of thick cardboard weighted with plasticine and finished with 5 red and yellow helichrysums.

Bottom row:
These candles are so decorative themselves that they need no further adornment. They are ordinary household candles, with a dribbled pattern made by melting children's wax crayons, used as you would sealing wax. Using two or three colors in this fashion gives this marbled effect when the candle is rotated slowly in front of a candle flame. But it is not a game for the children to play. It really is playing with fire.

Oriental Wall Hanging

The natural color and texture of the bamboo place mat—available for a few cents at any department store—is an ideal background for an arrangement of dried helichrysums (strawflowers) and grasses. You can choose flowers in pale, muted pinks and mauves, or sharp, stinging yellows and oranges.

You will need: A bamboo place mat approximately 12 by 18 inches (ours had a design on the front so we used the plain back); a thick bamboo garden cane; ½-yard lacing cord; 2 styrofoam balls, cut in half; fine string; about 42 helichrysum heads; oats; grass seed heads as available; clear Scotch tape; pins.

To make the wall hanging: Use the half styrofoam balls left over from the flower basket design. Make "ties" on each half ball as follows: thread a tapestry or darning needle with fine string and push it through from the flat side of the ball at the angle shown in Diagram 1. Then push back again, making a "stitch" on the rounded side about ¾-inch long. Repeat on the opposite side. Place in position on the plain side of the mat, as shown in Diagram 2, and then thread the ends of the string through to the back and tie securely.

Reserve three well-shaped, dark heads, then cover the balls closely with helicrysums, fixing securely with pins pushed through the flower centers. Allow the outer ones to overlap, and then fill out the arrangement with a few more heads, stuck to the mat with clear glue. Push oats or grasses into the balls at an attractive angle, as shown. Stick the three remaining heads in the lower corner as illustrated.

Cut the bamboo cane into two pieces long enough to overlap mat about 1 inch at each end: tie

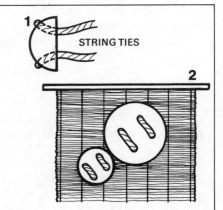

1 STRING TIES

2

neatly to upper and lower edges of hanging, hiding the knots at the back. Unravel each end of the lacing cord and tie securely to top bamboo. It is a good idea to secure the odd ends of string and cord at the back, and to reinforce the knots with a band of transparent tape behind the upper and lower edges.

TAKE A BUNDLE OF RUSHES

Think of rushes and you think of, what? Moses baskets . . . rushlights, their ends dipped in tallow . . . marshy waterways with wild fowl darting in and out of the edges . . . medieval houses with rushes strewn on the floor (changed only once a year!) or present-day room settings, with woven rush matting still providing a natural and practical floorcovering?

Certainly you will think, too, of table mats, shopping baskets, fruit bowls, lidded baskets—all of which are included in this section. But would you, as our contributor K. Whitbourn does, see rushes as an endlessly versatile artists' material?

To Mrs. Whitbourn, rushes have provided the inspiration for a variety of abstract and not-so-abstract pictures with, she says, the material "working like satin ribbon." We show two of her pictures in a color photograph. One of them is simply a panel of cross-weave which emphasizes the incredible, natural beauty of the material with all its different textures and shades. The other uses rushes, worked on a background of scrim.

To find your materials:
You can order rushes through craft stores or centers throughout the country; or you might be able to cut your own. Children love to wade into the water in their rubber boots. The rushes are ready in July, when the brown seed heads have formed; cut them as near the roots as possible, for the "butt" end is the strongest. The rushes can then be tied into bundles or "bolts" (you can see one in the color photograph and stood or hung in a cool, airy place. They will probably not be dried and ready to use until September, by which time they will have lost about half of their original weight.

Most of the small rushes, found beside ponds and along river banks, moorland rushes, and water iris are suitable for weaving and plaiting, too, and should be treated in the same way. Dark moorland rushes are particularly effective when combined with large rushes—see the fruit bowl on page 102.

The night before you want to use them, take out as many rushes as you will need. Wrap them in a damp blanket or old sheet, so that they absorb moisture right through the stem. Then, just before use, wipe each one separately with a damp sponge or cloth to clean it and remove the air trapped in the stem. If you do not do this, the rush will shrink too much at a later stage and leave ugly gaps in your work.

It is most important to grade the rushes before you start work, to obtain an even weave. The only exception here is the decorative panel, where the variety in the widths is part of the design. Generally, you will need large, thick rushes for big baskets and floor matting, and medium and fine ones for shopping baskets, flower containers and toys.

When working pairing weave, choose thicker rushes for the stakes (all of equal thickness) and uniformly thinner ones for the weavers. For cross-weave, both stakes and weavers should be of equal size.

Years ago I went to a basket weaving course deep in a cereal-growing region of the country. The instructor, a retired farmhand, constantly emphasized the importance of matching straw for thickness, so often, in fact, that he is teased about it to this day. "It doesn't matter what you do," former pupils will encourage him to chant, "so long as you select your straw." And Mr. Select-Your-Straw taught far more than the art of making the intricate, traditional shapes from the last season's harvest. He taught patience, the key to all craftwork, and the pride the craftsman has in handing on his skills to a new generation.

General hints on rushwork
Keep a damp sponge or cloth beside you, and wipe down each rush as you work. This minimizes the risk of splitting. Avoid the temptation to work in full sun or

in front of the fire or—less of a temptation—on a cold, frosty day. Any extreme conditions will adversely affect the rushes.

When measuring for the length required for stakes, allow an extra 4 inches at each side for border, unless otherwise stated in the pattern.

Begin working with the thin end of the rush.

If a weaver breaks, don't worry. It is easy to join in a new one. Place the thin end of another rush over the break, overlapping for at least 2 inches. Work them together until the new length is secure.

For a neat finish, trim all ends slantwise. This is less bulky and less obtrusive than a horizontal cut.

More on neatness: hold finished borders against a wooden block and tap gently with a wooden mallet to flatten.

Press plaits firmly beneath a thick, damp cloth before sewing into coils. Craftsmen used to pass them through a mangle, but not many of us have one in our kitchens nowadays.

When sewing a coiled plait together, be sure to keep the stitches in the center of the plait. Mats are meant to be reversible so the stitching must not show.

To keep your rush designs in tiptop condition, April showers are the answer. Stand or hang the articles in a light shower, then let them dry in a good strong breeze—never in front of a fire.

Tools You really do not need any special tools, but a football lacing awl, costing very little at a sporting goods store, is ideal for threading rushes. In addition, sharp scissors, blocks of wood or large flowerpots to use as molds, string and large-eyed needles for

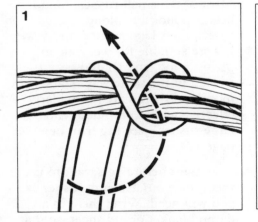

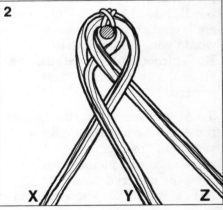

tying, and a wooden mallet are all useful.

Simple plaiting with rushes
The photograph shows two mats made of rushes and one, the oval one in the center, of water iris.

The round rush mat has a 12-inch diameter and takes about 6½ yards of three-plait, 1 inch thick. The oval iris mat, 15 by 11 inches, takes about 14 yards. For the oval rush mat, 17 by 12½ inches, allow

about 8½ yards of plait. A doormat is made on the same principle, and will require about 50 yards of thick plait.

To start, take three rushes of equal thickness and tie them in the center (see Diagram 1) with a long piece of 3-ply seaming string. This will be threaded into a large-eyed needle to join the plait into a coil.

Place mats, shopping bags, flower panels and containers, a cushion and a rug – all things to make from a bundle of rushes

To make "scrolls":

Diagram 2 shows the three lengths of rush tied in the middle, and now being used double.

Place the constrictor knot over a nail in the wall. Using the right hand only for plaiting, keep the rushes in place under the left thumb. Make a simple plait by taking the ends X over Y, and Z over X. Now bring Y over Z and continue in this way, keeping the plait even.

A curtain ring of suitable size may be slipped over the plait as a guide. If the ring fails to run freely, the plait is getting too thick and thinner rushes should be used.

Work in a new rush, overlapping the thin end, as required (see hints on opposite page).

Using the length of string with which you made the constrictor knot in the center of the rushes, start sewing the plait into a coil.

For the round mat, as shown on the left, form a tight coil with one end of the plait and hold it securely in place with stab stitches. Remember that the stitches must not show on either side of the mat, as it is to be reversible.

Continue coiling the work tightly and secure with strong stitches as you proceed.

To neaten the mat when you come to the end of the plait, weave the plait into the row below and sew it in position. In this way, the end will not show at all.

To make the oval mat, which is 15 inches long and 11 inches wide, fold over the first 4 inches of the plait.

Using a strong needle and string, as before, work up the length and back again, pulling the string tightly and bringing it back into position for stitching around the mat.

To establish the correct proportion for an oval (and you can, of course, make a mat of any size) subtract the measurement of the width from that of the length to find the length of plait you fold over to start the center.

Once you have made coiled mats like those on the facing page, you can add decorative motifs to your designs. The floor mat, above, has a 26-inch diameter, and is made from rushes plaited singly, not doubled as before. This gives a plait with ¾-inch thickness.

The plait is coiled until it measures 16 inches in diameter, then the scrolls are made.

For each scroll, take 45 inches of plait, mark the center, and coil from each end toward the marker, securing firmly with stab stitch (see Diagram 3).

When 11 scrolls have been worked, place them around the mat, stitch firmly, and then work another 7 rows to finish.

Rushes used as an embroidery thread and woven to show the color and texture to the best possible advantage – two highly original and decorative panels

Fruit Bowl Plaited in Cattails

It is impossible to talk in clearly defined terms of color when describing rushes, because in each type, indeed from each plant, stems will be found of a variety of shades.

But whereas the large rushes (*scirpus lacustrus*) are mainly green, the cattails used to work this fruit bowl are dull olive green; in other lights looking more like a heap of old autumn leaves.

These rushes are thinner than the large green ones and so, if one is to combine the two in one design, allowance has to be made for this difference in texture.

Here, the rim only is in the green rushes, which give a pale, contrasting finish to the work.

To work a raised shape for a circular bowl of this kind, or the base of a round basket (of the type popular for sewing baskets), start as for a coiled mat.

When you have formed a large enough coil for the base, raise the plait half a width for two rounds, then continue coiling, making sure that you keep the sides straight. To give a strong edge to the bowl, cut a pliable willow or hazel rod the length of the circumference of the bowl. Join the ends neatly with adhesive tape.

Thread four blunt needles with narrow green rushes, and weave them into the top coiled row of the basket until they are attached securely.

Place the hoop of rod on top of the basket (Diagram 1) and, using an equivalent of satin stitch, carry each rush forward, over and under the rod. Each "stitch" must be close to the previous one so that a continuous binding is formed and the strengthening rod is completely obscured.

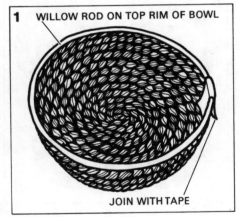

1 WILLOW ROD ON TOP RIM OF BOWL

JOIN WITH TAPE

This edge looks like a more complicated edging called a "four-rod wale."

Cross-Weave and Pairing

It takes only a few minutes to master the art of cross-weave (Diagram 2) and pairing (Diagram 3) with rushes, and then there is no end to the designs you can make. In this section, they include place mats, a cushion, a

2

flower container, a panel for dried flowers and a toy.

Cross-weave To make the place mat, shown ready for the border, below, start by cutting 10 medium-sized stakes each 18 inches long, from the butt end. Lay 5 stakes side by side on a table, thick and thin ends alternating, and hold them down with your left hand. Lift the second and fourth stake and insert the sixth one. Lift the first, third and fifth stakes, in turn, on each side of the one you have just positioned, and insert stakes 7 and 8. Now, in turn, lift the second and fourth stakes again, at the outside edges, and insert the remaining two. You will have an interlaced pattern just over 2 inches square. This is a cross-weave—and that's all it is.

Remember that your work is likely to shrink a little as it dries out, so take special care to push the stakes very tightly together, as shown in the sketch, below, left.

Pairing Weave   Take a fine rush, thinner than those used for the cross-weave stakes, and bend it in half. Loop it around the stake in the top left-hand corner of the work, as it faces you. Thinking of the two weavers as X and Y (see diagram below), pass X over Y in front of the first stake and behind the second stake. Pass weaver Y over X and in front of the second stake and behind the third stake.

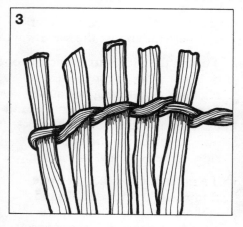

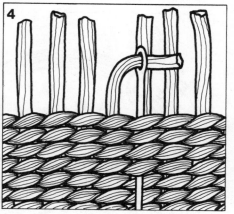

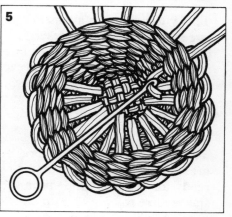

Use the rush weavers in this way until the mat is the size you require.

Turn the mat as you work, so that you are always working from left to right.

After the first two rounds of pairing, pull the corner stakes gently toward each other, to form a spiderweb type circle.

When you come nearly to the end of one weaver, there are two ways

of joining in another one. Either you can add another rush tip, having broken off the weak tip and, without letting the end show, work it double with the short one until the new one is secure. Or you can loop another rush over the stake you are to work next, as you did to begin, and work both ends double with the short ones. This is possibly more reliable. Cut off the ends, slantwise, as close to the work as you can.

To finish, push the eye of the awl up through four rounds and thread the stake before it (Diagram 4), bring it down and trim it close to the work. Diagram 5 shows how this is done.

Different Effects with the Same Weave

Yucca mat

The large wooden-looking leaves used for the center cross-weave panel in the mat below are yucca, a native plant of America. The leaves must be thoroughly dried before being woven, because otherwise a loose, untidy-looking weave would result.

This yucca mat has a panel of five stakes each way, worked exactly as described for the place mat on the opposite page. As each leaf is between $1\frac{1}{4}$ and $1\frac{1}{2}$ inches wide, the panel measures about $7\frac{1}{2}$ inches before the pairing border is added.

This, too, is worked as before, in green rushes. When the mat is ready for finishing, the yucca stakes have to be rolled up and twisted so that they will go through the eye of the awl. Then they are brought through four rows of pairing weave and cut off neatly.

Portable cushion

As neat as a handbag to take with you on a picnic, to your favorite sporting event, or to use as a kneeler when gardening (it's amazingly soft), this cushion uses the two techniques you have mastered already. And yet it looks so different from the yucca mat.

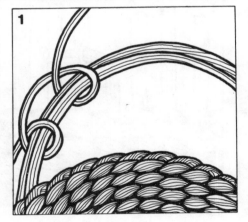

For the cross-weave stakes, take 7 *pairs* of stakes each way, using them double, one on top of the other. Weave them to make the center panel and then work 2 rounds of pairing. Now open the 4 corner stakes and use them singly, to give you a circle. After the next 2 rounds, open the second ones from the corner and so on until the middle stakes are opened last. Continue pairing until the circle is the size you require—this

one was 12 inches across. Work another side in just the same way.

To join the pieces together, lay one over the other, wrong sides together, and taking one stake from each mat, twist them around each other and thread the ends away, each down the opposite side, under six rows of pairing.

To make the handle, take one thin rush, bend it double and make a slip loop under three rounds of pairing. Thread the other two ends in and out of the pairing back toward the looped end, and tie them securely together, leaving a loop large enough to hold. Thread another thin rush and weave it through several rows of pairing, to secure it. Bind it tightly around the handle loop, as closely as possible. Diagram 1 shows this worked loosely, for clarity. Secure firmly when you reach the end.

Cone Doll Toy

Do you remember the cone dolls that used to be so popular? At first, they look just like cones with a stick in the middle, and then, magic, up pops a doll, as impudent as a jack-in-the-box.

To make the one shown here, which uses pairing weave, cut from cardboard a half-circle with a 6-inch radius. Wrap to form a cone, leaving a hole at the bottom wide enough to push a $\frac{1}{4}$-inch dowel through.

Cover the cone with rush stakes, thin ends at the bottom; allow an extra 8 inches for the border. Tie a piece of string around to hold them in place while you work.

Starting at the bottom, and again using thin rushes, cover the cone with pairing weave. As the cone gets wider, it will be necessary to add in extra stakes. To do this, simply slot new stakes over the ones you are working, and take your pairing weave over them singly as you come to them.

When you have covered the cone, work a double plait border, as described below.

Push the awl through the top 4 rows of pairings, thread each of the weavers in turn and bring them down under 4 rows of pairing, using the stakes.

To make the doll, you will need a $1\frac{1}{2}$-inch diameter wooden ball for the head, a 15-inch length of dowel and scraps of material. Drill a hole in the wooden ball large enough to take the dowel. Glue the top of the dowel and push it firmly in.

From the fabric scraps, cut a simple T-shaped dress, the width of the top of the cone. Attach the top with glue to the top of the dowel, just below the head. Cut out hand shapes from scraps of felt and glue to the arms of the

dress. To finish, add a few strands of wool for hair and with felt pens draw a face, either funny or serious depending on your mood!

To make the double plait border: The stakes will need to extend about 8 inches above the top of the cone for this type of border.

For the first row (Diagram 1), take each stake behind the next two, and leave outside. 2nd row: take each stake under the next two, and up (Diagram 2). To finish, take each stake behind the next two, and down. To do this, push the awl or large-eyed needle up, under four rows of pairing, thread each stake in turn, and draw it down through the plait and the pairing (Diagram 3).

Trim the ends slantwise, as usual.

An alternate way of finishing the top of the cone is the border for the place mat.

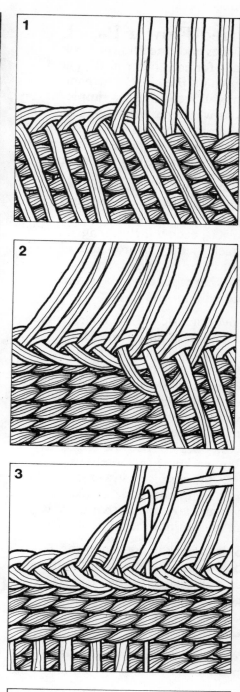

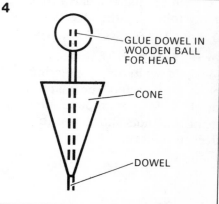

4

GLUE DOWEL IN WOODEN BALL FOR HEAD

CONE

DOWEL

Dried-Flower Panel

Rushes and dried flowers look made for each other in the panel shown on the right. The panel—you will recognize the simple cross-weave pattern—will last indefinitely. When they fade, the flowers can be replaced with a new arrangement, and so it goes on.

To make one like this, take a piece of masonite measuring 20 by 5 inches. Cut two $\frac{1}{4}$-inch dowels, each 7 inches long and attach them to the top and bottom of the board, using masking tape (it will be covered and will not show).

Cover one side of the board, which will be the front, with rushes pushed closely together. Bring them around the dowels, and across the back of the board, as if setting up the warp threads on a loom. Slip two more lengths of dowel under these stakes, so that the work does not become too tight. Remove these as you proceed. Join the rushes neatly at the back, with reef knots and, if necessary, add an extra one so that there is an uneven number.

Starting at the bottom of the board, work over and under in cross-weave until the board is covered. When the weaving tightens, then it is time to remove the two extra dowels.

Work up to the top and finish neatly.

To finish the panel make a rope handle following the directions given for the basket on page 109.

For the final flourish, make 4 monkey's fist knots, as described below, onto each of the 4 ends of dowel. A close-up photograph of one of the knots shows you the effect to achieve.

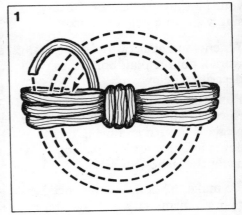

To make a monkey's fist knot:

Take a strong rush and wind three times around the hand, three times around the middle of the hank, three times through the loops of the first hank—see Diagram 1. Work the knot as tightly as possible. Using a strong knitting needle, push a hole in the knot, glue the end of one of the pieces of dowel, and secure the knot firmly. Make three more in the same way.

A Pretty Flower Basket

The indefinable green-yellow-brown tones of dried leaves, cones, seed pods and grasses form a perfect partnership with a rush container. And no matter how much one likes to have fresh flowers in every room, it must be admitted that there are times when they are too expensive to buy, or it is too wet to go out into the garden to pick them. And on those occasions it is a great comfort to be able to transform a room or a corner by an "everlasting" dried arrangement.

The basket we show here was made around a small cylindrical metal container, which now holds a block of dry artificial holding material (plasticine would do, but it is sometimes difficult to push the delicate, dried stems into it).

The base of the basket, and the lid, are simple cross-weave and pairing—where would we be without them?—and the sides of the basket are a continuation of the pairing.

Measure the stakes by laying one across the base of the container you are to work around, and up the sides to the top. Allow an extra 4 inches which will be taken up by the double plait border at the bottom, and 8 inches for the border at the top.

Our basket measured 5 inches in diameter, and was 3 inches deep. Each stake, therefore, was approximately 24 inches long.

Make the base by using a five-each-way cross-weave panel, and then enough rows of pairings (ours needed 6 rows) to cover the base of the container. Add in extra stakes, one at each corner, as you work.

To give the basket extra stability, make a double plait border at the base (following the directions given for the top of the cone doll but without threading in the stakes). Continue with the pairing weave up the side of the container, until you have covered the top. Work another row of double plait, this time bringing the ends of the stakes under 4 rows of pairing.

The lid is 6 inches in diameter, again started with a five-by-five cross-weave. The pairing rows are finished off with another double plait border. Extra care should be taken to finish this neatly, because when the basket lid is propped open (as in the photograph) the inside will show.

The lid is sewn to the back of the basket with a few firm stitches, using thick rushes—not string.

Three Strong Baskets

The first of the three is particularly versatile. Basically it is a picnic basket but is equally serviceable for taking swimming things, a book and other oddments for a lazy day on the beach.

Picnic basket

The base of the basket measures $7\frac{1}{2}$ by 5 inches and it is $12\frac{1}{2}$ inches tall, including the lid. It was made over a tin box. You would need to adapt your measurements to the size of your mold, or cut a block of wood to size, because baskets of this kind must be shaped around something solid. This is the only way of keeping the sides straight (see Diagram 1).

To find the length of the stakes you will need, measure once around the basket, underneath on the long side, up both sides to the top, and then add 8 inches. Now measure as before, but this time along the short side of the base, allowing an extra 8 inches again, for the border. Cut enough stakes to cover the base when closely packed side by side.

Set the stakes out as usual for cross-weaving, and make enough weave to cover the base. Now tie the base to the mold you are using or, if it is wooden, secure it lightly with thin staples. Before turning, strengthen the base in this way: with the work on its side, turn each stake under the next two, and back up.

Turn the stakes up the sides to begin the pairing and reverse pairing which makes the "fabric" of the design.

Diagram 2 shows reverse pairing which, used in alternate rows with the pairing weave you have used before, gives the appearance of knitting.

As you can see, this reverse pairing differs from pairing weave only in

that each weaver is taken under, instead of over the other one, before moving on.

Start in one corner with pairing and at the opposite (diagonal) corner, with another weaver, start with reverse pairing. Work these around alternately to the top of the tin box, and finish with a border as for the place mat already described.

For the lid, work in cross-weave, or a continuation of the pairing

reverse pairing pattern, whichever you prefer, until the work is slightly larger than the base.

Cast off 8 stakes in the middle of the long sides of the lid.

The "casting off" process is carried out in the same way as the simple border on the round mat, and a corresponding appearance is achieved in the "casting on" by pairing over each new stake halfway down its length, turning it

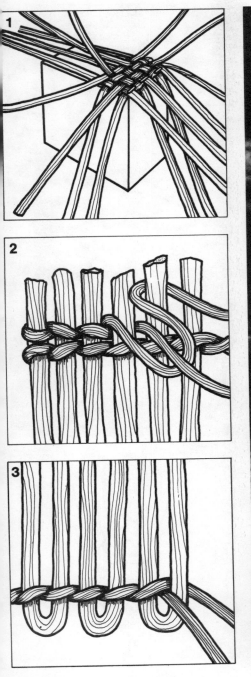

upward and pairing again (See Diagram 3).

Tie the lid onto the mold over the base and work 6 rows of pairing down the sides.

To work the rope handle, thread 4 good rushes into the basket, below the fourth round of pairing; pull them halfway through. Turn the basket with the opening facing you, and pick up the outside 4 rushes in your right hand. Twist them firmly to the right and place them in your left hand.

Now pick up the inside 4 rushes and twist them to the right; lift them over the others to the left. Change over in this way until the handle is a comfortable length and weave the ends away neatly into the same side of the basket, so that the handle will pass through the slit in the lid.

Make another handle in the same way.

Bucket-shaped shopping basket

This type of basket has a comfortingly familiar look about it—it is a shape that has been copied in all kinds of materials—leather, vinyl, canvas, denim—yet none looks as "right" as the rush basket we show below.

One of the signatures of Mrs Whitbourn's work is the surprising finishing touches she gives to otherwise everyday designs. On this basket, for example, the huge, flamboyant Turk's-head knot on the outside. (There is a smaller one, for comfort in carrying, on the other side.)

To make the bucket basket:
Even without reading the instructions you know you can begin by making a cross-weave and pairing weave circle.

The basket is worked over a 10-inch earthenware flower pot Measure underneath the flower pot and up the sides to determine the length and number of the stakes you will need, allowing an extra 8 inches for the border. Cut them, choosing rushes of equal thickness.

Take this measurement again, under the pot, up both sides and this time over the top, allowing enough for a comfortable hold. This measurement is for the handle, so remember that you have to put things into the basket and get them out without a struggle!

Using thick rushes, work this length in three-plait. Whip around both ends of the plait with fine string to prevent fraying and abut the ends firmly and sew them together (as shown in Diagram 1).

Work enough cross-weave and rounds of pairing weave to cover the base of the pot.

Turn the stakes up the sides and add the finished plait. Work up the sides in pairing weave covering the plait and two or three stakes with a long stroke.

Four inches from the top, make a Turk's-head knot from fine plaited rush over the plaited handle. Follow the Diagrams 2, 3 and 4.

First make your plait from the finest rushes you can find. The completed plait should be little more than $\frac{1}{4}$-inch thick and 2 or 3 yards in length.

Work 2 rush plaits at right angles

through the handle plait, giving 4 equal lengths (Diagram 2). Take each end over the next on the right and then each under the next one to the right (Diagram 3). With a blunt needle, thread each end and follow around, doubling each round and then tripling each round (Diagram 4). Pull the knot tight and draw all ends close to the thick handle plait, and trim.

Continue the basket in pairing weave without taking the handle into the work until the knot is passed. Then include the handle again and work to the top of the basket. Finish with a border as described for the place mat.

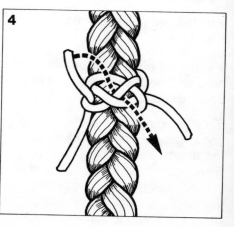

Close-up showing the Turk's-head knot which appears to secure the handle, but in fact just covers it—decoratively.

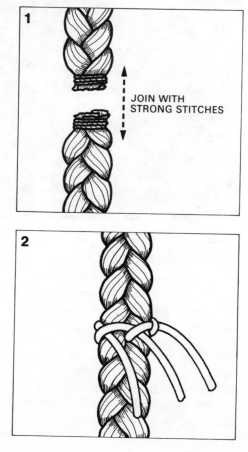

JOIN WITH STRONG STITCHES

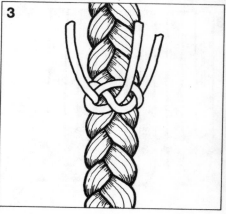

A five-sided book basket

Imagine any schoolgirl swinging along with her textbooks and notebooks in this basket, with that head-of-the-class feeling showing in every step! Its long, narrow shape is ideally suited, too, to carrying knitting, crochet, macramé, your favorite hobby material of the moment. And it is, in fact, the simplest to make of our three baskets.

Cut a piece of hardboard 17 by 11 inches. That is the measurement of the basket, taken from the highest point. Smooth away any rough edges.

Measure stakes around the length of the hardboard, to cover the back and front, allowing an extra 4 inches on each side for the border. Cut enough stakes to cover the board closely.

Using thick rushes, make a three-plait long enough to go right around the board, vertically, and to allow for a comfortable handle. This one was 49 inches long. Join the plait as described for the bucket basket.

Slip it into position over the board, join at the bottom, arrange the stakes, and tie them in place.

Work in pairing weave from the bottom of the basket, making a long stroke over the handle each time you come to it.

When you have worked 12 inches of pairing, start shaping for the top. Take the 2 end stakes together after each 4 rows of pairing, crossing the weavers over each other at the end of the row and working back in reverse pairing, that is, under the weaver instead of over it. Finish neatly around the plait.

Bring each stake down, on the inside of the work, in front of the one on the right of it and cut off, slantwise, close to the work.

A Picture with a Difference

Take a bundle of rushes, this section is headed. And, to make the picture shown on the right, that is almost all you do. Take a bundle of rushes, a handful of leaves (yucca leaves, in this case) and weave a picture.

As you can see from the color photograph, this panel of woven rushes illustrates, more than anything, the delightful range of colors, subtly blending, subtly contrasting, to be found in rushes.

The textures are interesting, too, from the graining on the wide, brown yucca leaves, like watermarks on a piece of darkened parchment, to the pure, faded gold of some of the rushes.

K. Whitbourn, whose inspiration this was, says that her work was influenced by Paul Klee. And, in its turn, we hope that this development of the rushwork you have practiced already will encourage you to use rushes in this totally different way.

To make a panel of this kind—this one measures 23 by 17 inches—work the design on a table or other flat surface. When it is finished, turn in the ends neatly to the back of the work and glue to a piece of board. In this case, the simple pine frame was made specially to fit the design.

This panel is a simple cross-weave design, which depends for its interest on the color and texture of the natural materials.

Embroidering with Leaves and Rushes

This pulled work panel is as intricate as a finely detailed pen and ink drawing, and every bit as expressive.

"It's only just a piece of builder's scrim," Mrs. Whitbourn explained, with heavy understatement. A piece of builder's scrim, stretched over a piece of hardboard, and framed in natural pine; a piece of builder's scrim with the threads drawn, using other threads pulled from the selvedge, to give the material a texture and appearance which lifts it right out of the utilitarian class.

The "embroidery threads" are leaves from the scarlet poker plant, used just as they are picked, without any preparation at all. For the raised "flowers," Mrs. Whitbourn has used fine green rushes in the way that English country craftsmen use hollow straw to make "corn dolly" lanterns, making an open plait with 5 straws at a time. Equally effective in this way would be a collection (make it an uneven number, for balance) of Turk's-head knots, as described for the bucket-shaped basket.

Just for the record, this panel measures 21 by 14 inches. However, as the composition of these panels is largely a matter of individual taste, yours will probably be quite different.

A piece of work like this, created in a highly individual way, is impossible to copy step by step. But it can be an inspiration to others to start a whole new adventure with these materials or similar ones which might be more readily available in some localities.

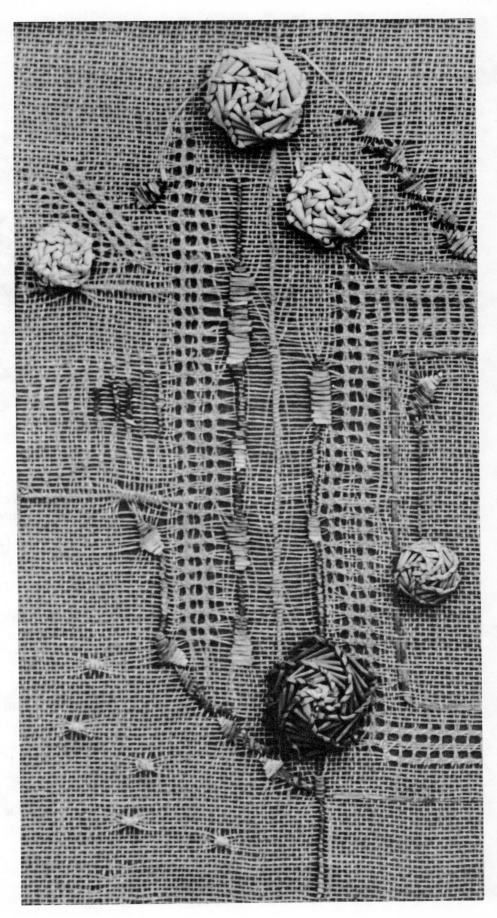

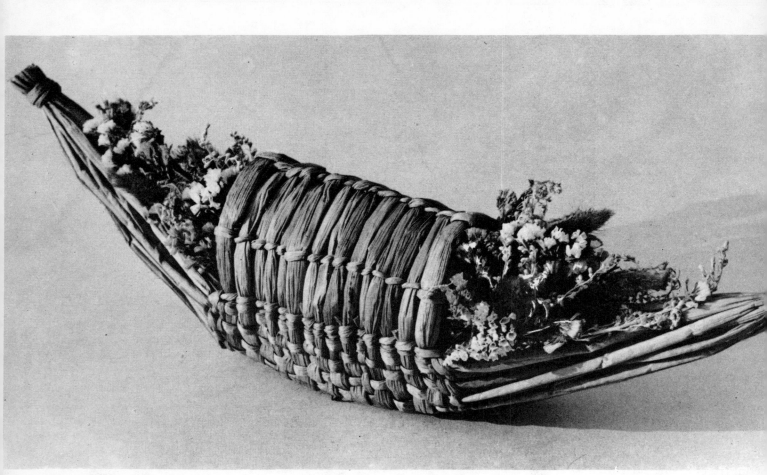

A Flower Boat

Perhaps because they grow by the waterside, rushes seem to have a natural affinity with shapes associated with waterways. One of Mrs. Whitbourn's most successful designs, a copy of Ra, the Egyptian style sail boat used by the Norwegian, Thor Heyerdahl, in his expedition across the Atlantic, looks as if it could set sail at once with its own crew of toy pioneers. Since the model, accurate down to the last detail, was too complicated for a novice to make, yet because we liked it so much, Mrs. Whitbourn designed a compromise for us, this sampan which can be now a toy, next a flower container or simply a beautiful ornament.

The total measurement, from tip to tip, is 19 inches, and the base is 6 by 2½ inches. You need 30 stakes each 20 inches long.

Make a cross-weave base, covering the whole area, and then work at least 2 rounds of firm pairing. Tie the side stakes together at each end. This gives you the boat shape.

Place a round tin can on its side on top of the base and overlap the remaining stakes over it. Make a row of pairing halfway up each of the sides and one along the top, weaving in the end to finish neatly.

Thread the ends of the stakes through the pairing in the base and trim.

Allow the boat to dry with the tin in place, so that it retains the round shape of the canopy.

To fill the boat with flowers, as shown in the photograph, wire to the base a small block of dry artificial holding material (such as plasticine) and push into it stems of statice, starflowers, dried grasses or any other small flowers. If you want to use your sampan for fresh flowers, it will need lining with a watertight container before the holding material is put inside the boat.

TAKE A PILE OF NEWSPAPERS

Papier-Mâché

Papier-mâché, the art form used to make many of the designs in this chapter, is, at its simplest, a method of combining paper and paste to make a material which can be either molded or modeled.

Like so many arts and crafts, papier-mâché is not new. Its origins go back at least two thousand years and can be traced to China. The characteristic properties of the material can be summed up as strength without weight. Even household articles such as chairs, stools and tables can be and are made from it. And, by contrast, it is used for carnival and religious masks all over the world—notably in the South American countries.

Paper strip method   There are two methods of making papier-mâché. One, known as the paper strip method, involves tearing paper—usually newspaper, because of its cheapness and availability—into small strips, soaking it first in clear water and then in a glue solution, and layering it over a mold. The work will shrink as it dries, so some kind of form is necessary. For fruit bowls, jewelry boxes or other hollow articles, the paper can be layered on to a suitable household object—a mixing or salad bowl, which can later be released, or a strong cardboard box which can be incorporated into the

material as it is built up. For flat articles, and since the soaked paper has first to be laid on something, a piece of cardboard will be adequate. And for figures and other models, an armature (rough working model) can be formed from twisted wire (coat hangers are ideal), crumpled chicken wire or even pipe cleaners.

Pulp method   The other method is to pulp the paper and paste, liquefying it so that it has almost the consistency of modeling clay. Newspapers or molded paper egg cartons give a paper clay with a rather rough texture, not unlike modeling clay. To make this, tear papers or cartons into small pieces, drop them one by one into a bowl of water and then squeeze out any further excess until you have a pulp. Put this pulp into an old pot or can (a galvanized bucket is ideal), just cover with water and boil for about 15 minutes, stirring occasionally with a stick. You can make this pulp in advance and store it well wrapped in plastic bags indefinitely. When you want to use it, knead it with enough wallpaper paste, mixed to a thick consistency, to make it easy to work, without being too sticky. The instructions in the following designs will give you full details about the quantities you will need.

A finer paper clay can be made using the same method, but with

toilet tissues or household paper toweling. This is sometimes recommended for a final surface on models built up initially of the coarser paper clay. In this way, the foundation of the work is quickly built up with the heavier material and the details and finishing touches worked on the smoother surface.

The properties of paper clay, whichever type of material is used, are surprising. For example, a small cardboard box covered with about $\frac{1}{8}$-inch paper clay will dry out with the strength of a wooden box, and will have an attractive, slightly rough appearance.

Finishing   A number of different finishes can be given to papier-mâché.

Paint or color stains can be used effectively. Again, details are given with each design. To give a "used" appearance to your work, try painting it over with white opaque watercolor (Chinese White). When this is dry, apply a coat of dark oak varnish stain, and while this is still wet, wipe off with a piece of rag. This will give a rubbed, "antique" finish. To make models resistant to water or even the elements, they can be brushed, when thoroughly dry, with three or four coats of linseed oil and then baked in a cool oven. It is important not to put the articles into a warm oven as this would cause cracking.

The Paper Strip Method

You will need: Three or four large newspapers; 2 pints cold water; 1 tablespoon of wallpaper paste; 2 large bowls.

Pour water into one of the bowls, sprinkle the wallpaper paste on to it, stir well and allow to stand for 15 minutes.

Tear up newspaper into strips and pieces, tearing as many thicknesses together as you can manage, to minimize the time it takes. Aim for narrow strips, about 10 inches long by 1½ inches wide. Tear off the cut edges of the newspaper so that all the edges are rough and vignetted. This will help bonding later.

Fill the other bowl with cold water and drop the strips of newspaper into it, one by one, making sure that they all separate. Don't try to save time by soaking them in bundles. This would greatly reduce the amount of water they would absorb. Remove the soaked sheets and dip them into the mixture, which should by now be a smooth paste, or brush them with it, whichever you find easier.

The Lidded Bowl

You will need: 3 or 4 large newspapers; 2 pints cold water; 1 tablespoon wallpaper paste; 2 large bowls (to use as instructions above). One 10-inch mixing bowl to use as a mold; 1 yogurt container or similar receptacle (the one we used was narrower at the top than the bottom); 2-inch paste or paint-brush; aluminum foil; stiff cardboard; glue; scissors; paint and varnish.

To make the bowl: Mix the paste, as described above, and leave to stand. Tear up the newspaper into strips and soak in cold water. Line the inside of the bowl with one layer of unpasted paper.

To do this, place one strip across the bottom of the bowl and extending up each side; then another strip, crossing the first one; then another, and another, star-fashion (Diagram 1). Continue until the inside of the bowl is completely covered with newspaper. Make sure that all the edges overlap. The paper should extend about three-quarters up the sides of the bowl to achieve the proportions of the design as shown.

Dip newspaper into the paste piece by piece, or brush it with paste, and continue layering the inside of the bowl. You will need five or six layers altogether. Leave the rest of the newspaper to use when the bowl is dry, the next day.

Leave the bowl in a warm place overnight to dry. Do not put it near direct heat, especially not in front of a fire, as this would cause too rapid drying and excessive shrinkage. Carefully remove the shape from the bowl.

Using strong, sharp scissors, trim the edge neatly, making the bowl about 4 inches high.

Glue the top (the narrow end) of the yogurt container to the outside center of the papier-mâché bowl, to form a stand.

Soak and then paste the remaining strips of newspaper, as before, and cover the bowl and yogurt container with another 8 or 9 layers of strips, "binding" the edge of the bowl (Diagram 2, page 119) to give a neat finish. Leave the bowl to dry.

Cut a circle of cardboard a little larger than the top of the bowl. Cut a long, narrow strip of foil, crunch it up so that it forms a strip of about the thickness of piping cord, and stick it around the circle of cardboard, about 1 inch from the circumference.

This will form the "lip" for the lid.

Cover the lid on both sides with at least 6 layers of pasted paper strips, binding the "lip" as described for the edge of the bowl (Diagram 3). Leave to dry.

Cut a long strip of newspaper 2 inches wide. Brush with paste and roll into a tight tube. Brush the end with paste, then glue it to the center of the top of the lid, for the handle. Now add pasted paper strips all around this, overlapping them well, so that they "bind" the handle to the lid.

To decorate the lid, cut some strips of newspaper ¾-inch wide by 3 inches long. Brush both sides with paste, or dip them into the mixture, then fold in half twice (Diagram 4). Curl one end around your middle finger, then attach as shown (Diagram 5) around the base of the handle. Lay the excess strips carefully along the top of the lid, and cover these with more strips of paper to bind. Leave to dry.

Finishing Paint the bowl and lid inside and out, in a dark color, such as forest green or black, giving two coats if necessary. When the paint is dry, paint light, bright flowers all over it, as shown in the photograph. Allow to dry.

Finally, paint the bowl with at least three coats of varnish so that it will be water resistant.

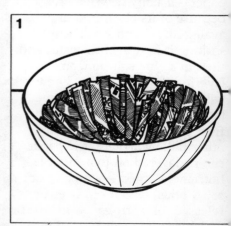

All from a few sheets of newspaper, a brightly painted candlestick, heavily weighted for safety, for children to make

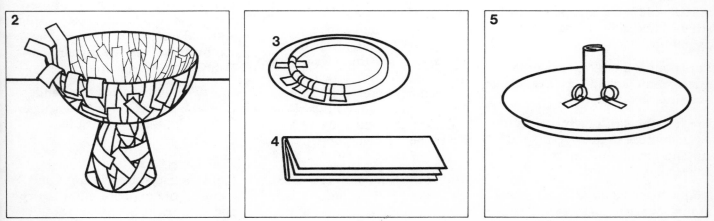

A nativity scene that looks like sculpture – the figures are made of crumpled wire forms covered with softly draped fabrics (see Plaster Section)

Arm Puppets

There's no need to aim at realistic sculpted profiles in toys of this kind—the more grotesque and unlikely they are, the more fun children will have playing with them, making up characters for them, and weaving stories and plays around them. The puppets illustrated here and in the color photograph are meant to bear a vague resemblance to Punch and Judy, probably the best-loved and best-known puppets of all.

You will need: Several old newspapers—about 32 large double sheets for pulping, and more besides (see below); 3 pints cold water; 4 level tablespoons wallpaper paste; thick stick; clear varnish; colored stretch-nylon sock; old cup; small varnish or paintbrush; turpentine (to clean brush); wool; household glue; lace doilies; large bucket; paints; adhesive tape.

To make the puppets: Tear up the 32 sheets of newspaper into very small pieces and put into the bucket. Pour very hot water over them, taking care not to splash yourself. Leave to soak about 36 hours, stirring occasionally, and pounding with the stick.

Remove the soaked paper, squeezing out as much water as possible (as this is a messy job, it is advisable to wear rubber gloves). Clean bucket.

Pour the cold water into the empty bucket, add the wallpaper paste, stir well and allow to stand for 15 minutes.

Put about 3–4 tablespoons of the mixture into an old cup. Leave on one side.

Break the soaked newspaper in the paste mixture in the bucket, and stir and pound until all the adhesive is absorbed.

You will need a large double sheet of newspaper to make each sleeve

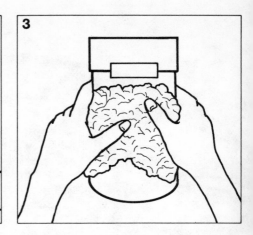

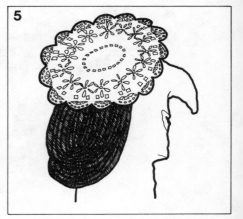

base for the puppets. Fold this in two, then curl into a tube large enough to fit comfortably over your arm. Tape the sides together. Fold over the top of the tube to make an envelope shape and tape along the top fold. This is shown in Diagrams 1 and 2. Make two of these, one for each puppet.

Stuff each sleeve with crumpled sheets of newspaper until it is full and firm. Take a handful of the

papier-mâché and press it around the sleeve (Diagram 3). Continue until the shape is covered with pulp. Build up more around the ears, and an exaggeratedly large amount for Punch's nose and chin. Follow the profiles shown in the photograph for these features. Leave in a warm place until quite dry.

Thoroughly paste one side of half a large sheet of newspaper, using the reserve mixture in the cup. Fold in half, paste the top of the paper and fold again. Then paste and fold once more. Smooth the top firmly to remove any air bubbles, then leave to dry.

Cut two pairs of arms and hands from the pasted, folded newspaper. Follow the shapes shown in Diagram 4.

Finishing

Paint the faces, bodies, arms and hands of the puppets, allow to dry and then varnish. If your paint is

quickly absorbed, you might like to apply a second coat so that you get a good strong color, before varnishing.

Clean varnish brush in turpentine, then wash in soap and cold water.

The hair of both puppets is made with thick wool—rug wool is best, but thick knitting wool would do. Arrange this over the heads in untidy strands and glue into place.

Judy's little dust cap is cut from a lace doily. Glue this in place, pinching it up at the center. Follow Diagram 5 for position.

No Punch puppet is complete without a large, stiff ruff at the neck. This one is made from three doilies. Cut out a hole in the middle, then pinch and pleat to make the collar stand out well. Alternatively, soak the doilies in the glue mixture after forming the ruff. Allow to dry and then glue

around the puppet's neck (Diagram 6).

His hat is made from the toe of a colored sock. Cut off just below the heel, turn cut end inward to hide the rough edge, then pull on to the puppet's head. Glue in place.

The puppets are now ready to play. Don't forget that Punch is often aggressive, and that Judy usually gives as good as she takes!

Easter Table Decoration

You can be your own Fabergé, and present the family with a dish of gaily decorated eggs to feast the eyes. The basic structure of the chicken was built up around household items covered with papier-mâché. Follow the instructions to put the technique you have already learned to a different use.

You will need: 6 large eggs; darning needle; small empty coffee can; small mixing bowl; newspaper; medium-sized styrofoam flower ball; medium-sized styrofoam flower cone; 18-inch length of strong modeling wire; large empty box of thin cardboard (cereal box is ideal); scissors; strong glue; lengths of cotton lace; paint; varnish; sequins; kitchen paper toweling; toothpick; sharp knife; small package of wallpaper paste; large bowl; paste brush if desired.

To make the decoration: Mix up the wallpaper paste according to the instructions on the package.

Push the toothpick into the top of the styrofoam cone, and then push the ball on top of it—see Diagram 1.

From the cardboard, cut out a diamond 4 inches long for the beak, and a pointed oval 2 inches long for the tongue. Bend both pieces as shown in Diagrams 2 and 3 respectively.

Using the sharp knife, make a cut in the ball where the beak is to go (follow Diagram 4 for position), spread a little glue across the fold of the beak and put it into the cut. Glue the tongue to the beak (Diagram 5).

Cut out a comb and wattle from the cardboard, following Diagrams 6 (a) and (b) respectively. Make slits in the ball as shown in

Diagram 7 and insert these pieces, gluing them in place.

Tear the newspaper into strips and pieces about half the size of a postcard.

Turn the small mixing bowl upside down and cover the bottom with a layer of newspaper pieces soaked in cold water. Dip the other newspaper strips in the paste, or brush them with the mixture if preferred. Lay the paste strips, first one, and then another, crisscrossing the bottom of the bowl and continuing up the side until it is covered almost to the top (Diagram 8). You will need 5 layers of paper. Dry in a warm place.

Remove the shape from the bowl and trim the edges, so that you achieve the slightly "dished" shape of the container, as shown in Diagram 9. Glue the shape firmly to the top of the coffee can.

Cut two thin strips of cardboard about 18 inches long, insert the wire between them and glue them together. Before the glue sets, curl them into an attractive shape to represent the tail feathers, then allow to dry. Glue the strip to the outside of the container shape.

Stand the body of the rooster, the ball and cone, next to the container shape, and glue them together at the top where they meet. Make two small tight balls of newspaper and glue to the face to make eyes.

Soak strips of newspaper in the paste, then cover the shape with 5 layers, making sure that they are all overlapping and the surface is evenly and completely covered. Tuck the untidy ends of the paper under the model. Cover the tail with only one layer of pasted strips.

Soak scraps of cotton lace in paste, squeeze to remove excess moisture, then cover the model

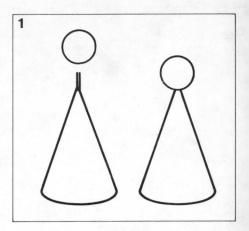

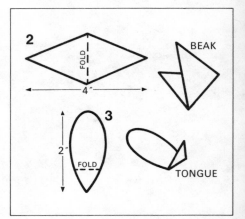

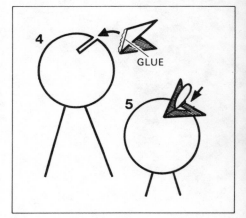

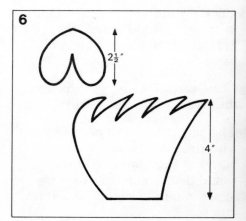

with overlapping strips, as shown in the photograph. Allow to dry.

Cut narrow strips of thin cardboard and glue in extravagant curls and spirals to the tail. To make the cardboard curl, lay the strip flat on a table, hold down one end and rub the blunt side of a scissor blade firmly down the length. The degree of pressure you exert will determine the tightness of the curl.

If you like the soft, creamy color of the lace, there is no need to paint the main part of the model, but you will want to paint the features and the comb in bright, attractive colors. Apply two coats of varnish, allowing the first to dry. To add a finishing, sparkling touch, glue sequins to the tail. Don't overdo this, though, or your model will look more like a peacock than a rooster.

To decorate the eggs   First of all, you will have to blow the

whites and the yolks out of the eggshells. To do this, pierce each end of the egg with a sterilized darning needle. Break away a little of the shell around one hole, using the needle to chip it away. Hold the egg over a basin or a cup, then blow hard through the smaller hole. The egg should come out easily.

Hold the blown eggshells under water, shake the water in the shell, then blow out. Repeat until the shell is clean inside, and the water you blow out of it is clear. Stand eggshells on end to dry overnight.

Dip a paper towel into the paste, then wrap it around an egg. You will need about three towels for each egg. Smooth the paper over the surface and set aside to dry. Paper egg cartons are useful as stands at this stage.

Using the brightest colors you have, paint the eggs in scrolls,

spots, geometric shapes, or with the children's names. Allow to dry and then paint over with a coat of varnish.

Eggshells decorated in this way make very pretty little vases for the Easter table. To do this, break away the shell at one end, until you have a hole about the size of a small teaspoon. Tip out the egg, wash the shell and decorate as described above. Fill the eggshell with water, stand it in an eggcup and arrange a miniature posy of tiny spring flowers, such as primroses.

Lucifer and Beelzebub Masks

The phrase "scared the life out of you" could well have some meaning if you encountered these masks unexpectedly. They are made—as menacing as possible—from shopping bags covered with pasted cloth. It is, in fact, the technique known as cloth sculpture, though perhaps that is too ambitious a term for the results!

You will need: 2 paper shopping bags; scissors; newspaper; 2 level tablespoons wallpaper paste; $2\frac{1}{2}$ pints cold water; large bowl; bucket; pieces of material, such as old sheets or pillowcases; dressmaker's pins; paint; paintbrush.

To make the masks: Pour the cold water into the bowl, sprinkle the wallpaper paste on to it, stir and allow to stand for 15 minutes.

Cut handles from the two shopping bags, and then cut out scoops from each side, as shown in Diagram 1, so that the bags fit over the children's shoulders. Try the bags on the children for size, and mark the holes for the eyes.

Take the paper bags off and cut out the eye holes. Continue for each one as follows:

Stuff the top of the bag with crumpled newspaper, then wedge it over the upside down bucket. This will hold the bag steady while you work.

Tear the material into squares, oblongs and strips, some large and some small. The shape is irrelevant. Soak in the paste, which should be smooth and creamy, and squeeze out some of the excess.

Arrange pieces of material over the bag (Diagram 2), molding it around the eyes to leave them free. Use plenty of material so that a really gnarled and wrinkled effect is achieved.

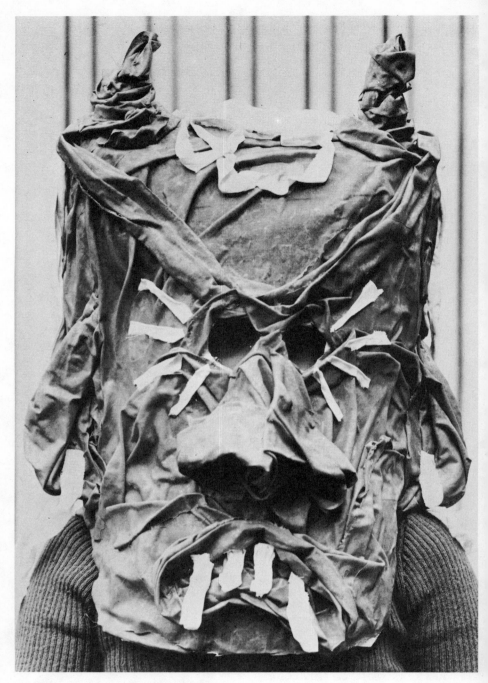

Crumple some pieces of material for the features, and hold them in position on the masks with dressmaker's pins (Diagram 3). Wind some more strips into cones, for the horns, and hold them in place with pins. Use narrow strips of fabric, or scraps of thick rug wool for the hair. The style is unimportant, as you can see from the photographs. Soak the fabric or wool in paste, squeeze out most of the excess, and position on top

of the masks. Hold in place with pins if necessary. Make the fanglike teeth from pasted strips of white fabric, positioning them as unevenly as possible.

Do not let the children try on the masks until they are completely dry and the pins have been removed. Then they can be painted, if white material was used. Otherwise it will be necessary just to outline and emphasize the features.

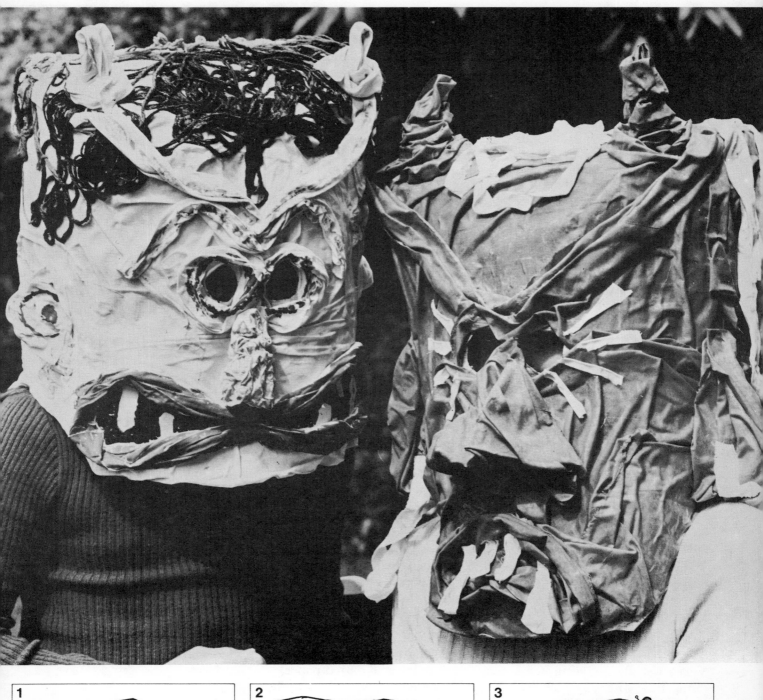

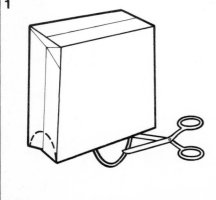

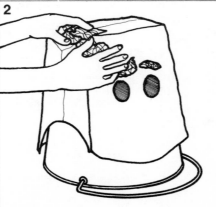

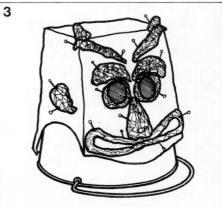

Lamp Shades Made with Newspaper

These lamp shades are very cheap to make—if you have to buy anything, it will probably only be the lamp shade ring, which costs a few cents. They let the light shine through in an interesting, softly diffused way and are therefore suitable for any room in the house. You can vary the style of the shade as you please—the way you decorate it determines whether it will look more at home in a modern or traditional setting, a bedroom or a living room.

For the conical shade
You will need: 6-inch diameter ring from an old lamp shade; large sheets of newspaper; 1 heaping teaspoon wallpaper paste; 1 pint water; bowl; spoon; paste brush, clear household glue; paint; trimming as required.

To make the shade: Pour the water into the bowl, add the wallpaper paste, stir well and allow to stand for 15 minutes. This will give a thick paste which helps to strengthen the paper.

Brush the paste over one large sheet of newspaper. Smooth a second sheet on top, pressing out any air bubbles. Repeat three times more so that your papier-mâché is five sheets thick. Smooth over to release air bubbles again, then leave flat to dry.

Very carefully and accurately mark out a circle with a 13-inch radius and, using the same center point for your compass, a concentric circle with a 4-inch radius. Cut away a wedge shape, of about one quarter of the circle (Diagram 1), and cut out the inner ring.

Curl the paper into a cone section and glue the ends together. Check to see that the shape is even all around.

Glue the lamp shade ring into the

top of the cone, as far down as it will fit. Leave until the glue dries.

Tear some newspaper into narrow strips, about 4 inches long and 1½–2 inches wide. Paste the strips or dip them into the paste, and stick them over the ring to hold it in position. Cover the inside of the shade with one layer of pasted paper, pressing out air bubbles. Leave to dry.

Cover the outside of the shade with another layer of pasted paper, and paste narrow strips over the bottom edge to neaten it, overlapping them all the way around. Leave to dry.

Paint the shade thickly with paint and, when dry, glue lamp shade trimming or fringe around the outside edge.

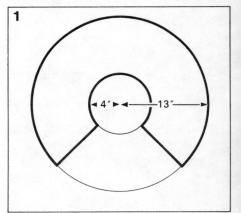

For the Tiffany shade
You will need: 6-inch lamp shade ring; large sheets of newspaper; 10-inch diameter mixing bowl; glue; 1 pint water; 1 heaping tablespoon wallpaper paste; bowl; spoon; paste brush; cereal box; paint.

To make the shade: Mix the paste as already described, and let stand for 15 minutes.

Tear newspaper into strips. Cover the inside of the mixing bowl with pieces of newspaper dipped in clear water.

Now cover the inside of the bowl with 5 layers of pasted paper, extending it beyond the edge of the bowl by about 4 inches (Diagram 2). Leave to dry, and then carefully lift the shape from the bowl.

Cut a circle in the top of the papier-mâché shape, slightly smaller than the ring. The hole would therefore have a 5½-inch diameter.

Carefully measure around the circumference (using a compass is the easiest way to do this) and divide it into 8 equal sections. Mark into scallops, using a compass or a saucer or small plate to give you the arc, and cut out (Diagram 3).

Glue the lamp shade ring into position over the hole.

When the glue has dried, cover the ring with narrow strips of pasted paper to keep it in position. Two layers should be enough.

Using a piece of cardboard from a cereal box, cut a strip 1½ inches wide, long enough to fit around the top of the shade and make a "collar." Glue the strip to make a circle, fit it in position (Diagram 4) and cover it from front to back with overlapping strips of pasted newspaper. Leave it to dry.

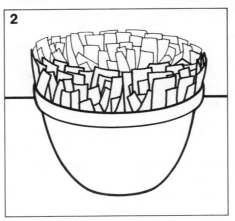

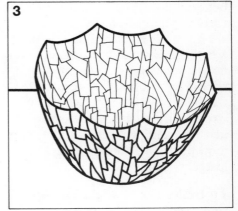

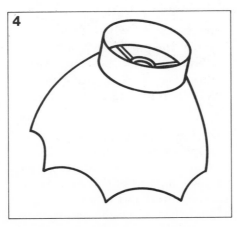

Paint the shade as you like. If drawing and painting flowers is not your strong point, cut pictures from seed catalogues or magazines with color pictures and paste them onto the shade in a decorative arrangement.

Viking Ship Centerpiece

With children these days growing less and less fond of birthday cakes, it is a good idea to make a table centerpiece instead. This Viking ship, with realistic sailors and crested waves, could come out year after year and become almost a family heirloom.

You will need: 16 large double sheets of newspaper; 1½ pints cold water; 2 level tablespoons wallpaper paste for papier-mâché; plus 2 further tablespoons filler (such as spackle); one 24-inch-square used cake stand or a piece of stiff cardboard that size; a scrap of red and white striped material; 2 pieces of strong florist's wire, one 12 and one 8 inches long; strong thread; needle; one thin strip of wood (batten) 30 inches long; gummed tape; bowls and spoons for mixing; paint; clear varnish; strong glue; half of a date box; thin cardboard (used cereal boxes will do); large supermarket carton; piece of plastic sheeting; several large sheets of newspaper; 5 lengths of very thin cane or flower sticks for oars (bamboo stick); paste brush; X-acto knife; felt pens; two 12-inch lengths of strong wire or thin stick, assorted licorice candies, fudge candies and toothpicks for Vikings (see instructions).

To make the model: Mix up some papier-mâché, using the recipe given for the arm puppets on the preceding pages, and allow to stand. It will be used for molding around the cardboard shape of the ship.

Cut out two shapes for the sides of the ship from the supermarket carton. Follow Diagram 1 for the measurements and shape. You will need to use the sharp X-acto knife for this, so if the children are helping to make the model, this is a job that you should reserve

for yourself. Tape the two sides together at the front and back so that you have a hollow boat shape.

Glue the half date box between the two sides to wedge them apart and to give strength to the model. Stand the ship on a piece of plastic sheeting.

Curl the 12-inch length of wire to form the base of the spiral bow of the ship and the shorter, 8-inch length into a similar shape to make the spiral stern.

Pour 1½ cups of water into a bowl, then add 3¾ cups of spackle to the water. Stir until the mixture is smooth. Pour enough of this mixture into the bottom of the ship to cover the date box.

While the mixture is still wet, push the 30-inch strip of wood (batten) into the center of the ship to make the mast. Now fix the shaped pieces of wire to the fore and aft of the ship, using the thick spackle mixture to hold them in position (Diagram 2). Leave to set.

Pour 2 pints cold water into a bowl, then sprinkle 2 level tablespoons wallpaper paste into the water. Stir well, then allow to stand for 15 minutes.

Tear the newspaper into strips, soak them first in cold water, then either dip into the paste or brush with it. Wind these around the wire shapes at each end of the ship (Diagram 3) for the figureheads.

Now cover the whole ship with a layer of the papier-mâché mixture, molding it carefully around the figureheads. Leave until quite dry, which may take at least 24 hours.

If you wish, you may then sandpaper the surface to make it smooth, but this is not necessary. In fact, models of this kind look more natural and weather-beaten if they have a rough surface.

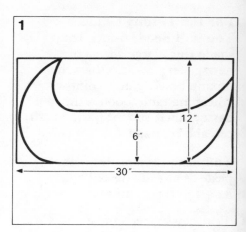

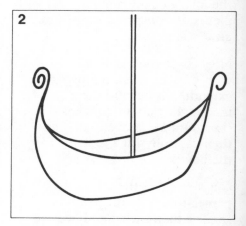

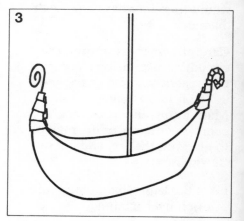

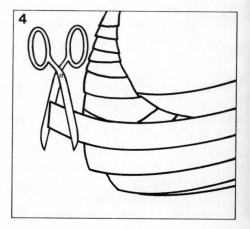

Cut some strips of newspaper 8 inches wide and a little longer than the ship. Brush paste on both sides, or dip them in the paste, and fold them into three, smoothing the top firmly with your hands to remove any air bubbles. Brush the top with a further layer of paste, then arrange in layers around the sides of the ship, beginning at the bottom, and overlapping the edges to make a "clinker" finish (the appearance of wooden planks). Cut off excess at both ends (Diagram 4).

Leave to dry, then paint and varnish the vessel.

Cut an oblong of red striped material, 10 by 20 inches. Glue the ends over the two 12-inch lengths of strong wire or thick stick. Brush the sail with paste, then hang from a table edge in a curve, using heavy stones or books to hold the wire in position while the sail dries (Diagram 5). Cut a pennant from striped material, dip into paste, then leave to dry. Wind the end of the pennant around the top of the mast and glue into position.

Sew a length of strong thread through the center of the top and bottom of the sail. Tie the sail to the mast, gluing into position (Diagram 6). Add the rigging, tying to the top of the mast and attaching the ends to the ship with a dab of glue.

Mix up a bowl of spackle, using $2\frac{1}{2}$ parts filler to 1 part water.

Spread this over the cake stand or board to a thickness of about $1\frac{1}{2}$ inches. "Whip" with a knife into waves, following the shapes you can see in the photograph. Stand the boat in these waves, and then add any more you need so that they come realistically up the hull.

Arrange the oars in position, gluing one end to the edge of the ship and pushing the other into the plaster waves before they set. Now leave to dry.

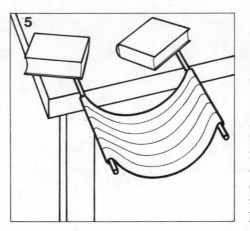

The shields are cut from circles of cardboard, 3 inches in diameter, decorated with felt pens. Glue them over the oars, overlapping the edges as shown in the photograph.

To make the Vikings: The fierce-looking Vikings are really quite sweet when you get to know them! They are made from assorted licorice candies, fixed together with pieces of toothpick. Use a pink candy for the face.

Make holes with the end of a toothpick or similar instrument (awl) for the eyes and nose, then push in slivers of licorice for the eyes and a round candy or nut for the nose.

Make hair and mustaches with yellow and orange coconut icing found on some of the licorice candies. This can be molded quite easily when softened between warm—and clean—fingers. The helmets and horns are made of square fudge candies rubbed and molded into shape (Diagram 7).

As the whole decoration cannot be eaten, it is a good idea to make enough Vikings for each guest at a birthday party to be able to eat at least one.

Children's Candleholder

Now that so many children make candles, they want to make decorative holders for them. Here is an amusing one that they will enjoy making from the simple papier-mâché technique. It goes without saying, however, that its use, when the candles are burning, must be supervised; and that the holder must be heavily weighted to prevent it from toppling over.

You will need: Wallpaper paste; newspaper; bowl; measuring spoons; water; paste brush (2-inch paintbrush will do); 3 small foil baking cups; 16-inch length of strong wire (or part of a coat hanger); skewer; strong adhesive; a very heavy stone or piece of scrap metal to weight the holder; 9-inch styrofoam flower cone; 2-inch diameter styrofoam flower ball; stirrer or long matchstick; piece of thin cardboard (cereal box).

To make the candleholder

Pour 1 pint of water into the bowl, sprinkle on to it 1½ teaspoons wallpaper paste, stir and allow to stand for 15 minutes.

Push the skewer through the cone, about 4 inches from the tip, to make a hole from side to side. Push the wire through, bend the sides slightly upward for the arms and then curl the ends for the hands.

Gouge a hole from the base of the cone and insert the stone weight (Diagram 1).

Cut a base from the cardboard, a little larger than the circumference of the base of the cone, giving it 6 "scallops" (Diagram 2) and glue this to the base of the cone (Diagram 3).

Push one end of the matchstick or stirrer into the tip of the cone and the other end into the styrofoam ball.

Tear up some newspaper into strips and brush each side with the paste. Cover the whole shape with one layer of paper strips, overlapping each piece.

Crumple some pasted newspaper and build out the folds in the dress. Now continue to cover the shape with about 6 layers of newspaper, building out the shape of the arms and sleeves until they are thick enough to hold the foil cups. Press all the pieces of paper firmly as you work, to make sure that no air bubbles are trapped.

Put the three baking cups in place, one on each arm and one on the head (Diagram 4). Cover these with pasted paper strips, making sure that they are well pressed down underneath the cups, so that a firm bond is made.

To make the hair, tear some 2-inch squares of newspaper. Paste on one side only, fold in half, paste again, and fold once more, to make narrow strips. Press firmly. Stick these to the head to make hair. (You will see from the photograph that the hair is combed upward, and not hanging loose.)

Make the cuffs in the same way, using a narrow strip of pasted paper stuck around each arm. For the collar, start with a 2½-inch square of newspaper, folded and treated in the same way.

Leave the model in a warm place until it is quite dry. When it is ready to paint, you can choose between gloss enamel, oil paint, lacquer, or poster paint, which must be varnished.

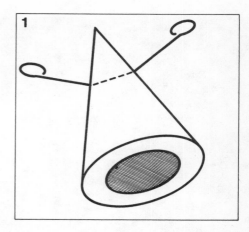

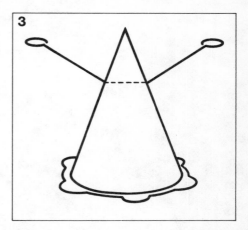

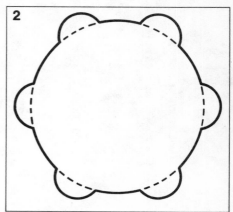

Knight on Horseback

More ambitious modeling can be attempted—and, as you can see from the photograph, achieved—using the paper-clay technique.

A wire armature (framework) was made for both the horse and rider. In the case of an animal or figure which is going to be required to stand, great care must be taken to achieve balance in positioning the legs. Most amateur craftsmen would need to copy a model of a horse, perhaps a toy one, or at the least a realistic drawing or painting, to obtain the correct proportions.

Paper clay (using newspaper, in the method already described) was used to model the horse, and paper strip layers to model the figure.

Trimmings were made from scraps of felt and fabric, cut lengths of knitting wool and scraps of paper.

The papier-mâché model was brushed over with a thin mixture of spackle, allowed to dry, then painted.

TAKE A PACKET OF PLASTER

A craftsman, it is said, is only as good as his tools and his materials. Skilled artists, sculptors and stonemasons, sure of their ability, can create designs using materials which offer no opportunity for second thoughts or correction of faults—which set or harden almost immediately.

But by using present-day materials, we can all enjoy the effects which their work has taught us to appreciate, without necessarily aspiring to their standards of craftsmanship.

In this chapter, we have used a spackling compound; this powder is available in packages at hardware stores under the trade name of Spackle. It has a number of advantages over plaster. It has a longer working time—plenty of time for the artist to think— strength and good adhesive qualities.

It can be piped in a similar way to sugar icing, using a syringe or pastry bag to produce simple line drawings which stand out as a relief design. The appealing, feathery owl and the Christmas decoration with a stained-glass window effect have been worked in this way, with a smooth, creamy mixture.

Using the mixture a little stiffer, and dribbling it from the end of a stick, you can achieve a rougher, more nubby outline, of the kind

shown for the colorful parrot.

We have used this material as a sculpting medium, casting it first into blocks and then carving out simple designs to make ornaments, paperweights and book ends. The trio of fish, animal and abstract shapes shows how effective this can be. As the plaster crumbles easily away under light pressure, this technique is simple enough for a child.

The model of a monk, Brother Dominic, was set in a liquid detergent bottle. As the material easily sticks to itself, it is simple to build up a model, adding hair, hands and other features after the main mold has been formed.

Blocks of the material cast in a similar way to those used for sculpture work can be inlaid with inks, colored paints, melted candle wax or solder. The outlines for the design can be scooped out of the block using a screwdriver or linoleum cutting tool and then filled with the chosen material. The lion and the graceful water carrier, on pages 140 and 141, show the effects that can be achieved.

Modeling with the cloth sculpture technique can be done with a thin mixture of the filler used to "paint" the pieces of cloth over a wire frame. The finished result, rather like papier-mâché, yet rather like plaster casts, can be extremely professional.

The material can be colored with concentrated color such as dyes, food coloring or poster paint, and—for lighter colors—with other household paints. The large-scale model village, shown in the color photograph, has been both colored and overpainted to give a striking effect. The consistency of spackle varies according to the technique, and quantities are given in the appropriate section.

How to Work in Bas Relief

A decorative plaque can be quite simply made using small pieces you can pick up in the garden to give the dimension and pattern. If you cover the whole design with wet spackle and leave it to set, it will look as if you had carved the pattern out of solid plaster.

The simple plaque on the next page was designed (using the same technique) to give a beginner a "feel" for the medium.

To make the flower plate you will need: Paper plate, 9-inch diameter; twig; pebbles and stones; 12-inch length of strong string; fir cone; spackle; paintbrush; paint (oil, emulsion, gloss enamel paint or acrylic); water; bowl. Make 2 holes in the plate, at equal distances from the outside, and toward the top, so that your plaque will hang upright. Thread the string through the holes, tie the ends inside the plate.

On a table, arrange the pebbles, stones and cone to make a flower design as illustrated.

Pour 4 cupfuls of water into the bowl and add 9 cupfuls of spackle. Stir to a smooth paste. Pour into the plate, making sure the string is well embedded. Leave for about 5 minutes to thicken a little.

Transfer the pattern you have made with the pebbles and cone, pressing them firmly into the wet mixture. Then, push the twig in place and set aside to dry.

Wash mixing bowl. Pour into it $\frac{1}{2}$ cupful water and an equal amount of spackle. Brush this mixture over the plaque to fill in any cracks and give a smooth surface. Allow to set.

Paint any color you choose. If you are using a water-based paint, cover the surface first with a coat of clear varnish.

Impasto: Texture Painting

There's something immensely satisfying about painting with a trowel . . . or a spatula . . . or with your fingers. Described here is another form of "finger painting," this time using spackle, water and poster paint. The effects are pleasingly thick and have an interesting three-dimensional quality. And, somehow, the standard of the designs does not seem all-important: after all, we are not pretending it's fine art!

Creating a picture   To create an impasto picture, choose a design of our own, either one you can draw freehand, or can trace from a textbook or from a picture book, as in the case of this Egyptian head. Look, in the beginning, for simple subjects with fairly well-defined areas of colors. It is a longer, slower job to have to deal with more than four or five colors at a time.

The directions given are to make the picture of an Egyptian lady, as shown here, and in color. You can insert string for hanging into the back of the cardboard before beginning work (see directions on the next page) or have the picture framed.

You will need: Piece of strong cardboard 20 by 28 inches; bowl; tablespoon; spackle—remember to carefully check following directions for proportions with manufacturer's instructions; poster paint; ice-cream stick; small teaspoon.

To make: Draw the outline of the head on the cardboard. Mix 4 tablespoons water with 8 level tablespoons spackle. Stir in 2 small level teaspoons of dark green paint. Spread the now-green filler over the background, smoothing with your finger tips and slightly overlapping the outside edge of the drawing.

Between each different color application, thoroughly wash the bowl and spoon.

Mix together 9 tablespoons water with 18 tablespoons of spackle. Add 3 teaspoons brown paint and mix well. Smooth over the face, neck and arms, building up above the background. Wash utensils.

Mix together $1\frac{1}{2}$ tablespoons water, 3 level tablespoons of spackle and 1 teaspoon yellow paint. Color the dress with this.

Now build up the collar, mixing up a little water, spackle and paint at a time, cleaning the bowl between each mixing.

For the hair, mix 20 tablespoons water, 40 level tablespoons spackle and 10 teaspoons black paint.

For the blue band around the hair, mix 2 tablespoons water, 4 level tablespoons spackle and 2 teaspoons blue paint.

Cellulose filler dribbled from the end of a stick gives the parrot a nubby outline and an appealing, ruffled appearance

Add any other detail you wish. Outline the design with black-colored spackle, using the side of an ice-cream stick to make a thin line.

One general point to bear in mind: when coloring compounds such as spackle, do not be sparing with the paint you add, because the mixture dries several shades lighter than it appears when wet.

Creating a "Mood" Picture

The designer says that anyone who can make a mud pie can make this picture. And, she might have added, it is just as much fun, though need not be nearly as messy! The abstract subject lends itself to free adaptation—it really is something to make up as you go along.

You will need: A box lid (the one shown measures 14 by 18 by 2½ inches deep); 4 bowls and spoons; cellulose filler (such as spackle); any paint of your choice (acrylic, oil, poster or powder); 24-inch length strong cord or string for hanging the box; masking tape.

To make: Pierce 2 neat holes near the top of the box, using the point of a pair of scissors. If children are working the design, it might be advisable for an adult to supervise this exercise.

Thread the string through the holes from the back to the front, so that the ends are inside the box. Adjust the length by pulling up the string outside the box, until it is the right length to hang your picture. Tie a knot firmly at the appropriate place.

Paint the sides of the box, which will form the "frame" for your picture, any color that will blend with your design.

Pour 5 cupfuls of water into first bowl, then 1 cup of water into each of the other 3 bowls. Add 9 cupfuls of spackle to the first bowl

and stir into a smooth paste. Add 1½ cupfuls of spackle to each of the other bowls and stir.

Add paint—any colors you choose —to the 3 small bowls, stirring well and adding a little more of each color if you think it is not deep enough. (Remember that it will dry much lighter.)

Pour the first bowl of uncolored filler into the box, smoothing it well over the surface and making sure that the string is firmly embedded.

Pour the bowls of colored filler over the uncolored layer in a random pattern. Using a teaspoon, scratch a pattern—any pattern!— into the colors, revealing an outline in the uncoloured filler underneath.

Don't worry if some of the filler spills on to the sides of the box— if the shapes are interesting, leave them.

If you wish, you can paint your picture, once it has thoroughly dried, with a clear varnish.

The first, uncolored, layer of filler has been poured into the box and is now being smoothed out over the whole surface. Use a wooden spoon, spatula or even your hand.

Simple Sculpture

You don't have to go to art school to learn how to carve ornaments that would be attractive around the house as paperweights, book ends or—just ornaments. If you make a simple cast, as described below, and let it set, you can work the design by working the plaster away with a penknife. Made a mistake and taken too much off? Just add a little more spackle to the outline, wait for it to set, and be more careful next time!

The three designs shown, all simple shapes, were made by schoolchildren. And if you really

A project on a large scale, suitable for school groups or holiday hobby classes, a village made from supermarket grocery cartons and household scraps

can't draw a fish or rabbit, or find one to trace, then don't despair. Abstracts are still very much "in."

You will need: Cardboard box, any size: it depends how many objects you wish to carve, and what sizes they will be; a sheet of vinyl plastic; spackle (or similar filler) or plaster; bowl; water; strong penknife; linoleum cutting tools or small pocket screwdriver; sandpaper; poster paint.

To make the cast: Line the box with the sheet of plastic. Mix some spackle in the bowl, using 2 cups of the powder to one cup of water. The quantity will depend on you. If you want your carvings to be colored, stir in some poster paint at this stage, making sure that the color is well mixed in.

Pour the mixture into the box and allow it to set for about 4 hours.

Carefully lift out the block from the box, gently peel the plastic sheet away from the sides, and leave the block standing on it for several hours more, until it is completely hard—overnight, if possible.

For beginners, we recommend a simple design like the fish shown in the photograph. They are flat, two-sided creatures without any awkward limbs to worry about!

Draw the outline of the design on one side of the block, as shown below, then, using the penknife blade, begin carving away the parts of the block outside the design.

As you work, keep holding the object away from you to judge the effect—all artists do this, of course! When you are satisfied that the first side is roughly what you want to achieve, turn the block around and work on the other, constantly turning to the first side to insure that you get them more or less identical. (Of course, if you chose an abstract shape, this is immaterial: only you can say what it is and what it should look like!)

Once you have carved the rough shape, smooth the surface with sandpaper, then, using linoleum cutting tools or a small screwdriver, add the detailed markings, such as scales, wings or whatever.

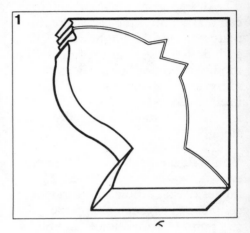

Diagram 1 shows a block of plaster with the outline of a fish drawn on one side, the design being chipped away with a penknife blade. It is important to make sure that the base of your design is wide enough to stand upright.

"Dribbled" Outlines

Polly Parrot has outlines nearly as bold as the coloring on her feathers—lines "dribbled" on so that they make an uneven, interesting texture. As you can see from the color photograph she is painted in colors that really give her something to sing about.

You will need: 1 large sheet cardboard; 1 cup cold water; 1 cup spackle; poster paints; fine brush; thin twig or cocktail stirrer; bowl; spoon; paper; pencil.

To make: The backing from a large sketching pad was used for this picture. You could use a large box lid, or the side of a box. Cut a piece of paper the same size as the cardboard. Draw the parrot and her perch on the paper. If you cannot copy our parrot well enough for your liking, either find one to trace or, failing that, make an exotic bird outline of your own.

Scribble on the back of the drawing with a soft pencil, covering the whole outline.

Place the drawing on top of the cardboard, the scribbled side down. Clip paper and board together to avoid the paper slipping, then redraw the parrot, following the same lines (Diagram 1).

When you remove the drawing, you will find that it is repeated on the cardboard (Diagram 2).

Pour the water into the bowl, add spackle and stir.

Dip the twig or stirrer into the mixture; it will run off the end of the stick in the way that ink runs from a pen, but in an uneven, more pronounced line (Diagram 3). Redraw the lines in this way, refilling the stick as necessary.

Leave the drawing to dry. Wash the bowl and spoon before the plaster sets.

Now carefully color the sections between the outlines, using thick paint and taking care not to get paint on the lines.

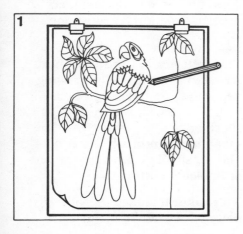

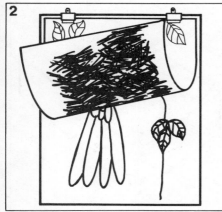

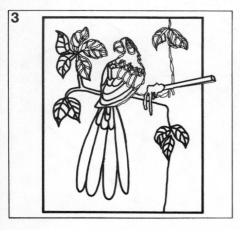

Interesting Inlays

Craftsmen for hundreds of years have been carrying out beautiful and intricate designs using the technique of inlaying one material into another, producing interesting combinations of color and texture. Here, on these two pages, you see examples of the simplest possible form of inlay—a spackle cast carved with a design on one surface and the outlines filled in with ink, melted solder or wax. The effects are never less than dramatic and always satisfying.

Leo the Lion

You will need: Cardboard box, 8 by 11 inches; piece of drawing paper the same size; ball-point pen; 6 cups cold water, 12 cups spackle; bowl; spoon; colored inks; fine paintbrush; sheet of plastic; small pocket screwdriver or linoleum cutting tool.

To make: line the box with a piece of plastic. Pour the water

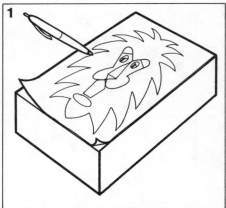

into the bowl, add the spackle, then stir well with the spoon until the mixture is smooth and creamy. Pour the mixture into the box, and clean bowl and spoon before the mixture sets.

After about 4 hours, lift out the block from the box. Gently tear the plastic from the sides of the block and leave it standing on the plastic for several hours more, until it is set hard.

Draw a design on the piece of paper, copying something from a book, comic or photograph, or enlarging the drawing of our friendly, happy lion. The design should be mainly composed of well-defined lines.

When you are satisfied with your design, place the paper on the top of the block, then redraw the lines with a ball-point pen, pressing fairly hard so that they are lightly scored into the block (Diagram 1).

Now carve the lines into the block, using the screwdriver or linoleum cutting tool (Diagram 2). The depth and width of the lines will depend on what your design is.

Carefully color the lines with the inks, applying them with a fine paintbrush. You can use just one color, or many colors as we did.

Once you have completed one inlay block, using inks, you might like to try filling the lines with melted candle wax, working quickly before it sets hard again, or with melted solder.

Aquarius, the Water Carrier (*right*)
Here is another design, using exactly the same technique but, as you can see, a little more intricate. This is the kind of design you might find in a history or geography book, or on a travel poster or catalogue. It looks as if it could be a valuable piece of early carving, doesn't it?

Simple Outline Designs

Children watching their mothers icing a birthday cake invariably want to try their hand at guiding the pastry bag along, and producing designs, however wiggly, of their own. Here is a way that the whole family can enjoy the fun of squeezing a design out of a nozzle or a tube, to make a nursery picture or a traditional Christmas decoration.

You can use pre-mixed spackle, piped straight from the tube, or a mixture of approximately 3 parts spackle to 1 part water. In this case, put the mixture into a pastry bag or syringe to obtain a similar effect.

To make the owl
You will need: A piece of cardboard or stiff paper; spackle compound (powder form or pre-mixed); pastry bag if tube not used; black paint; chalk.

Cover the board with black paint and leave to dry. Any type of paint will do—watercolor, poster, acrylic, oil—it depends on whether you want a matte or a shiny finish and, of course, on what you happen to have in the house.

Draw the owl on the board with the chalk. If you are not satisfied with your first attempt, it is easy to rub out the chalk line, paint over the smudge and start again as soon as the paint is dry.

Now follow the lines you have drawn, with the tube or bag of mixed spackle, as shown in Diagram 1. You will soon get the "feel" of making your outline as thick or as thin as you want it to be.

You will notice from looking at our owl that the more uneven the lines are, the more ruffled and appealing his feathers look!

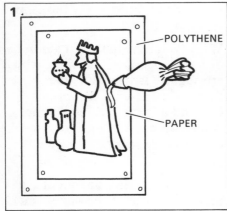

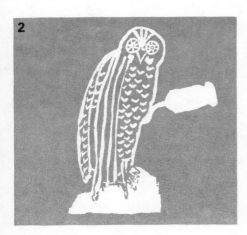

To make the Christmas Crèche You will need: Paper for drawing; pencil; transparent sheet of plastic; piece of board or cardboard as long as your design and 4 inches wide; paint; small beads and Christmas baubles for trimming; colored cellophane paper; package of "glitter," if desired; glue. Pre-mixed or powdered spackle as for owl.

Copy the lines of the design on the paper (notice that all the lines for each figure or the creche interconnect) or copy or trace a Christmas card with a similar design. Pin the paper to a board. Cover the design with the plastic and pin this in place, too.

Follow the lines of the drawing, over the plastic sheet, with spackle. While the outline is still wet, you can press baubles or sequins into it to represent the gifts. Leave to harden.

Carefully remove the plastic to leave the outlines of the design. Glue pieces of colored cellophane to the back of each shape to obtain the interesting stained-glass effect.

Cover the piece of board or cardboard with spackle and press the figures and crèche onto it while it is still wet, so that they stand up. At this stage, you can sprinkle glitter on the ground.

If you place this crèche—where children or animals cannot reach it, because it is fragile—so that a light shines through it, you will have a doubly pleasing effect, from the decoration itself and the shadow it throws on the wall behind it.

You can, of course, use this technique for a number of other decorations: a Christmas tree, with glowing candles and baubles; a doll's house with colored cellophane for lighted windows; a vase of flowers, with each one a different color.

Be Your Own Town Planner

It is sometimes fun for children to work on models on a fairly large scale—and in any case some children, like some adults, are more suited to working with large surfaces, rather than with smaller items.

This model town or village is an ideal project for schoolwork, or for families who have room to house it. The scale is such that small toy automobiles can be wheeled along the road and plastic dolls can stand at the garden gates or sit on the bench on the village green.

The model is built up on a large box, the kind one might be given in a supermarket, with another used as the background scenery. Both of these are strengthened and given textural interest by being covered with spackle, colored where necessary. The models, too, are cardboard based and plastered over, so that the whole townscape should have a playlife of a number of years.

Here is a list of the basic materials you will need to make the model as shown here and in the color photograph. But, as with all kinds of creative work, you will want to add your own finishing touches, such as paper flowers, a piece of glass inset into the base to represent the village pond, and so on.

You will need: For the base and the background, 2 large supermarket grocery boxes, approximately 26 inches long, 20 inches wide and 6 inches high. For the houses—4 are shown in our model—cereal, cake mix, sugar or other grocery boxes with, in each case, one slightly larger from which to cut the "overhanging roof." For the church, a larger cardboard carton, and for the steeple and belfry, a kitchen foil roll and a

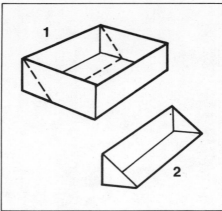

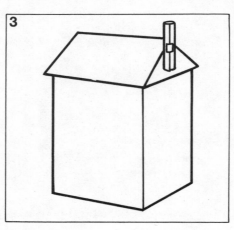

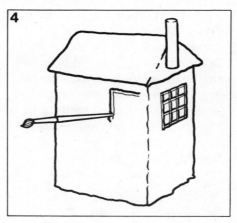

concentrated orange juice container (or other tube with slightly larger circumference than the roll). For the church gate, porch, weathercock, house gates and chimneys, pieces of cardboard according to the measurements given in the detailed instructions for each item. For the fences, used wooden matchsticks; for the trees, twigs, scraps of green woolen fabric and short lengths of cut knitting or rug wool in green.

For the weaver vane, drinking straw or thin twig.

The plaster type material used throughout is spackle, mixed in the proportion of approximately $2\frac{1}{4}$ cups of the powder to each cup of water. This is mixed separately for the different stages of making the model.

Other materials needed: wallpaper paste; strong glue; masking tape or Scotch tape; poster paint colors—green, brown, blue, black and others for the houses; scissors, paintbrush and bowl for mixing plaster.

To Make a House

As in so many towns and villages at home and abroad, houses are of different shapes, sizes and styles, but they all have one thing in common—they look like nice cozy, friendly places to live in. They can be made from a selection of empty boxes, ones that have held cereal, cake mixes, granulated sugar, dried fruits—any boxes in that kind of scale.

When you have gathered a number of boxes together, find some which are slightly larger than others; put them in pairs, with an upright box and a larger one from which you could cut a "slice" to make the overhanging roof.

Cut a strip from each of the larger boxes, so that they are about $\frac{1}{4}$ to $\frac{1}{5}$ as deep as each of the boxes you will use, upright, for the houses. Mark and cut the roof pieces, and stick them so that they form triangular sections, as shown in Diagrams 1 and 2. Glue the roofs firmly to the houses, using gummed tape to help secure if necessary. This will not show in your finished model.

To make the chimneys (Diagram 3), use tubes rolled from pieces of cardboard or heavy paper, and secure them with gummed tape. Stick the chimneys to the roofs of

the houses in the different positions shown in the photograph.

Mix up some spackle using $2\frac{1}{4}$ cups of powder to each cup of water, and stir well. Cover each house with a layer of the wet filler, spreading it on with a spatula or your fingers.

While the plaster is still wet—it sounds like building real houses, doesn't it?—score lines to represent windows, doors, roof tiles and brickwork as shown in Diagram 4. To do this, use the handle end of a paintbrush or a matchstick. Leave the houses to dry before you decorate them.

To Make the Church

Naturally, the church will have to be a great deal larger than your houses, so you might have to ask for a box at the supermarket to get one in the right proportion. It

needs to be about three times the size of a large cereal box.

Cut a slice from the top of the box—you will probably not be able to find one just a little larger than that one—and make the triangular roof section as described on the opposite page. Glue it in place.

The church needs a long, important-looking tower. To make this, glue the cardboard roll from a box of kitchen foil to one end of the large box (see Diagram 5). Attach it by binding with sticky tape to hold it firmly. Slide the cardboard part of a concentrated orange juice container over the roll to make the belfry.

Cover the church and tower with wet spackle, as described for the houses. While it is still wet, score in the windows—you can make the church from any period of history you like when you do this—the door and the clock.

Build the plaster mixture up into a cone shape at the top of the belfry and press a straight stick or drinking straw into the center of the cone (Diagram 5). Smooth plaster around it to strengthen.

Cut out the shape of a bird in cardboard, dip it in wet plaster and fix this to the top of the stick or straw for the weather vane. Leave the church to dry thoroughly.

To make the gate   The church needs a good, solid-looking pair of gates, and a porch to provide rest and shelter for weary travelers.

For the gates, follow Diagrams 6 and 7. Cut a piece of strong cardboard 5 inches long and 3½ inches deep. Draw a flowing curve, like a bracket on its side, to make the shape of the top of the gates, and cut out carefully around the line.

To make the gate stand up properly, glue the shaped piece of cardboard to a small box—a long matchbox is ideal.

To make the porch   Cut a long piece of cardboard 24 inches by 1½ inches. Measure 7 inches in from each end, score vertical lines with the back of a scissor blade. Measure to find the center of the length, 12 inches from the end, and score a line down there, too (Diagram 8). Fold in these three places so that the card bends into the shape of an arch (Diagram 9).

Stick the porch firmly to the sides of the box to complete the gate.

To make the tombstones, cut out pieces of cardboard, some for the headstones and some for the gravestones.

Cover the gates, porch and the tombstones with a thin layer of spackle and leave to dry.

To make the seat   On the left of the church, in front of the parsonage, you can see a seat. Perhaps it was given to the village by someone who lived there many years ago, or it might be in memory of a former minister.

To make the seat, cut a small piece of cardboard 5 inches long and 1 inch high.

Measure 1 inch in from each side, score the cardboard vertically, and fold it so that the two sides make the legs of the seat, as shown in Diagram 10.

For the back of the seat, cut a piece of cardboard 3 inches long by 2 inches. Fold it lengthwise (Diagrams 8 and 9) and glue the lower half firmly to the top of the seat you have made. You can see the shape of the finished seat in Diagram 11.

Cut gates for the houses around the green from pieces of cardboard varying the shapes as shown in the photograph.

Cover the seat and the gates with a thin layer of wet spackle and leave them all to dry.

Putting Them Together

When you have made all the models, of the houses, the church, the seat, the tombstones and gates, you are ready to build your village.

Using the top of one of the large supermarket boxes, mark it out with the "ground plan" of the area, as shown in Diagram 12. To do this accurately, draw around the models you have made, so that you have the exact outline of each one.

Mark in pathways, fences, where the trees will be, and any other features you wish to add.

Divide some wet spackle mixture into two, leaving half of it colorless. Color one half of the remaining mixture with green poster or other paint, for the village green and lawns in front of the houses, and the rest of the mixture brown, for the pathways and the road in front of the church.

Now work over your ground plan with the wet spackle, using the colorless mixture where the church and houses will stand, and the appropriate colors for the other areas.

While the spackle is still wet, press all the models into position,

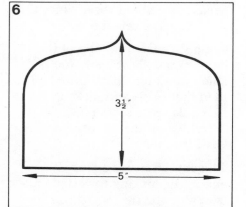

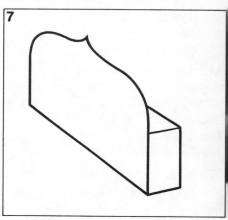

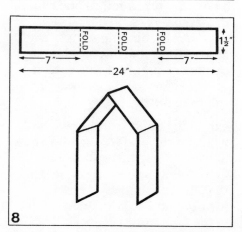

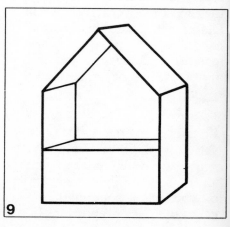

pushing them firmly but carefully in so that they are well anchored.

Push matchsticks or small pieces of twig in to represent the fences around the houses, and some larger twigs for the tree trunks.

Build up a ridge of the brown-colored spackle to make the church wall, taking it around the side of the model. Try to give this a good rough-textured finish.

To make the background Use the second large supermarket box for this. Mix up some spackle in the usual way, and color it with poster paint to get a good, strong blue so that your village enjoys a permanent summer. Use some of the colorless mixture for the light, fluffy clouds, and some of the brown for a range of distant hills. You will find that if you blend each color into the other one as you are putting them on, you will get softer, more natural looking lines.

You can press twigs into the "distant hills" to make trees. Stand the background behind the village model and smooth a layer of wet spackle along the joints. Let stand until it is completely dry and set firm.

To make the trees and hedges No town or village is complete without some well-established trees, and this one is no exception.

You will need some scraps of green woolen material, and some short lengths of green knitting or rug wool.

Put $\frac{1}{2}$ pint water into a bowl and sprinkle $\frac{1}{2}$ level teaspoon wallpaper paste into it. Stir well and leave to stand for 15 minutes.

Soak the wool and fabric scraps in this mixture. Squeeze out the surplus paste, then arrange on top of the twigs in the model to make foliage. You can also arrange some

of the cut wool behind the garden fences to make hedges.

The finishing touches Now comes the fun of painting your model with any colors you like. Use poster paint for the brightest effect.

Paint the houses, gates and the church first, making the roof tiles a different color from the walls. Paint the church gate and porch to make it look like oak that has "weathered" for hundreds of years, and use the same color for the seat.

When the first coat of paint is dry, add colors for the doors of the houses, putting in any finishing touches you like, such as curtains, roses around the door, and so on.

With black paint, outline the windows of the houses and the church, the shape of the church gates, the belfry and, of course, the clock tower.

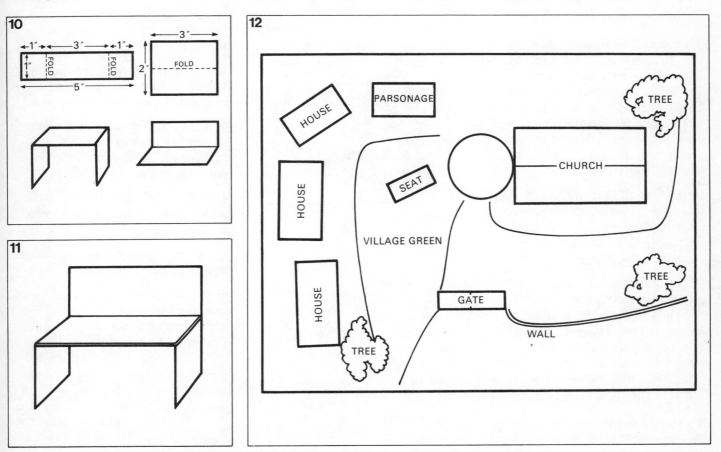

Cloth Sculpture with a Plaster Look

Using a thin, creamy plaster mixture, you can "paint" pieces of fabric so that they drape in natural folds over wire frame "armatures" to give gentle molding to figures. The couple shown in the photograph on the left, called The Flight into Egypt, could be made for a very special Christmas decoration—so special, indeed, that you would be most reluctant to pack it away after the holidays.

You will need: To make each figure, you will need a piece of lightweight chicken wire 9 inches high and 24 inches long for the body; 28-inch length of firm modeling wire for the arms; cocktail stirrer; ping-pong ball for the head; scraps of materials such as old sheeting, cheesecloth, lace and scraps of wool, string and cord; silver spray paint; wire cutters; scissors; glue; spackle. Each figure is 12 inches high.

To make the figure Wrap the chicken wire around to make a tube (the 9-inch measurement is the height) as shown in Diagram 1. Crush the top with your hands until you have formed a cone with evenly sloping sides and crush it gently to make a hard, compact shape (Diagram 2).

Repeat for the second figure. At this stage it is not important to give much more detailed shape to the "armature," as this can so easily be added later.

Wind the modeling wire once around the body, then loop back the ends to form the foundation for the hands (Diagram 3). Push the cocktail stirrer into the ping-pong ball (Diagram 4) then wedge it into the crushed wire forming the top of the cone.

To shape the clothes Tear up the scraps of fabric into

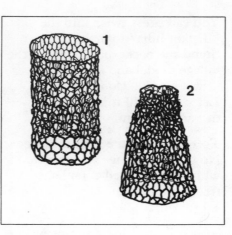

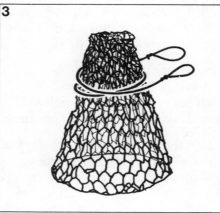

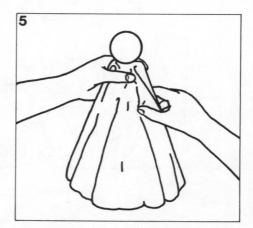

convenient-sized strips and squares—approximately 9 or 10 inches long, with some shorter ones.

Mix the spackle, using 2 cups powder to 1 cup of water. Stir to a smooth, creamy consistency as usual.

Dip the pieces of fabric into the spackle mixture so that they are completely covered with the wet substance. Drape, wind and arrange over the framework for each figure (Diagram 5), building up the thickness by winding more material around to give the width of the shoulders, skirt, etc.

When the figures are the desired thickness (compare yours with those in the photograph), you can start arranging the material that will represent their clothes. You will find that the plaster-covered fabric drapes easily and this is not difficult to do.

Dip the scraps of wool into the spackle mixture, squeeze out excess moisture and arrange for the hair.

Cover the ping-ping ball heads with a fine layer of the mixture, shaping it roughly into features.

Spread some spackle over a length of flexible wire to make the staff, and pass it through the wire loop forming one of the hands.

Cover the "hands" of both figures with spackle until you achieve a natural shape.

Leave the figures to dry overnight and then paint or spray.

You can either make these figures freestanding—and this is not difficult with models which have draped floor-length skirts like these—or can stand them on a board, as we have done, pressing them into a thin layer of wet spackle. Then the base should be painted or sprayed along with the figures.

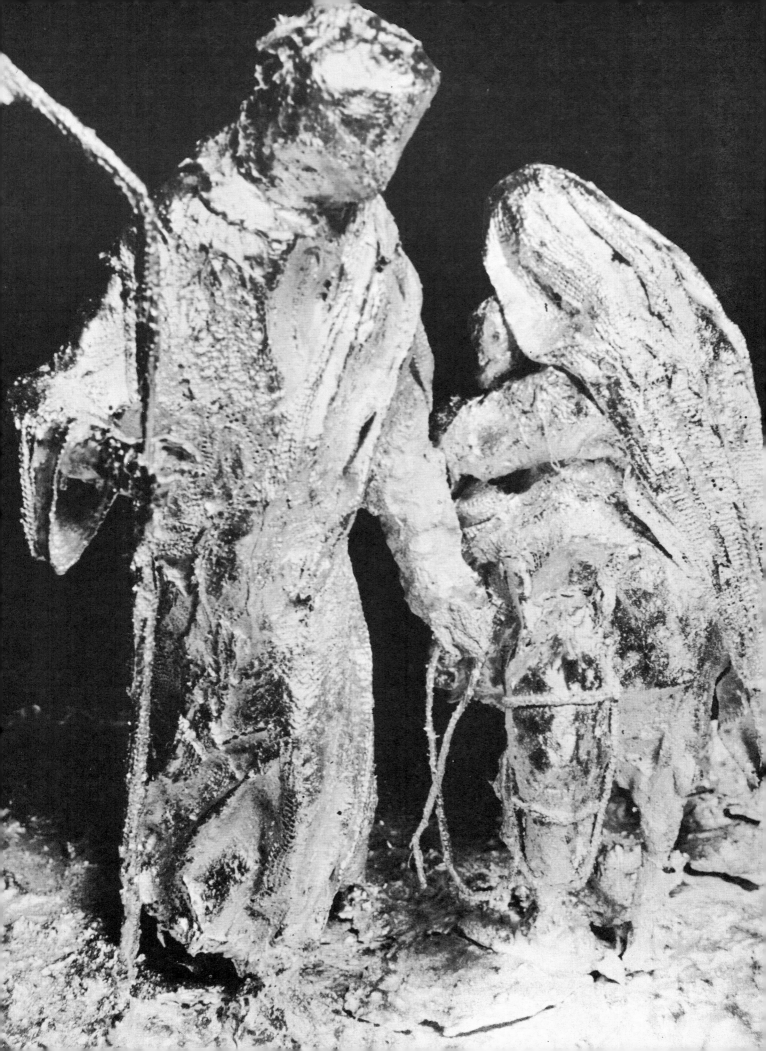

A Model Monk

Modeling from a simple shape, like this cylinder, a variety of interesting and amusing figures, such as "Brother Dominic," can be made. The shape was molded in a plastic liquid detergent bottle, allowed to set, and the mold cut away. The features were added to the cylindrical mold and the top built up for the head.

The basic rules for this type of work are few and simple: if using a mold other than a plastic one, line it with a sheet of plastic to make removal easier; use a mixture of 2 parts spackle to 1 part water; shake the mold constantly when filling with the liquid mixture, to remove any air bubbles. Then let your imagination run away with you!

You will need: 1 large liquid soap container; 3½ cupfuls cold water; 8 cups spackle; turpentine; small brush (varnish or paintbrush); bowl; spoon; small

Mix 1 cup water with 3 cups spackle, making a thicker consistency. Use this for modeling the monk's bald pate by building up the top of the head, working with your fingers, the spatula or knife (Diagram 2). Model the fringe of hair around the monk's head (his tonsure) and continue by modeling his nose, chin, eyebrows, arms, cross and cowl (Diagram 3). Follow the photograph closely for these details, and take care to give him a beatific smile! Set the model aside to dry. Clean bowl and spoon before the mixture sets.

To finish When the model is set, carve any other details you wish to add.

Finally, paint the monk's habit and his fringe with brown paint, high light his cross in gold or yellow paint and color his features. When the paint is dry, cover the model with a coat of clear varnish.

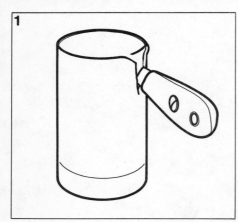

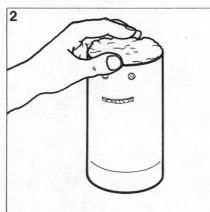

pocket screwdriver or linoleum cutting tool; scissors; tape measure; spatula or flexible knife; leftover paint.

To make the monk: Cut off the shaped top from the container. Pour 2½ cupfuls water into bowl, add 5 cups spackle, then mix together. Pour the mixture into the container and leave for 4 or 5 hours. Clean bowl and spoon.

Carefully cut away the container

to remove the tubular block (Diagram 1). Leave the block in a warm place overnight to harden right through—near a radiator is ideal.

Now begin the carving. Gouge out two small holes for the eyes, 1½ inches from the top edge and 1¾ inches apart. Score a line around the front of the block to separate the head from the body, 3 inches from top. Score a curved line for mouth.

Clean the varnish brush in turpentine, or paint thinner, then wash in soap and cold water.

TAKE A POT OF PAINT

Paints are irresistible to most small children. They love the colors, the freedom, the instant results, and if given the chance will squeeze, brush or smear them on paper, fabric, wood or any other available surface.

Many schools offer children marvelous facilities and plenty of time to get out their equipment, use it and put it away again, and against this background their enthusiasm and ability develop. So much so that when children come home from school waving their latest work of art—not necessarily a drawing or a painting, but perhaps a new technique— parents become interested, and the family starts a project together. This section is for just that situation—the ideas are for children and adults, at home and at school.

If children are less fortunate, and have little opportunity to use paint at school, encouraging parents can be a great help if they provide some space to work in, lots of newspaper to put on the floor and adequate painting materials.

Everybody can be an artist. Lack of drawing ability is no handicap to using paint successfully in many ways. Ideas can be carried out as simply or ambitiously as desired. Some readers will already be able to draw well and may have drawings on which to base designs for linocuts, block prints and so on. The simplest ideas are often the best. You can get inspiration from anything, anywhere; at home, in the city or country, at the beach, in the sky, looking at people, reading books or listening to music.

It is necessary, before starting to use the various types of paints, to know how to use them and what they can be used for. The following paragraphs will serve as a reference, both for the illustrated instructions in this section and for general guidance about paints, brushes and color-mixing.

Oil Paints

Oils come in a vast range of beautiful colors. They are based on linseed oil and have a high degree of permanence. Artists' oil colors are the finest made, using the best ingredients, regardless of cost. Students' oil paints are less expensive, and are therefore much more suitable for beginners. They can be used straight from the tube, squeezed, brushed on or applied with a palette knife, or thinned down with a little purified linseed oil and turpentine. Linseed stand oil can be used instead of purified linseed oil for a slightly shinier finish. Paint can be scraped after it has been applied to obtain a texture, or blotted to lift off surface paint. Oil paint is a slow-drying medium, so it is important to make sure that one layer is quite dry before applying the next.

You can paint on: paper, canvas, canvas board, cardboard, wood, plaster, plywood, masonite, styrofoam, etc. If you use unprimed canvas, first attach it to a canvas stretcher and pull smooth and taut using thumb tacks or staples around the outside edges, then prime the surface with canvas size and 2 coats of white lead or linseed oil or undercoat primer.

Acrylic Paints

These have the same consistency as oil paints, but are used with water for thinning purposes, *never* oil or turpentine. They can be used straight from the tube, then they will closely resemble oil colors, or mixed with water to resemble poster paints. If used very thinly, they become almost transparent. To get the greatest degree of transparency, use a coat of special white primer first, which will make the colors appear very intense. These paints dry extremely quickly, which is their chief advantage. They are also adhesive and can be used in collages of paper, fabric, wood, beads and so on.

You can paint on: paper, canvas, cardboard, wood, plaster, hardboard, newsprint, modeling clay and fabric. No special preparation or priming is required.

Water Soluble Paints

Watercolors are transparent paints, used mostly for fairly small-scale works. As their name implies, they are water-based. If you want to do a picture with large flat areas of wash when you will be using a lot of water, the paper must first of all have the stretch taken out of it in the following way: Choose a piece of watercolor paper, soak it in cold water for a few seconds, lay it on a flat board and tape the paper to it until it is dry and ready to use. If you plan to use drier paints, it is not necessary to stretch the paper by soaking. White should be used very sparingly in watercolor painting as it is not transparent.

Gouache, poster paints and powder paints are also water-based, but are opaque, unlike watercolors. Gouache paints are sold in tubes and are the best quality in this range. They come in the greatest variety of colors and have the best covering power.

Poster paints are sold in tubes or jars, and are also used with water.

Powder paints are a powdered form of pigment, sold in cans or large bags, and are mostly used in schools as they are economical. The paint is slightly inferior to poster paints. A small quantity should be spooned onto a palette or in a jar and mixed to a thick, smooth paste with a little water. Then you can add a little more water, without making it too runny. All these paints are suitable for painting large areas.

You can paint on: newsprint (cheap and good for school work); coarse drawing paper, and high-quality watercolor paper or board.

Linoleum Block Printing Inks

These are really poster paints with added glycerin to keep the colors moist when printing. The water-based variety is greatly preferable to oil-based colors, which tend to give a blurred edge to the finished print. They are sold in tubes and the colors should be squeezed onto a glass or plastic surface without any water being added, and rolled out with a brayer onto an area slightly larger than the width of the roller. The colors, which can be mixed on the glass surface, will take a few hours to dry after printing.

You can print on: practically any paper, thick or thin, plain or colored.

Paint Dyes

Paint dyes are made from a type of pigment different from poster paints, and are washable and color-fast. They are mainly used for painting and printing on fabric, but they can also be used successfully on paper. They are sold in jars and can be used as they come for block printing and stenciling, or diluted with a little water for painting directly on fabric.

You can use paint dyes on: natural fabrics like cotton, silk and linen. Don't use stiff, starchy materials as they don't wash well. To fix the color, let the painted fabric dry and then iron it on the reverse side.

Care of Paints

Tops must always be put back on tubes and jars, or the paint will dry up and be unusable. Always squeeze paint from the bottom of tubes (like toothpaste!); otherwise it has a habit of suddenly gushing out of the bottom.

Brushes

The best brushes are made of finest quality sable and hog bristles. They are expensive, but there are good brushes made of sable, hog bristles, squirrel hair and ox ear hair at reasonable prices. Don't waste money on cheap, thin little brushes. All the hairs will come out, and probably onto what you are painting. Brushes are made in a variety of widths, lengths and shapes for different purposes; fine for details, large for big areas, and any number in between.

Always clean your brushes after use and between using one color and another. Oil-painting brushes should be thoroughly cleaned with turpentine and then washed in warm, soapy water before putting them away. Brushes used for any watercolor painting should be cleaned in water, and *never* left in the water jar to become like little hockey sticks. Brushes used for acrylic paints should be cleaned *immediately* in water after using, as the paint dries so quickly.

Colors

The primary colors are red, yellow and blue. The secondary colors are
(1) red and yellow = orange;
(2) red and blue = violet;
(3) yellow and blue = green. In painting, all colors can be made from these six, except white and a true black. Probably the most useful colors to buy are black, white, blue, both Prussian and cobalt, red, both scarlet and crimson, and bright yellow and yellow ocher. Brown can be made from mixing the three primary colors. Of course, you could save yourself the trouble and buy it! Pale colors should be made by adding a strong color in a tiny amount to a larger amount of white; for example, a dash of red plus white makes pink.

A final word of encouragement before you go ahead. Don't be frightened of making mistakes. It is most unlikely that you will get everything right the first time. Sometimes it takes hours—or even days—to produce something you are pleased with. But when you do time just doesn't matter: it's the pride of achievement that counts.

The speed and power of an owl in flight is effectively conveyed in this dramatic linoleum block cut by a thirteen-year-old pupil. Below Once a smoothly rounded piece of granite, now a colorful, ornamental paperweight, transformed by blurred stripes of bright poster pain

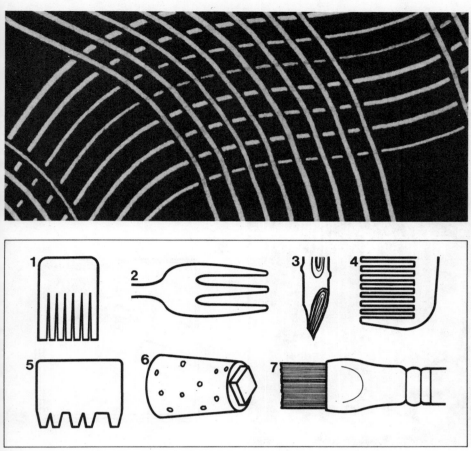

1. A specially made metal comb
2. A table fork
3. A sharpened stick
4. A piece of a comb
5. A homemade comb, cut from cardboard
6. A cork with a pattern cut out of the top
7. A stiff painting brush

Combed Patterns

Decorative papers can be made by painting paper with a mixture of paint and paste and "combing" patterns on while the paper is wet. When dry, the finished papers make attractive folders, book jackets or covers for boxes or other containers. Practice on small pieces first, and don't exceed a size of about 18 by 24 inches, as the paint/paste will dry in some places before the whole area is covered.

Use fairly stiff paper with a smooth surface. Dampen the paper with a wet sponge and then pin or tape it onto a wooden board. A colored paper can be used to give a two-tone effect.

To prepare the paint/paste mixture, either mix powder paint to a stiff, smooth paste or use poster paints/watercolors in tubes. Put the paint on a small palette, or an old saucer, carefully add a few drops of water at a time, and stir well.

Then add a white liquid glue such as Elmer's or Sobo in a slightly larger quantity than the paint. First put it into another small palette, and pour it onto the paint. Mix well. The object is to get a thick but flowing liquid. Be sure to make enough to cover your paper. Dampen the paper again immediately before covering it with the mixture, as this makes the color go on more easily.

Cover the paper very evenly with the mixture, using a large, floppy brush. Go first from top to bottom, then from side to side.

When the paper is covered, use whichever tool you like, doing crisscross, straight, wavy, zigzag lines, squiggles, or stamping patterns.

As you can see from the photographs on this page, you can make waves, swirls, S-shapes and so on.

Fabric printing at its simplest – bold colors and random repetition of an 'A is for Apple' design, cut from a foam block. Below: Marbling – floating oil paints on a layer of size – a fascinating technique which makes designs suitable for covering books, blotters and boxes

Combing with Linoleum Block Printing Inks

There is another method of making combed patterns or shapes, using linoleum block printing inks instead of the paint/paste mixture.

For this you use a glass pane, and roll out linoleum block printing ink evenly over its surface, using a rubber-covered brayer (Diagram 1).

Then comb or scrape the pattern on the glass pane. Now lay the paper on top of the inked pane and very carefully rub the reverse side. Be sure that the paper does not move. Peel it off (Diagram 2) and hang it up to dry.

Remember that the pattern will be reversed on the paper so if, for instance, you wanted to reproduce your name you would have to do it in mirror writing.

Lucy Forrest, aged 6, used this technique, but with finger paints, to print this smug-looking cat.

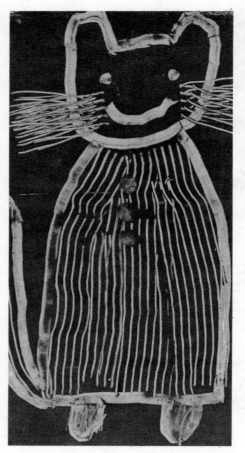

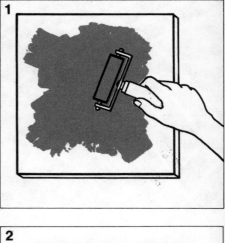

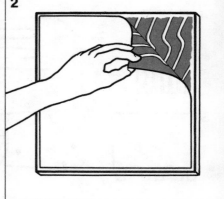

variety of effects. You can use combs, glue-spreaders, ice-cream sticks, etc., to "lift" the paint from the paper. This is what Lucy Forrest did to make the design of the dragon in the photograph on the left.

To print the cat shown on the left above, she rolled finger paints onto a glass pane, worked out the pattern with a stick, and then printed it off onto paper, using the flat of her hand to get an even impression.

Finger paints come in wide-necked jars big enough to get practically the whole hand in.

Ice-cream sticks or twigs are ideal to scrape the paint off and leave a big, bold outline.

Finger Painting

This is the best medium ever invented for children up to about six years old. After all, as someone somewhere has surely observed, fingers were made before brushes.

The best paper for this is a shiny surfaced one specially sold for the purpose, but any non-absorbent paper will do. Not only can the paint be put on the paper with the fingers or the whole hand, but it can also be taken off to get a wide

Vegetable and Fruit Cuts

Potatoes are often used, cut into shapes, as a medium for printing because they are large and cheap. However, they ooze liquid if cut and used immediately. It is advisable, therefore, to leave them for several hours, or overnight, after cutting and before using. Turnips, parsnips and carrots are better, as they can be used right away. And once you have decided to experiment with vegetable cuts, who wants to wait till tomorrow to do it?

Cut your vegetable into a big enough piece for easy handling. See that the edges of the pattern are cleanly cut, as in the examples illustrated above. Use one or more shapes to give you an interesting, composite pattern, like the one in the photograph on the left.

The following paints can be used for this technique: water paints,

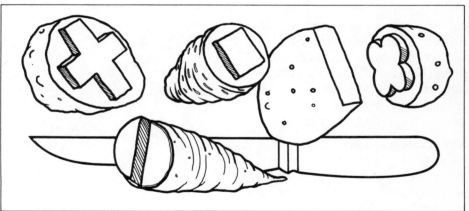

poster, gouache or powder paints mixed to a stiff, flowing paste; linoleum block printing inks, or dye paints.

Mix your color in a palette or flat plate and dip the patterned end of the vegetable in the paint. Making sure that no drips will follow onto your paper, place the vegetable firmly down to print, and lift off carefully.

Fruit cuts   You can also use certain fruit, cut in half, for printing. Try oranges, lemons (see the photograph on the right), apples, strawberries (as long as they are slightly under-ripe and firm), pears, slices of pineapple or tomatoes.

The photograph on the left, above, shows four different shapes, which were cut and printed by Rebecca Gregory, who also produced the lemon print, above right.

Spatter and Stone Painting

Paint spattering is a marvelous way of getting a textured look with water paints. But be warned—it spatters not only the paper, but you and your immediate surroundings too, so wear a smock or old clothes and choose a table or floor away from furniture and walls. Lay down masses of newspaper. Use poster, gouache or water paints in tubes. Mix the colors you want to a fairly fluid consistency, in shallow containers. Wet your papers (not too thin a paper) under the cold water faucet for a few moments, then pin or tape them to a flat surface to dry before using. Use an old toothbrush and dip it into the first color. Scrape the surplus paint off on the side of the container. Run a finger along the bristles to knock the paint off in showers—here's where a little restraint comes in! (Diagram 1).

You can make patterns by placing cutouts (particularly good in foam rubber) or objects on the paper and spattering the paint around them (Diagram 2). The shapes can then be lifted off, moved around, and interesting areas of varying paint density created.

The photograph on the right was "spattered" by Rebecca Gregory in three colors. As with combed patterns, this would be attractive as a book cover.

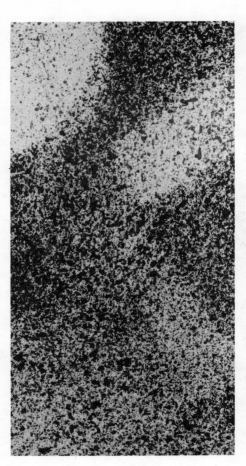

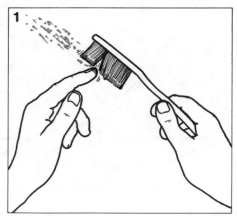

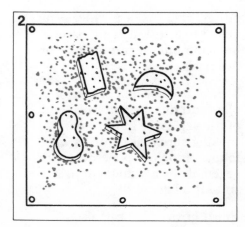

Painting Stones

This is a fascinating pastime which produces some lively and surprising effects. The stones can afterward be used as paperweights or singly as ornaments. And a collection of them, in blending colors, makes a most attractive feature displayed in a shallow bowl.

Choose stones that have a smooth surface. They can be of a regular or quite irregular shape, depending on what you want to achieve. A stone with a hole in it, for instance, is good material, for the hole can be the focal point for the design. Wash the stones well and dry them before painting.

Use poster, gouache or acrylic paints. The paints can be used quite thickly; or, to let the grain of the stone show through, quite thinly.

One interesting way of using the paints is to let one color run into another. Or you can cover the stone in one color, and drop splashes of paint in other colors while the first coat is still wet. This will give you a soft, vignette effect.

You can also draw a design and paint it in with a fine paintbrush. In this case, the shape of the stone should determine the pattern.

A coat of clear varnish greatly enhances the colors.

The stone photographed opposite is painted with a random design in yellow and muddy green = brown. The lines in the lighter color are outlined with the darker one.

Stripes of red, blue and pink, with a touch of white, make up the striking color scheme of the stone on the far right. This is also shown in the color photograph.

If you have painted a stone which you think really looks like a work of art, you can mount it on a piece of plywood, using a strong contact adhesive, and hang it. A small collection mounted in this way looks most attractive.

Painting with Straws

This is a very free way of painting; apply the paint to the paper, then blow it with straws.

You will need: Water paints (poster, powder, gouache or watercolors in tubes); some straws; some strong white paper such as Bond paper.

Method: Mix your colors to a flowing consistency with water. Don't add too much water, or the results will be disappointingly faint. Four or five colors should be enough to start with.

Drop little puddles of color, one at a time, onto the paper, and blow with a straw. The paint will race over the paper and make weird shapes, like those in the photograph above. As you have more practice, you will soon learn to control the pattern to a large extent by the direction and the strength you blow. You do *not* fill the straw with paint and blow that.

Printing on Fabrics

Equipment:

1. Paint dyes
2. Styrofoam $\frac{1}{4}$-inch thick
3. A block of wood slightly larger than the design
4. Strong glue
5. Scissors
6. Kitchen knife
7. Sponge

Method 1: Block Printing

You can print on cotton, linen or silk. A piece of old cotton sheet is ideal. Don't use stiff, starchy fabrics as they do not wash well. Wash, dry and iron the fabric first, and then pin it on a flat, wooden surface with pushpins. Put several thicknesses of newspaper underneath. Work out a very simple design that can be easily cut. Draw it out on the piece of styrofoam with a felt-tip pen, cut it out and glue it to the block of wood.

Knife some paint dye onto the sponge in an area corresponding to your design and squeeze it a little. Press the styrofoam printing block onto the color on the sponge and then press it hard on the fabric in order to print. When the paint dye has dried on the fabric, it should be ironed on the reverse side to "fix" the color.

Ten-year-old Susannah Critchley used this method to print her design of apples, which you can see in the photograph above and in color. Her red, white and black color scheme is strikingly simple.

Method 2: Stencil Printing

You can also print using a stencil. To cut a stencil you will need only a pair of sharp scissors and some lightweight cardboard such as tagboard, one- or two-ply Bristolboard, or pebble board. Draw a simple design on the cardboard leaving some space on all sides.

Using Paint and Art Masking Fluid

Art masking fluid, or liquid frisket, is a pale yellow liquid, sold in most art supply stores; when used on paper and allowed to dry, it forms a thin protective film that paint cannot penetrate. The colors go right over the art masking fluid and when they, in their turn, are dry, the fluid can be peeled off very easily, leaving the paper blank underneath.

You can use art masking fluid in the following ways: with a paintbrush, spattered with a toothbrush, blown with a straw or done in conjunction with folded paper butterflies, all of which techniques are described in this section.

Method: Use strong paper or white cardboard. Use any of the methods described above to mask out the areas you do not want colored. Allow it to dry thoroughly.

The paints (water-based) should be used fairly wet. Once the colors are dry, rub the places covered with the art masking fluid with your finger, and it will easily peel away.

In Diagram 1 you can see the paint being brushed over the whole area, with the lines drawn in art masking fluid showing through.

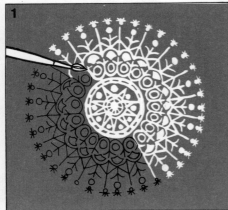

Put the point of the scissors through the design and cut out the shape, taking care not to cut the surrounding cardboard.

Pin the fabric down and place the stencil on it. Tape it in two or three places to keep it steady. Brush in the paint dye using a stiff brush. Carefully lift off the stencil. It should reveal a neat shape with no blurred edges.

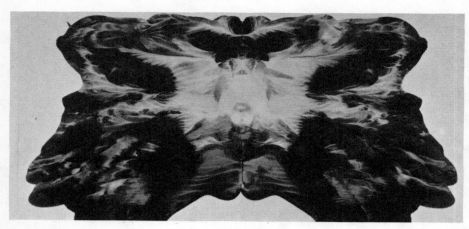

Folded Paper Butterflies

There can't be many people who have not tried their hand at folded paper butterflies. They are very easy and great fun to do. Take a piece of paper—coarse drawing or construction paper is good—and fold it in half. Choose any size and any shape of paper you like, square, oblong or circular. Paper butterflies come in all shapes, sizes and colors!

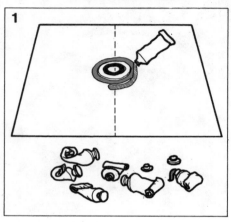

Method 1: This is a good way of using up odds and ends of tubes of watercolors. Over the center of the fold, squeeze a circle of one color. Repeat, making a larger circle with another color. Make three or four circles, or more if your paper is very large.

Now fold the paper in half again where the crease was made, and with the side of your hand, push the paint toward the outside edges. This should be done quickly, before the paint sticks to the other side of the paper and becomes difficult to open up.

Now unfold the paper, and both sides will be "printed." Place on a flat surface, with weights on each side, until dry.

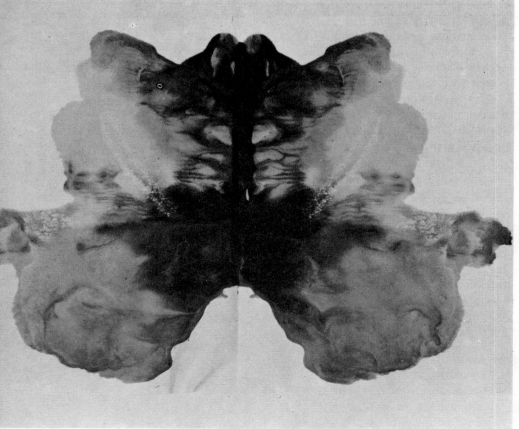

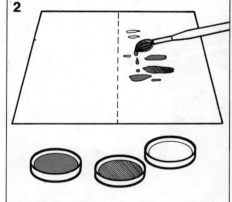

Method 2: To get a very blurred effect, use poster, gouache, powder or watercolor paints mixed with a little water. The paint should be of a runny consistency.

Mix two or three colors ready for use, and drop a blob of each about one inch away from the central fold. Don't put too much on—it will run out of the paper! Fold the paper over, push with your hand and then open and leave to dry.

Using Linoleum Block Printing Inks

To print simple objects with linoleum block printing ink you will need: a tube of linoleum block printing ink, preferably in a dark color; a brayer; a glass pane, and paper to print on (practically any paper will do—newsprint, wrapping paper, etc.).

Squeeze about ¾-inch of printing ink onto the glass. Roll the roller over the ink at different angles in order to cover the roller completely and evenly.

Have ready any soft, flat article with interesting markings or texture, like a leaf, small piece of fabric, lace or canvas, a frayed rope end or a discarded bit of knitting.

Lay down some newspaper and put your object on it. Roll the inked roller right over it, backward and forward until it is evenly inked. For delicate leaves, roll only very lightly so that the veins show.

Now lift the inked article up and put it, inked side down, on a piece of clean paper. Place another piece of paper on top, and rub over the article with your fingers or a spare brayer.

The result will be a sharply defined impression.

The photograph right shows a rock geranium leaf; the picture above shows some openwork fabric.

Diagram 1 shows a piece of glass with linoleum block printing ink on it, and the roller being evenly coated. Diagram 2 shows the ink being transferred from the roller to a leaf, ready for printing.

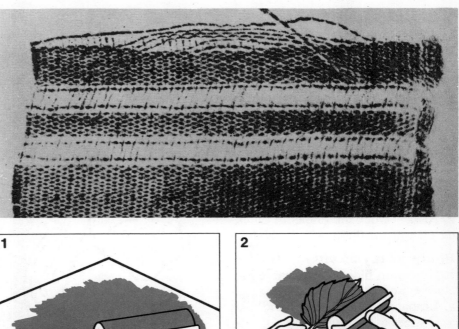

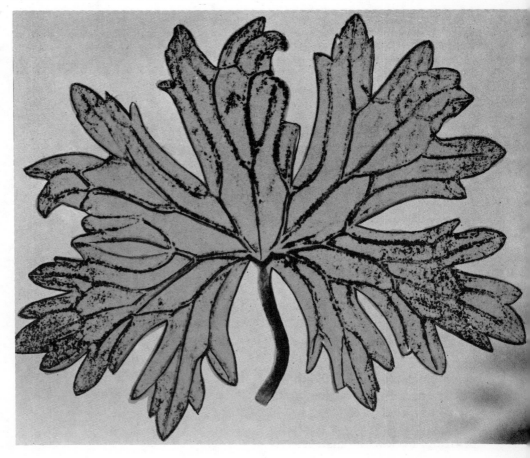

Linoleum Block Cutting and Printing

This technique is not suitable for very young children, as the linoleum cutters are sharp, but children of nine and above should be able to manage if taught the correct way to do it.

It is essential to:
1. Keep the hand that is not cutting the linoleum block out of the way of the cutter.
2. Always work the linoleum block cutter toward the block of wood.

Equipment you will need:
1. Linoleum blocks, obtainable in a variety of sizes
2. Linoleum block cutter handle
3. Cutters of various sizes and shapes for different uses. For beginners, two or three cutters are sufficient: fine, medium and one spoon-shaped one
4. Rubber-covered brayer
5. A glass or plastic palette
6. Paper to print on

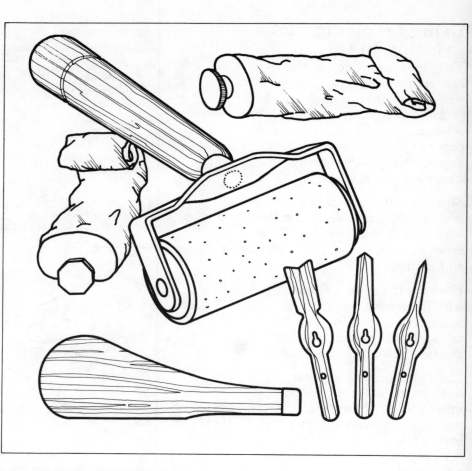

Method 1: Color Printing
1. Work out a simple design on paper, to the size desired. It is best to color in with crayons or felt-tip pens the required color area. Remember that the pieces that are cut out will *not* print—only the areas that are left.
2. Then make a tracing of your design, including the surrounding area, and leave enough tracing paper at the sides so that it can be pinned down over the linoleum. *Either* put a piece of carbon paper, shiny side down, on the linoleum before tracing, *or* pencil on the reverse side of the tracing. Now trace onto the linoleum.
3. Start cutting the linoleum. Don't cut too deeply, as you might dig a hole right through the linoleum. Note (Diagram 1) the position of the hands, and the wood block. Cut just enough so that the areas to be printed are a little raised.
4. The linoleum is now ready for printing. Follow the instructions

given for rolling ink on the previous page.
5. Lay down several sheets of newspaper and put your linoleum over it. Quickly roll the inked roller over the raised surface until every part is evenly covered.
6. The very best way to print at home is: Put one newspaper down on the floor. Put your linoleum on it, *inked side up.* Lay the paper to be printed on top, and give it a roll with a spare roller or rub with the back of a wooden spoon. *Then* put one or two sheets of newspaper on top and stand on it. Don't jump around, though!

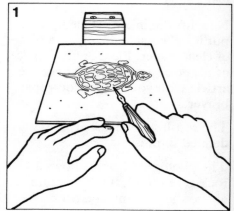

Method 2: Using more than one color

Work out a design on paper using not more than three colors.

Make a separate tracing of *each* color, i.e. three colors = 3 tracings. Draw a line around the four sides of the block each time a tracing is made to position each color accurately. Print the first color in the way described previously. Let it dry for three or four hours before printing the second one in a different color on top.

For successful linoleum block cutting

1. Cut out all the outlines first with a fine cutter.
2. Use the cutter with a slight wriggling movement of the hand. This will give greater control than ploughing along in a straight line.
3. Don't try to cut too much linoleum off at one time. Smaller cuts are easier to manage.

For successful inking

1. The ink on the slab should be tacky, not slimy. If it is overinked, scrape a little ink off, and roll again.
2. Foreign matter, on either the roller or the slab, should be lifted off before printing.
3. Before each printing, ink the roller up again, adding more ink when necessary.

The photograph above shows a tortoise design, printed in one color, using Method 1.

The owl, which you can also see in the color picture, was designed, cut and printed by a 13-year-old schoolboy. This is a three-color print, using Method 2, and is painstaking work.

Marbled Papers

This method, using oil paints floated on a layer of size, is the best way of making marbled papers at home or possibly at school.

The more professional and less limited way of making them, with Carragheen Moss Size and specially prepared colors, is so complicated that it has not been described here.

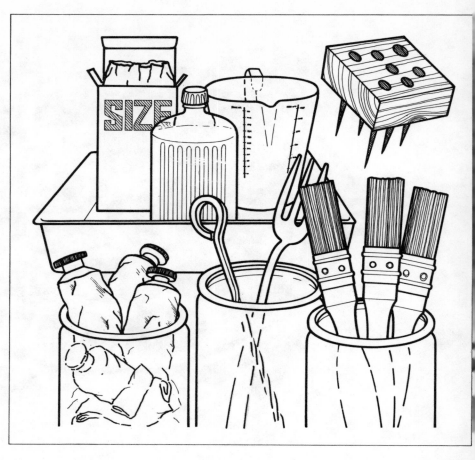

Equipment you will need:

1. An old square or oblong baking dish, a zinc trough, a sink or similar receptacle to hold the size
2. A package of powdered size
3. Tubes of oil paint
4. A measuring cup or milk bottle
5. Jars for mixing paint
6. Turpentine
7. A large brush for each color
8. A tool for combing the colors, like a fork, meat skewer, piece of wood with a few nails driven through it
9. Clean paper of any kind (not glazed)

To prepare the size:

1. Measure out 2 oz. of powdered size, such as rabbit's-skin glue, into a container large enough to hold 4 pints.
2. Add 1 pint boiling water and stir until the size is completely dissolved. Then add 3 pints of hot water, stir again for a minute or two, and let cool. The size, once prepared, will last for about six days.

To prepare the colors:

1. Generally, two colors or, at most, three will be enough for each printed paper. Squeeze about 2 inches of each color into separate mixing jars.
2. Add about a teaspoonful of turpentine to each, and stir the colors until they are completely mixed and free of lumps.

To prepare for marbling:

1. When the prepared size is cold, pour some to a depth of about $1\frac{1}{2}$ inches into the receptacle.

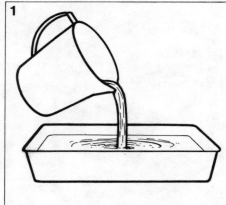

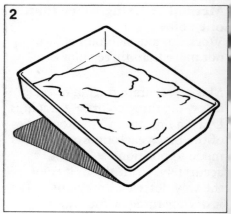

2. Put plenty of newspaper around your working area and on a flat surface nearby, where you will put your printed papers to dry.

3. To check the consistency of the size, tilt the receptacle a little (Diagram 2). If any part is like jelly, add a little hot water and stir to get rid of the stickiness.

4. Cut several pieces of paper, smaller than the receptacle. To begin with, it is better to use quite small pieces, say 6 to 8 inches.

Method of marbling:

1. With a different brush for each color, drop blobs onto the size mixture (Diagram 3). If the color sinks to the bottom, it's too thick; add more turpentine. If the color loses its intensity the moment it is on the size, it is too thin; add more oil paint.

2. With your combing tool, very gently work up a pattern on the surface of the size (Diagram 4). Don't do it quickly, as the colors

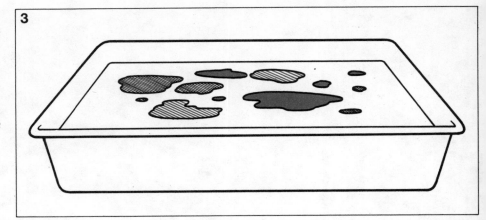

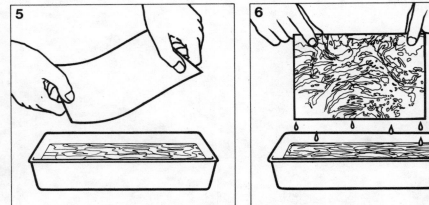

will drop to the bottom, and the pattern will also whirl out of sight before you have had a chance to print.

3. When the distribution of colors and shapes is to your liking, pick up your piece of paper at both ends, and gently lower it into the middle of the size, so that it floats on top (Diagram 5).

4. In a few seconds, a definition of the pattern will be seen on the reverse side. Lift it off carefully, by two opposite corners, and let any surplus size drip off before putting it flat to dry (Diagram 6).

Notes on Marbling

After each printing, the size can be cleaned by leveling the color off with a folded-up newspaper.

When completely dry the design can be ironed on the back. This will flatten it completely. Try not to get large patches of just one colour. The results are more interesting when the surface is broken with other colors.

Any combination of colors can be used: Prussian blue/scarlet, raw sienna/black/emerald; these 5, worked out in different combinations and different quantities of color will give an enormous range of effects.

See the example in the color picture.

TAKE A TIN OF DYE

An Introduction to Tie-Dyeing

Have you ever thought how useful it would be, if you were a fabric designer? Every time you wanted some material for new clothes or furnishings, you could dream up just whatever you liked, and go right ahead and create it for yourself.

There's no need to go to art school, or even to have any particular flair to produce your own fabrics, for the art of tie-dyeing, which so many young children now learn at school, is as easy as it is fun. It's a cheap and cheerful way of creating pattern and color combinations in any mood and on any scale.

Just as the name implies, first you tie the fabric, then you dye it. The fabric will resist the dye in the parts that are tightly bound; depending on which method you use, you can create designs with circles, stripes, checks, waves, squares, anything.

At first, before you are very experienced at tie-dyeing, unwrapping the fabric after dyeing will have as much of an element of surprise as opening a birthday present. Later, you will have the thrill of controlling the dye and making it do exactly what you want—then you will really be a fabric designer.

Without any special skills, you can achieve effects that look as if an artist had washed his paintbrush out on the material; lengths of fabrics that appear to have gotten caught in a shower of colored rain; designs as delicate as a piece of cracked porcelain or as dazzling as a burst of sunlight.

There is such a vast range of colors available in dyes for home use that it's hard to know which to choose. Part of the fun in tie-dyeing is in creating your own colors by dyeing one on top of the other. Everyone knows that blue and yellow will produce green: yellow and red make orange, and blue and red will give you purple. But you can experiment for yourself, over-dyeing two or more colors so that the finished product shows traces of none of them: your fabric can't be more individual than that!

The instructions on the following pages are easy to follow and fully illustrated. There are many different ways you can make the fabric resist the dye, and the ones described here are the beginnings of a fascinating and thoroughly practical hobby. If, as you progress, some of your earlier efforts do not meet with your approval, nothing is lost: you can remove the color and start again.

Try the simpler methods first, copying the patterns we show on small pieces of fabric. Then you can graduate to dyeing lengths of fabric to make into skirts and dresses, scarves, screens, curtains and so on. You can see examples of these in the two color pages in this section.

You need the very minimum of equipment for tie-dyeing; you will have practically all of it at home already.

Suitable Fabrics

We recommend that you start by using Rit cold-water dye or Tintex, which is colorfast and suitable for all types of cotton, from fine lawn to unbleached cotton fabric. All the instructions in this section are based on the use of this type of dye. Other fabrics that can be used successfully with it are muslin, toweling, linen, rayon, wool/cotton mixtures, light woolen fabrics, pure silk, cotton and silk velvets and corduroys. Cotton fabrics with a crease-resistant or drip-dry finish tend to repel the dye. For beginners, lightweight materials are best, because they are easier to fold, pleat, bunch up and knot.

Synthetic fabrics—rayon and all nylons—need special dyes; other polyester fibers resist some dyes.

There is no need to stick to white or cream fabrics; try pale blue, pink, green and others, using dyes that are complementary to the background.

Before tying, wash the fabrics in hot, soapy water, and let soak for an hour or two, before rinsing and drying.

Tying

It is important to tie fabrics as tightly as possible, to prevent the dye from seeping in. Children might need help.

Different types of tying produce different results. An area bound heavily with cotton gauze will produce a broader effect than one that has been crisscrossed with string: this will emerge with a finely textured pattern.

You can tie with any of the following: string, raffia, strong cotton and linen threads, cord, yarn, tape, strips torn from old sheets, bandages and wide elastic or rubber bands.

Equipment you will need

Choose a container deep enough to cover the articles to be dyed, a pot, bucket or basin made of plastic, glass, china or stainless steel, but not of aluminum. For large quantities, use a sink, bathtub or washing machine.

Then you will need: a 1-pint measuring cup or milk bottle; table salt; a package of cold-water dye fixative; tablespoon; wooden spoon or stick; rubber gloves; waterproof apron; sharp scissors; pencil; needle and thread for some designs, and string or tapes, as above.

About dyeing in general

Always prepare your dye just before you need it, as the addition of baking soda or the dye fixative makes the dye liquid react immediately. The dye retains its potency for a limited time.

Generally, two dyes of a different color are needed to get the best results, the second one enriching the effect. A third color can be used as desired.

Once you have tied your fabric, you can dye it either wet or dry.

Wetting the bound areas first gives the design sharper definition.

On a fine day, you can do your dyeing out of doors. If you do it indoors, it is as well to spread a few old newspapers around the area where you will be working. It isn't every surface in the home that you want to change color!

Preparing the dye   Always weigh the article, dry, before preparing the correct amount of dye. One can of Rit cold-water dye will dye $\frac{1}{2}$ lb. of dry material. Therefore, if a garment weighs 1 lb. and is to be dyed with two colors, you will need two cans of each color. In any case, follow the manufacturer's instructions carefully and, if necessary, adjust our directions accordingly.

Pierce can and dissolve each can of powder in 1 pint warm water. Stir well. Pour into the dye vessel and add enough cold water to cover the articles to be dyed – about $1\frac{1}{2}$ to 2 pints for $\frac{1}{2}$ lb. of dry material. Make a note of the amount used, in case you want to match the color later.

Next, add 4 tablespoons of table salt and stir, using a wooden spoon or stick. Dissolve 1 package of cold-water dye fixative in a pint of very hot water. Stir it well, making sure that all the particles are melted. Add this to the container, and stir again for a minute. When dyeing woolen fabrics, add $1\frac{1}{2}$ cups of vinegar to the dye vessel and use medium-hot water instead of cold. This keeps the fabric soft.

Dyeing

The dye is now ready to use. Submerge your tied-up cloth (details of how to do that later) either wet or dry, into the dye, and stir the dye with a wooden spoon or stick for about ten minutes so that all the fabric is equally exposed to it. Leave the articles in the dye for an additional 50

minutes. Lift out of container, using the stick or a pair of tongs. The dye can be poured away or used a second time, when its color will be less intense.

Rinsing

The articles need rinsing very thoroughly in several changes of cold water, squeezing the excess dye out at the same time. Remove all or some of the bindings, soak the articles in hot, soapy water for five minutes, and then rinse again until water is clear.

Cutting the cords

This is perhaps the most exciting part of the whole operation, when you will be able to see the results of your work. Children should be reminded to cut very carefully, and get the point of the scissors through and out of the binding before cutting; otherwise, they might snip the fabric.

Retying

Hang the articles up to dry, and then tie up again for the second dyeing. Follow the instructions given for the first dyeing, and after rinsing, soaking in hot, soapy water, rinsing again and cutting the ties, let them dry a little. Then iron while still damp.

Helpful Hints
Below: How to tie a square knot

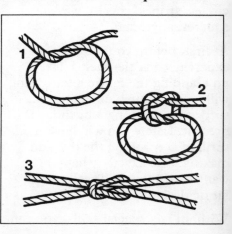

Showing the versatility of a piece of plain cotton and a can of dye – a batik (wax-and-dye) picture and two tie-dyed dress cotton lengths

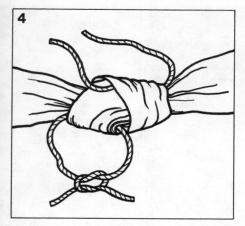

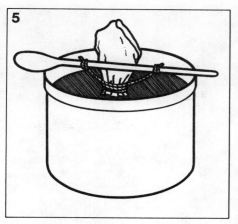

Above: We all know how difficult it is sometimes to untie a knot in string or, even worse, in wet fabric. You will have to do this many times in tie-dyeing. To make it easier, tie two additional lengths of string into both parts of the knot before tying the fabric. Then you can simply pull these apart.

Above: Where there are large areas of a fabric that you do not want to dye, tie a plastic bag very tightly over them. Suspend from a handle, or from a wooden spoon or stick lying across the top of the dye-vessel, so that only the fabric that is to be dyed comes into contact with the color.

Above: When children—at home or at school—are using the same dye-vessel, it is a good idea if they tie an extra length of string to their tied article and attach a thread spool, pair of scissors, etc. It's like a grab bag, but in this case they will know which "prize" is their own!

Simple Knotting

To produce a pattern of wavy lines, as shown in the photograph on the right, take a piece of fine cloth and fold it once or twice lengthwise, depending on its size. Roll it into a loose "sausage" shape. Tie knots in the "sausage" as closely together as you can. Following the directions on the opposite page, dye the fabric, untie the knots and, if you want to use another color, tie it up again and redye. The photograph is of fabric after one dyeing, showing "waves" of the background color.

To make a pattern of circles, as shown in the photograph, lower right, take a piece of fine cloth and mark the center. Pull the cloth up at this point and knot it tightly. Tie the four corners as well, and dye. Untie and, if desired, retie for a second color. The photograph, showing the circle in the center of the cloth and part of those at the corners, was taken after only one dyeing.

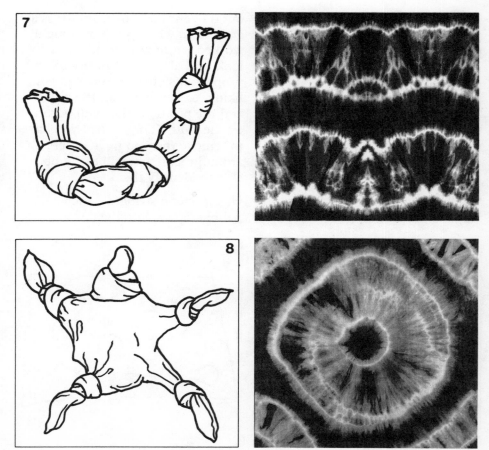

The skirt and scarf show striped and check effects that can be achieved by first pleating and then dyeing the fabric

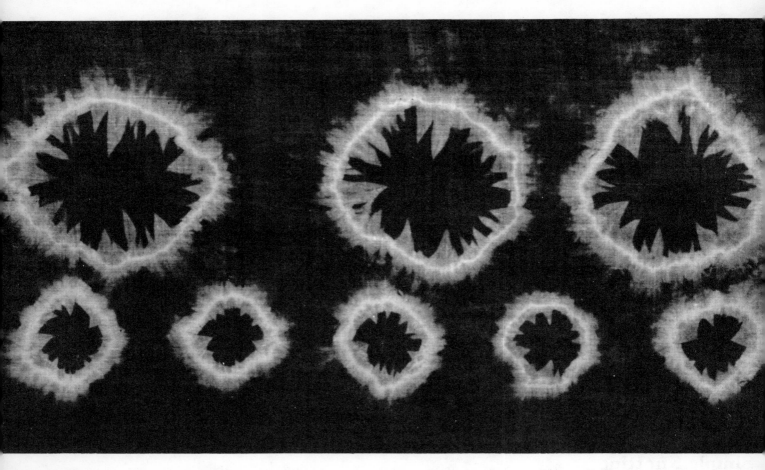

Patterns with Pebbles

It is difficult to believe that a handful of pebbles could produce the design you see on the fabric in the photograph above. Any small, hard objects can be tied into the cloth—you can try using corks, thread spools, buttons (they must be rustproof), marbles, shells, small pieces of wood, and so on. Vary the size and shape according to the kind of effect you want.

Lay the pebbles or other objects out on your piece of fabric. It is a good idea, when you have roughly worked out how your design will look, and altered the positions and proportions of the pebbles to your liking, to number both the objects and the positions they will occupy on the cloth. Then, when you have to remove them to tie in others around them, you will easily be able to identify them.

Using strong string, tie each pebble tightly into the fabric, winding the string around several times until you are quite sure that no dye can seep in past it. The size of the pebble or other object determines the size of the circle or shape that will resist the dye, where the string is tied, and so with only a little practice you can easily visualize how your finished work will look. The photograph above was taken after one dyeing.

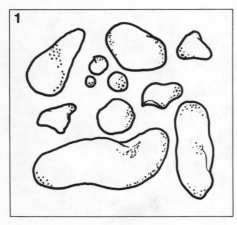

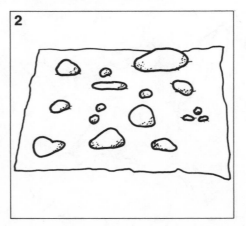

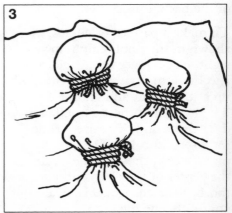

How to Make a "Sunburst"

Take a square of cloth, and fold it into four so that you have a smaller square. Hold the inside corner of the fabric with your left hand, as shown in Diagram 1, shake the cloth out, and smooth it down with your right hand. You have seen magicians doing this with a handkerchief when they want to convince you that they have nothing hidden up their sleeve!

Now tie the strip of cloth in various places, as shown in Diagram 2. Use thin string or thicker cords according to the width of the "sunburst" circles you want. Dye the fabric, untie the bindings. Following the general instructions on page 170 retie the cloth and dye again for a second-color effect.

The photograph above was dyed twice and now shows a yellow sunburst on a dark blue ground.

Just to show how easy it is, this fabric was tie-dyed by a six-year-old.

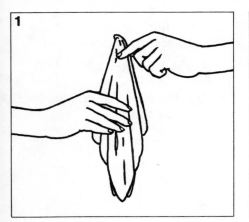

Stripes and Checks

A girl of 11 achieved the soft, stripy effect shown in the photograph with two dyeings.

The skirt worn by our model was dyed with cold-water dye using Radiant Pink and French Navy. Her scarf used the same French Navy but, as the fabric was of a different type, took the dye in a different density.

Both the skirt and the scarf use the pleating method, shown on these two pages, to give an effect of stripes. You can also see them in the color photograph.

To give your fabric a striped effect, work like this: Fold it in half lengthwise. Lay it on a clean, flat surface and, using a pencil and ruler, mark every two or three inches along the folded edge and the top outside edge. The spaces must all be equal. Pleat the fabric, using the pencil marks as guidelines. Hold the fabric tightly as you work along it.

If your fabric is particularly large, it is easier to do it this way: Fold it in half lengthwise, as before, and make the pencil marks along both long edges. Thread two needles, and run the needles in and out of the pencil marks. Pull the thread taut until the pleated cloth is tight at both ends (Diagrams 3, 4, 5).

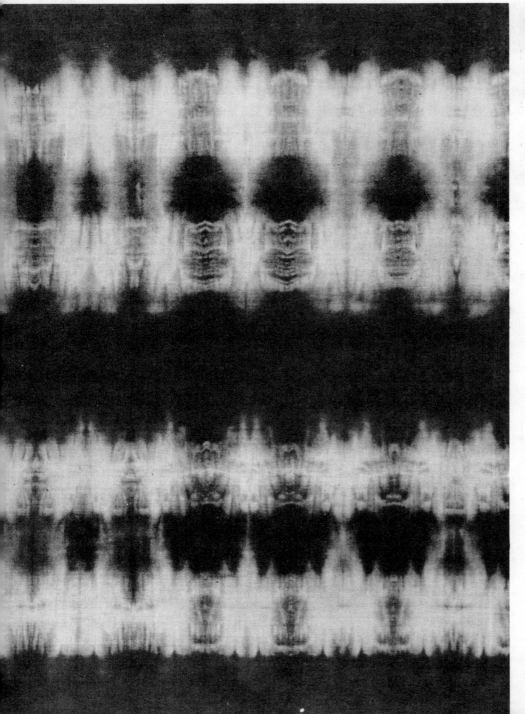

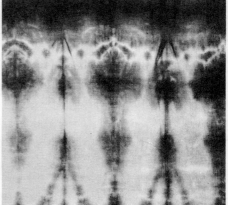

Whichever method of pleating you have used, tie the strip of fabric in various places (Diagram 1, opposite), remembering that where you bind it, it will resist the dye and give a striped effect. If you used thread to help with the pleating, pull it out before dyeing. Dye the fabric, untie the binding. For a second dyeing, retie in different places, using the same pleats as before.

You can see the effect in the close-up photograph and the garments shown opposite.

To obtain a checked effect, fold the fabric in half crosswise, pleat it in this direction, tie and proceed as described above.

Twisting and Coiling

This method was used for the two lengths of fabric shown in the color photograph and for the one below, which has been dyed only once.

You need to twist the fabric as tightly as possible. To do this, get someone to hold one end, pin it to a vertical surface, or knot the end to a doorhandle. Now twist until there is no more "give" in the length of fabric (Diagram 2).

Let the strip double back on itself, from the middle, to form a ropelike coil. Tie it in various places, and dye.

After dyeing and before retying (if you wish a second color), it is a good idea to fold the fabric once lengthwise, and put a basting stitch here and there to show where the patterns match on the edges.

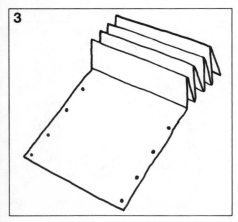

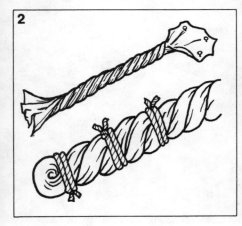

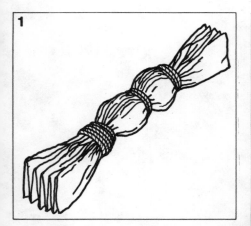

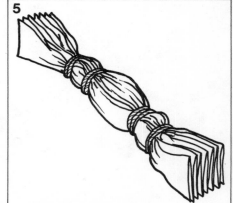

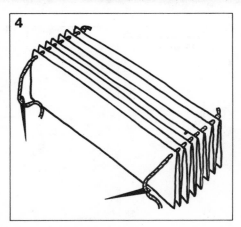

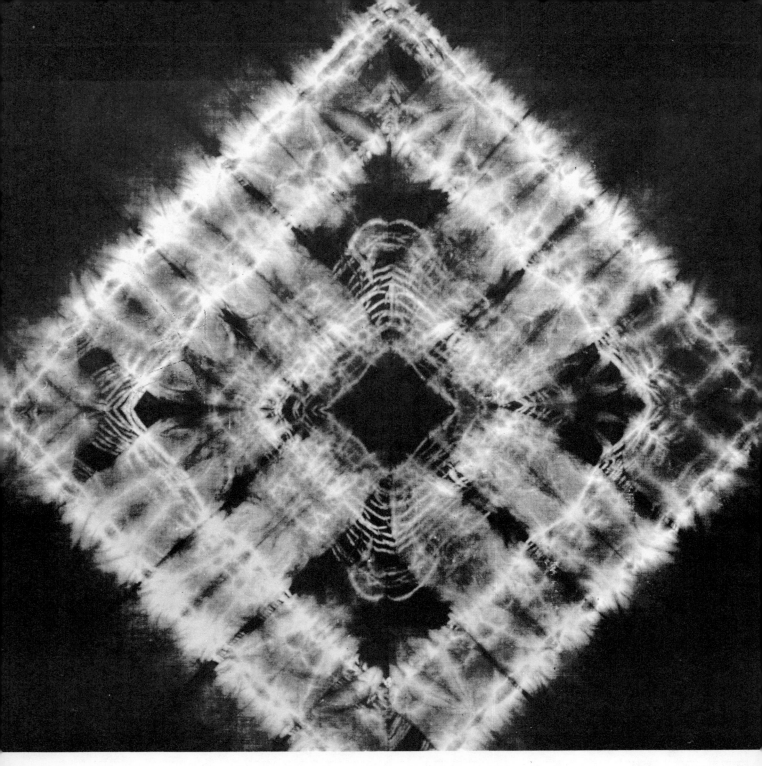

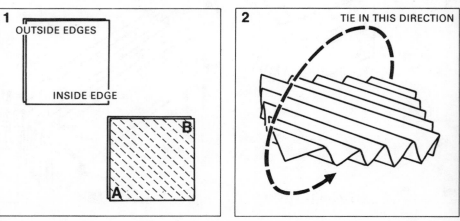

1

OUTSIDE EDGES

INSIDE EDGE

B

A

2

TIE IN THIS DIRECTION

Squaring Up

For this method, you need to fold diagonally. To do this, take a square of fine cloth, and fold it in four, so that you have a square a quarter of the original size.

Pleat or roll the cloth diagonally, from A to B, according to Diagram 1, below, left.

Now tie the cloth in the *opposite* direction to the folds, as shown in Diagram 2.

Dye, untie and retie, binding in the same direction as before, but in slightly different places. Dye a second time.

A third color on this type of design can be most attractive. If you want to do this, untie the binding, retie in other places and redye.

Imagine how smart a tablecloth would look if you dyed it with this pattern, centering the design in the length of a rectangular table, or making it to fit a square table. Napkins could repeat the design in miniature, or be dyed in one of the plain colours.

The material shown on the left has been subjected to two dyeings.

Another way of folding squares diagonally

To obtain a cross effect, instead of a square, as described on the opposite page, you need to fold the fabric in the opposite direction.

Take a square of fine cloth, as before, and fold it in four. Pleat or roll the square from A to B, diagonally, as indicated on the sketch, right.

Tie the fabric in the *opposite* direction to the folds, and dye. Untie. Retie and dye a second time.

This pattern gains in effectiveness with a second or third dyeing.

Quite different effects can be achieved by varying the strength

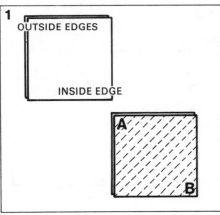

of the colors used and mixing bold and pastel shades, or by using two or three strong, dark colors together.

Paula Critchley, who designed all the tie-dye patterns in this section, says that the one on the right is her favorite. She used cold-water dye colors of nasturtium and bronze rose. The finished fabric has all the colors of a chestnut tree in the autumn sunlight!

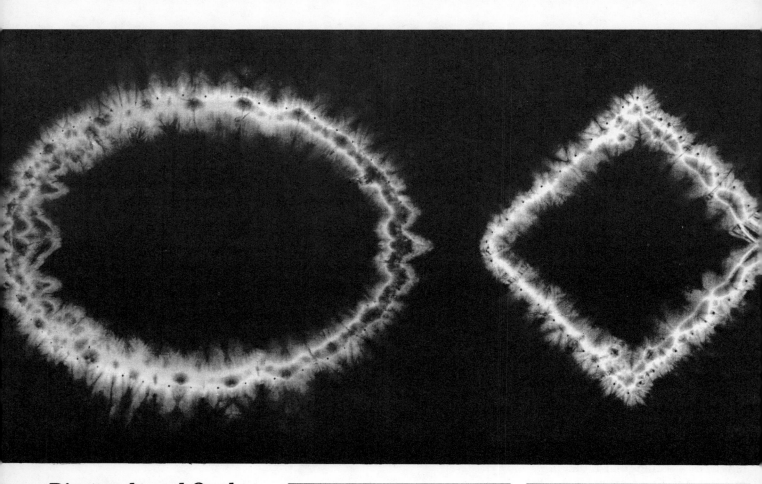

Diamonds and Ovals

The fabric photographed above has been dyed once with a diamond and oval pattern.

To do this, fold a piece of cloth in half. Along the folded edge, draw half a diamond and/or half an oval with a pencil (Diagram 1).

Keeping the cloth folded, run a safety pin in and out of the drawn lines, and fasten it (Diagram 2).

The sketch above shows the cloth pinned for only one design. If you copy both the diamond and the oval, of course, you will have two sections pinned and bunched up.

Bind the cloth just below the pin, to secure it; remove the pin, and tie above the other row of binding, pulling the string as tightly as you can (Diagram 3).

Dye, untie and examine the pattern you have made. If desired, retie and dye again with another color.

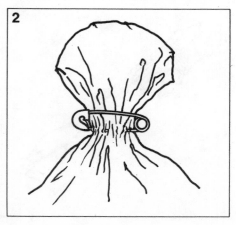

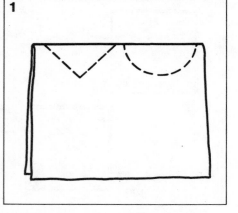

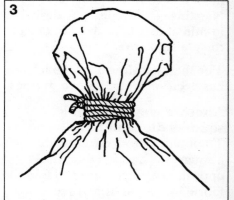

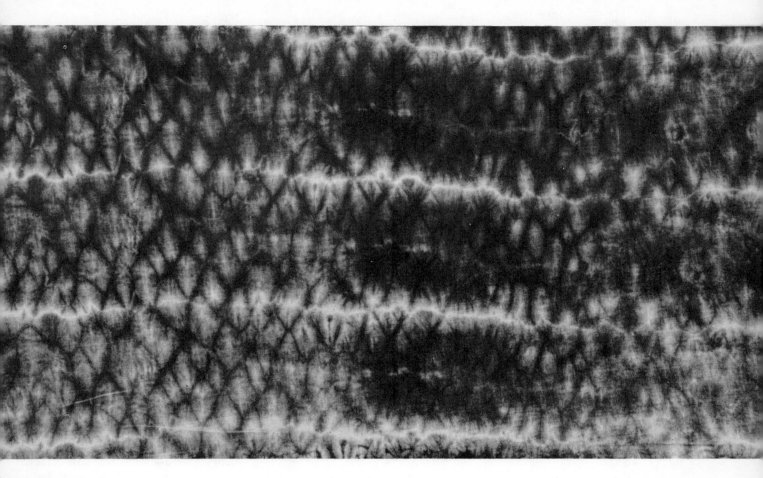

Roping It In

A most attractive pattern made up of tiny diamonds and narrow stripes can be made by tying a length of rope into your fabric.

Take a piece of fine cloth and lay it on a clean, flat surface. Place a length of rope on one side of the cloth, as shown in Diagram 1.

Roll the cloth tightly around the rope, center left, and fold the strip in half, tying the loose ends of the rope together (Diagram 2).

Now push the cloth up the rope, and tie both sides together (Diagrams 3 and 4). Dye; untie. Tie again, placing the rope first on the opposite side (the darker side) and dye again.

The fabric illustrated above has been dyed only once, so that you can clearly see the allover pattern.

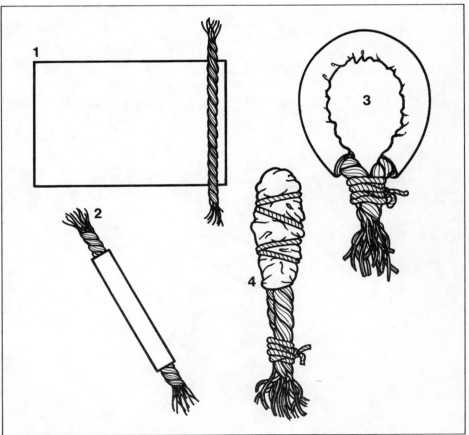

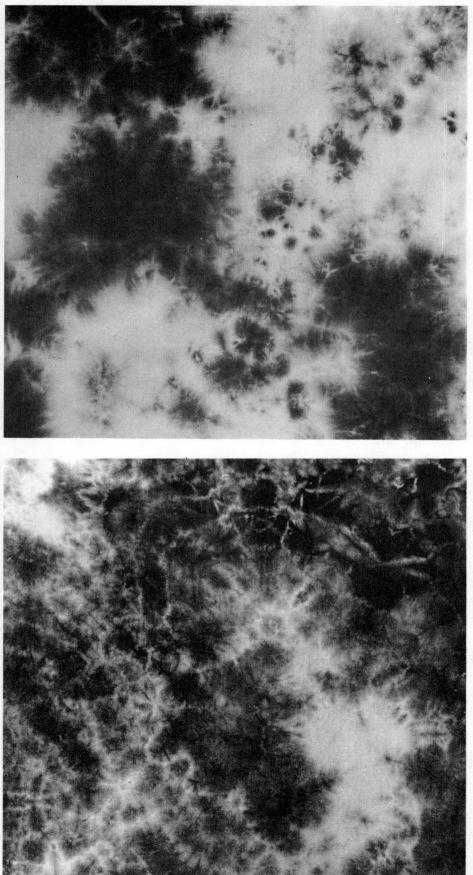

Marbling

This is the pattern which, in the introduction to this section, we described as looking as if the fabric had been caught in a shower of colored rain.

It is easy to do: you simply crumple up a piece of fine cloth in your hands until it forms a tight ball (Diagram 1), tie it very tightly with string or wide rubber bands and dye. Untie, tie again and dye a second color.

Another method is to push the cloth into a small plastic bag (Diagram 2), twist the top and tie. Put into a second plastic bag, twist and tie again. Prick holes in bags with sewing needle, then immerse in dye. Repeat for second dyeing.

The fabric shown at the top of the page has been dyed once, and the lower photograph shows it after a second dyeing. Both the methods described above give this effect.

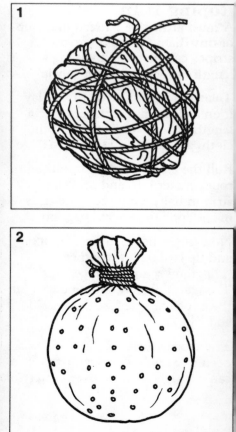

Painting with Dye

In the preceding pages, we have been talking about tying fabrics in such a way that, when immersed in dye, they will accept the color in some places and not in others. As you can see, the scope of this craft is enormous, but not quite limitless.

By using a dye that can be brushed on to fabric like paint, the horizons are wider still, for any design that you can paint can be transferred on to fabric in this way.

The baby's T shirt in the photograph was painted with cold-water dye, plus a dye paint thickening agent, plus cold dye fixative. It is permanently color-fast and, although it is a dye, it behaves just like paint. It can be applied with ordinary paint-brushes.

For best results, use it on cotton, linen or silk, but not on synthetic fabrics. Always wash fabrics before treating them, in the same way as for tie-dyeing.

Remember that these colors are dyes; pale blue used on white will, of course, stay pale blue, but pale blue on yellow will give you a shade of green.

Method of working: Empty the contents of 1 can of cold-water dye and 1 packet of paint dye into a jar. Add ½ pint of hot water and stir well to dissolve. Leave for a good 15 minutes. Then add one package of cold dye fixative and stir well. Leave for a further 5 minutes. The dye properties last for 4 hours. Carefully check these directions with the manufacturer's instructions on the packages of dye products.

If you are painting an article of clothing, put a board between the top and bottom layers (sketch, near right). Using a soft pencil, draw or trace your design on. The more color you apply, the deeper it will be. After painting, allow to

dry for 6 hours, away from heat.

When it is completely dry, rinse first in cold water to get off excess dye. A small nailbrush is useful to scrub off any stubborn bits.

Then wash the article thoroughly in hot, soapy water and rinse twice in cold water.

Dry before ironing.

Painted with cold-water dye, dye paint and fixative by Drika Collins.

BOARD INSIDE SHIRT

Batik, The Art of Wax-and-Dye

There's nothing new in treating fabrics so that they resist dye. The art of batik has been used in the Orient as a means of decorating cloth for many centuries. One of the earliest known examples of batik is Indian screens, created in the eighth century, by which time the art was highly developed. And the Javanese people of Indonesia have been waxing and cold-dyeing cloth for hundreds of years, some with intricate designs which took years to produce.

These designs were stylized and classical, but now that the art has been revived, any design that you can draw—and that includes geometrics and abstractions, as well as pictures of all kinds—can be created on fabric.

In the way that tying produces a resistance to color in tie-dying, so does the hot wax in batik, when dyed in cold water dyes. After the first waxing and dyeing, a second waxing is added and the article is then dyed a different color which, combined with the first, will make a third color. You can do as many waxings and dyeings as you wish, but beginners may prefer to experiment with two, or at most three, colors to start with.

Batik is not a suitable medium for very small children as the wax must be kept at a constantly high temperature.

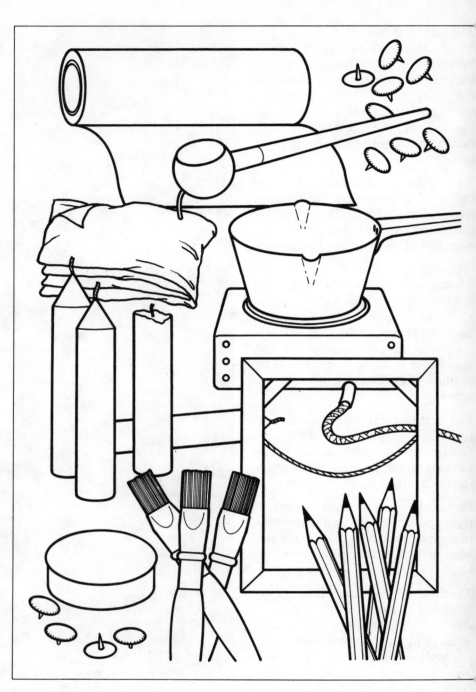

You will need:

1. Cotton or silk fabric (cotton sheeting is ideal). Synthetics are not suitable.

2. Batik wax.

3. Heavy saucepan to melt the wax in.

4. Hotplate (or other suitable heating apparatus).

5. Ordinary bristle paintbrushes in various sizes.

6. A tjanting (see opposite page) is useful for trailing slender lines or making dots in series.

7. Soft pencil.

8. Paper, tracing paper.

9. Old picture frame or canvas stretcher.

10. Pushpins.

11. Absorbent paper.

12. Plus the equipment needed for cold-water dyeing. This, and the method, are described at the beginning of this section.

Batik in three colors

Wash the fabric first and iron it carefully. Then pin it to the frame with thumb tacks (Diagram 1). If you do not have a suitable picture frame, pin the cloth to a drawer so that the fabric is flat and taut. Spread old newspapers or a sheet underneath to catch any drips.

You can work out your design on paper beforehand, and trace it on to the fabric (to do this, scribble with a soft pencil on the back of the tracing paper, then redraw over the design so that an impression is left on the fabric). The more confident can draw the design straight onto the fabric, using a soft pencil.

When you are ready to start waxing, melt sufficient wax in a heavy saucepan on the hotplate to cover the bristle end of the brush.

The wax must not boil, or the brush will frizzle! The right temperature to maintain is one that keeps the wax transparent when applied to the fabric.

Remember when applying the wax for the first time, the waxed area will resist the dye and retain the color of the background fabric.

If you intend to do a lot of batik, and decide to buy the special tool called a tjanting, here's how to use it: dip the little scoop into the hot wax, tilt it slightly to let a thin flow come out of the channel underneath and follow your pencil outline carefully. This takes practice, so it is as well to experiment first on an old sheet.

Follow the instructions already given at the beginning of this section for dyeing. Rinse thoroughly in cold water afterward but do not wash in hot soapy water. Hang up to drip dry.

Repeat the process, waxing in the same and different places,

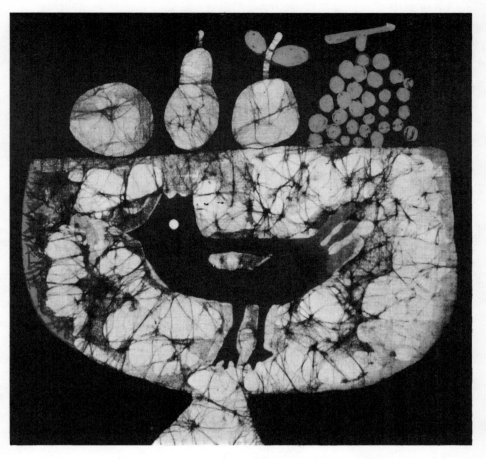

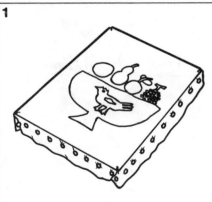

depending on what you wish to keep white (or the background color of the fabric) and what you want to retain of the first color.

For a cracked or crazed effect: When the wax has dried and before dyeing the article, lightly crumple parts of the material with your hands. This breaks the wax in an uneven way and lets the dye penetrate. It can be very effective, giving the fabric a pattern rather like a piece of old, crazed china.

To get the wax off the completed batik: Let the fabric dry after the final dyeing and then iron it quickly between two wads of absorbent paper, such as wrapping paper. Do not use freshly printed newspapers; the ink might transfer onto your batik.

Wash the fabric in detergent and very hot water, rinse, hang up to dry and finally iron.

A little girl of 7 proves that batik is child's play. She worked this decorative fruit bowl in weekend art classes, entirely from her own design. As a concession to her tender years, the teacher handled the hot wax, but strictly under the child's instructions. You can see her design in the color photograph.

Step-by-Step Guide to the Picture

Follow these stage-by-stage instructions and you will be able to create a picture like this fruit bowl and bird.

First waxing   The bowl, eye and wing of the bird were waxed. The wax was cracked slightly on the area of the bowl.

Dye: Yellow cold-water dye.

Second waxing   Two apples, one pear waxed out. Wax slightly cracked on fruit, to give appearance of the texture of the skin. Bowl, eye and wing remain from first waxing.

Dye: Pale blue cold-water dye.

Third waxing   Bird, bunch of grapes and two leaves on apple stalk waxed out.

It now looks like this before being dyed for the third time.

Dye: Hooker's green cold-water dye.

TAKE A ROLL OF FOIL

It is not surprising that the designs in this section have a festive feeling about them. Most of the items will have a short life but, as the saying goes, a gay one. In that time they will lend a cheerful sparkle to the celebrations. The frosty shimmer and glitter of silver, red, green and gold foil, by candlelight especially, will be an effect worth recapturing every year.

Although Christmas comes most readily to mind—and the designs shown in the color photograph were chosen for that occasion—it is not the only appropriate festival for this type of craftwork. With a little ingenuity, it will be possible to adapt these designs to suit many occasions. How about wedding anniversaries, for example? Gold, silver and ruby celebrations would be naturals for much of the decorative work.

Foil is available in different qualities, each with different properties, and it is a good idea to try the various types so that you are aware of the working potential.

The most common type, of course, is the roll of household foil. It does tend to tear rather easily, and in some cases it is advisable to paste it to a sheet of thin cardboard to strengthen it. This does not apply to any work where the foil is pushed or brushed into a design; for this method of working it must be flexible. When using household foil to cover a model, it is best to crumple it up first and smooth it out again. In this way, the foil will more readily take up the contours of the design and will give a much better finish to the work.

Some foil comes ready-mounted on paper and is available in many colors at arts and crafts stores.

A thicker type of "heavy duty" foil, with a number of possibilities for very interesting craft work, is also available. Covering boxes with this "super" foil, one really gets the feeling of working with metal. It needs most careful handling, however, as even the slightest pressure will mark the material and, if in the wrong place, spoil the effect.

Tools for the job
A minimum of tools are required for foil work—most of them can be found in any household.

First of all, scissors. A small pair for the more intricate cutting, and a larger pair for general use are all that you will need. To cut long, straight edges, an X-acto knife will be useful. One with disposable blades—the type that snap off to leave a permanently sharp cutting edge—would be ideal. X-acto knives should be used with a metal straightedge, not a ruler. Nothing is more annoying than a "straight" line that develops a large dip in the middle where the wood ruler has been pared away. In order to cut the foil evenly, it is important to have a durable, flat surface. A sheet of glass is the best, but a smooth piece of hardboard or a spare piece of Plexiglas will do. Do not cut on permanent surfaces, such as the top of a kitchen unit, for obvious reasons.

You will need cardboard to make the basic shapes for some of the models; look first at any packaging materials you may have on hand. It is wasteful to buy cardboard when you have cereal packages or other boxes which will serve the purpose perfectly well.

You will also need adhesive. Household or all-purpose glues like Elmer's or Duco cement are excellent; so is rubber cement. If any tube glue is left on the surface of the foil, be sure to wipe it off before it dries; otherwise it will make the surface dull.

To finish the models, you will need a variety of craft materials, such as poster paints, India ink and spray paints—black and brown are useful, all-purpose colors. It is interesting to experiment with the different effects you can achieve with these paints. Try spraying the surface of your work, allowing it to dry slightly and then wiping it off with a tissue, cloth or rag. This can give most exciting results and, if done well, make the foil look like old pewter. To seal the surface and make your models last longer, paint them with one or two coats of a wallpaper protective or polyurethane lacquer.

Making your ideas work

You are bound to have many ideas of your own for decorations, models and gifts to make from foil. Plan them first and make them up in scrap paper or newspaper to see if they work. Adapt the pattern until you are satisfied with it. Nothing will be wasted, not even your time, for you will be learning with every improvement you make. Transfer the final design to foil and proceed, following the techniques explained in this section. With only a little effort, you will find that this modern medium is full of exciting potential and can be an interesting material with which to work.

It must be stressed that foil work is vulnerable and should be handled with extreme care. Fingernail tears, for instance, are very difficult to disguise.

Decorative Jars and Bottles

Foil-covered jars have many uses and will make their contents, whatever they are, seem just that much more precious. They can be made quickly enough to be mass-produced for charity sales and bazaars.

You will need: a collection of jars with interesting shapes; once you have made a collection, the rest is clear sailing. The only extras you will need are string, leaves, odd pieces of cardboard and an adhesive, not forgetting a roll of silver foil.

Try "stringing" jars first. Draw a simple design on the jar with a felt-tip pen (Diagram 1) and glue along the lines. Follow the line of glue with string, pressing it on firmly to make sure that it adheres. This design is an S-shaped coil.

Cut a piece of foil large enough to go around the jar with an inch or so to spare at the end, plus an overlap at the top and bottom. Crush and smooth out the foil and glue it on one side. Most foils have a bright and a dull side; choose which you prefer to be showing, and glue the reverse side.

Cover the jar with your strip of foil and press it on gently with your thumbs to bring out the details of the stringing. Tap with the bristles of a clothesbrush if necessary to bring out extra detail, and complete the jar by folding the top and bottom over neatly and sticking. Other decorations such as ribbons, tinsel, labels, can be added.

Jars with leaf patterns are made in the same way. Stick the leaves to a piece of stiff paper or cardboard. When dry cut out each one and stick to a jar. This mounting on cardboard gives

more depth of detail to the finished jar (Diagram 2 next page). After covering with foil, spray with a contrasting color of spray paint to add interest to the jars.

Treasure worth diving for – crumpled foil covering a simple cardboard box gives the look of antique pewter to a child's jewel case

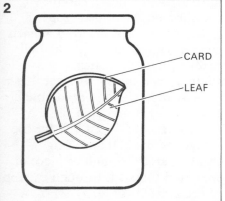

2

CARD

LEAF

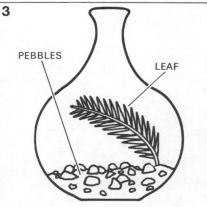

3

PEBBLES

LEAF

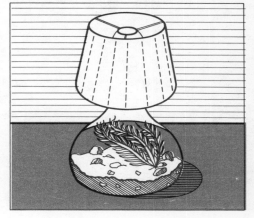

Bottle lamps

Bottles covered in the following way can be converted into lamp bases very easily. Fill the bottom of the bottle with small stones or dry sand to lessen the risk of toppling over and put a standard lamp fitting into the mouth of the bottle. (These are inexpensive and can be obtained at most hardware stores.) Cover the bottle with a fern leaf and then with foil (Diagram 3).

If you wish to tone the silver down a little you can do this by adding a layer of India ink, poster paint mixed with a little polyurethane lacquer or by using a spray paint. The added color should be wiped away before it dries, and will then leave some silver highlights. The amount you wipe away depends on the effect you wish to get. A layer or two of wallpaper protective, lacquer or spray varnish completes the work and will preserve the foil for a longer period.

The excitement of Christmas is reflected in a table set with woven foil place mat, silvery roses and intriguing parcels

Christmas Decorations

Try making these simple decorations to get the "feel" of working with foil papers. The ideas can easily be adapted to make many other kinds of decoration for festive occasions.

Bells

These are based on empty yogurt or similar, small containers wider at the top than the base. Make cuts $\frac{1}{2}$- to $\frac{3}{4}$-inch long around the top of the container and bend the pieces out. Hold them in position with pieces of masking tape stuck on the outside and pressed down and around into the container.

Crumple up a piece of foil to make a mound at the top of the bell; glue this on the base (now the top) of the container. The bell is now ready for covering with strips of foil. The strips should be $\frac{1}{2}$-inch wide and long enough to reach from the bottom of the bell inside to the top outside. Glue each strip and, starting on the inside, paste it down carefully, finishing on the outside top (Diagram 1). Make sure that each strip has stuck firmly to the bell before you add the next one, slightly overlapping. Repeat this process until the bell is completely covered. Crumple up a piece of foil into a small, tight ball for the clanger of the bell and hang it from a narrow ribbon or piece of wool and thread it through the top of the bell (Diagram 2). Make a second bell in the same way and tie it to the first with a decorative ribbon bow.

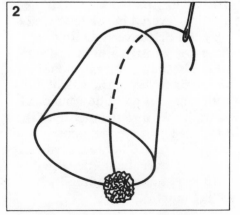

Lanterns

These little Christmas tree decorations are made from luster (foil) paper of various colors. The "hooded" lantern is made from a piece of paper 2½ by 6½ inches. Divide up the paper into ¾-inch strips, leaving ½-inch top and bottom; there is ½-inch overlap at the side to allow for pasting (Diagram 1).

Carefully cut the strips with an X-acto knife. Cut a 1½-inch strip of paper of another color and weave it in and out of the slits (Diagram 2). Glue the ends of the strip down at each end, bend the whole body of the lantern around and glue it.

The top of the lantern is made from a circle 3¾ inches in diameter. Cut this out and make a straight cut into the center, then bend the circle around to form a cone shape. Add a small strip of foil paper for a hanger. Use strips of masking tape to fasten the top in position. Stick these inside the body and press the top down, putting your fingers up inside to press it firmly to the tape.

The base is made from a circle 2¼ inches in diameter. Inside this circle, draw another 2 inches across, with the same center. Make a series of cuts all around the circle to meet the inner circle and bend them upward, with the foil side underneath. Glue the little tags formed and paste inside the base of the lantern (Diagram 3).

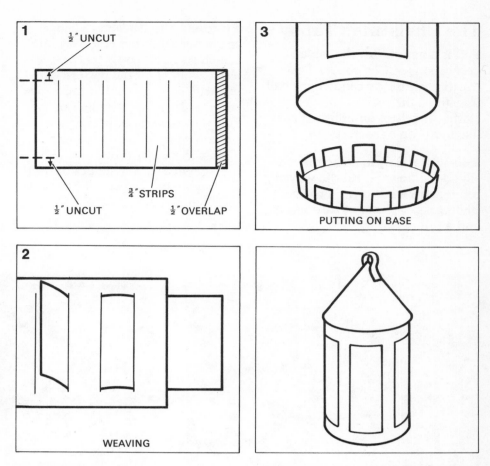

1   ½" UNCUT   ½" UNCUT   ¾" STRIPS   ½" OVERLAP

2   WEAVING

3   PUTTING ON BASE

Chinese lantern

The inner cylinder for this lantern is made first from a piece of foil paper 3½ by 8 inches. Glue to form a cylinder allowing a ½-inch strip for the overlap. The outer part is made from a paper of a different color, 5 by 8 inches. Divide this piece into ½-inch strips, allowing 1-inch space top and bottom; cut as for the previous lantern. Paste to the top of the outer part around the top of the cylinder. When this has stuck, repeat at the other end, pushing up to form the curved sides. A "handle" can be added by pasting a narrow strip of paper to the top.

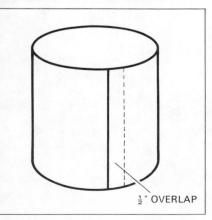

½" OVERLAP

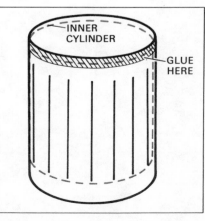

INNER CYLINDER   GLUE HERE

The Christmas Table

Foil is a natural for the table decorations at Christmas. The frostlike glitter by candlelight will transform the plainest of white cloths, or reflect on polished oak like lights on a frozen pond.

You will need, to make the silver-foil flowers and the woven foil place mats shown in the color photograph, pieces of cardboard and a roll of foil.

To make the flowers: Using graph paper, or paper drawn into 1-inch squares, copy the two leaf-shapes from the pattern below. You will see that these give you the shape for only half of the flower in each base. Make your pattern completing the other side. Transfer each of these four-petaled flower shapes to thin cardboard and cut out. These are your templates.

Each flower takes two of the larger and two of the smaller sets of petals. Using your template, cut out two thicknesses of foil in each size. Paste the four layers of foil together, with the two smaller ones at the top (Diagram 1). A dab of all-purpose glue between each petal in the center will secure them. Now gently mold and shape the petals to make a flower with soft, natural curves, as shown in the photograph. Finish the center of the flower, if you like, with a

cluster of small silver baubles tied together and stuck on top, or threaded through the foil.

These flowers make expensive-looking decorations for the Christmas tree or—if you have room on the table—are pretty to have beside each place setting.

To make the place mats: You can cover old cork mats, or pieces of thick cardboard. If using the latter, cut to a suitable size (these mats are 11¼ by 8¼ inches). Now

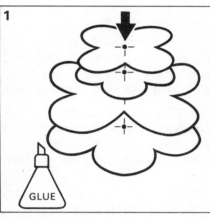

cut enough strips of foil, 1-inch wide, to cover the mat in each direction, allowing an extra 2 inches on each for turning. This means that for the mat illustrated, you need eleven strips 11 inches long and eight strips 14 inches long. (There is a very slight gap between each strip in the "weaving" process.)

Place the longest strips side by side on the cardboard, then fold over 1 inch at the top and stick to

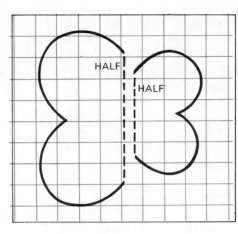

the back with a strip of masking tape. Place the mat on a flat surface and weave one of the shorter strips under and over at the top edge, leaving 1 inch projecting at each side (Diagram 2). Put a ruler or book over this strip to keep it in place, then lift up each alternate long strip (Diagram 3) so that your next piece of foil goes over and under to form a basket-weave effect. Repeat this weaving until all the strips are used up, making sure to press them closely together as you work.

Finally, fold the three edges back and paste them down on the reverse side of the mat.

When you have made a mat in this way, you can design others with quite different effects using different colored foils; by varying the weave, or using strips of different thicknesses. Thick and thin strips woven alternately make an interesting pattern.

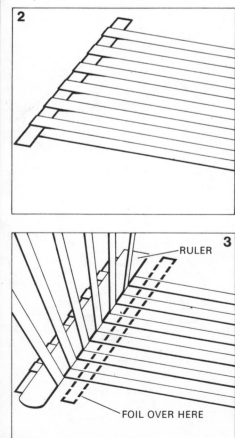

Figures from Cones

A simple way of making figures is to base the bodies on a conical shape—this avoids the problem of making them stand up! This is formed by making a circle of foil and cutting out a section. The size of this section will depend on the kind of figure you are making: generally a third of a complete circle is sufficient for one figure. Diagram 1 shows how to divide a circle accurately. The distance A—B, the radius, is equal to CB, a one-sixth segment. Here are some suggestions for different figures based on cones. They will probably set you thinking along other lines: don't hesitate to experiment with your own ideas.

Santa Claus

This is an ideal decoration for a Christmas tree. A 5 or 6-inch circle of stiff red foil will make cones for three figures. Enlarge the pattern for the body and arms and transfer it to stiff paper or thin cardboard. Cut this out and stick red foil on both sides; trim to shape. Push a length of thread through the top of the shape. Divide and cut the circle into three, as shown. Make two slits (Diagram 2) for the arms to go through; these should be about halfway down. Before pushing the arms through, place the length of thread on the center of the sheet so that it will come out through the top point of the body cone. This thread will serve as a hanger when the figure is complete. Now bend the outer piece to form a cone (Diagram 3), fastening the sides together on the inside with a strip of masking tape.

Santa Claus is now ready for strips of fluffy cotton to be stuck on the ends of his sleeves, around his hat, the bottom of his coat and the top of his boots. Paint the boots black; or, if your have black paper, paste that on. His belt is made in the same way with a silver buckle cut from foil and stuck on the front (Diagram 4). Finally, make his whiskers from a piece of cotton, cutting them as shown in the pattern. These are then stuck to the face shape, which is cut from colored paper, and fixed into position on the cone figure (Diagram 5).

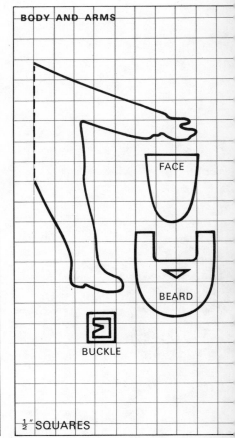

BODY AND ARMS

FACE

BEARD

BUCKLE

½" SQUARES

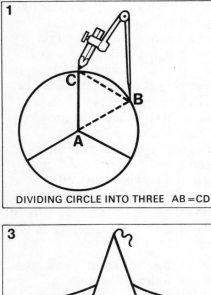

1 DIVIDING CIRCLE INTO THREE   AB = CD

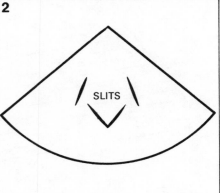

2 SLITS

3

4

5

Christmas angel

You will need a length of green plant support, or something similar, and a styrofoam ball with a diameter of 1½ inches. A gold paper was used for the angel, but of course the color choice is up to you.

Begin by making a cone in gold (or other color), as in the Santa Claus figure, but this time cut a circle with a radius of 8 to 9 inches. Push the styrofoam ball on to the end of the stick and push that through the top of the cone. Secure the stick inside the cone with a strip of masking tape (Diagram 1). Enlarge the other parts of the angel pattern and transfer onto gold paper. Cover the reverse sides of the pieces in gold.

Starting with the hair (Diagram 2) paste the pieces carefully in position; wings, arms and finally hymn book. Paint the angel's face carefully with poster paints and add the features (Diagram 3). To give more interest to the robe of the angel why not try adding pieces of paper doily?

Choirboy

The choirboy is made in a similar way. We used a red foil paper and constructed the head and body as for the angel. The shorter hair of the choirboy is made up in two pieces transferred from the pattern (Diagram 4) and pasted on the head. Part of a paper doily makes the robe and collar. The arms are covered with red foil, then with pieces of doily stuck on the outside. Now paste the arms to the body; when they are dry, stick the hymn book in the figure's hands. Finally paint the features.

What an angelic pair they make!

CHOIRBOY
CUTS
HAIR (CHOIRBOY)
CUTS
CUTS
HYMNBOOK
FOLD
ANGEL
CUTS
A
HAIR (ANGEL)
ARM
(CHOIRBOY & ANGEL)
PART 'A' HAS LUSTRE BOTH SIDES

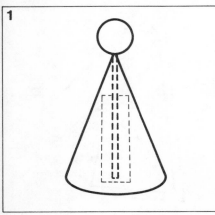

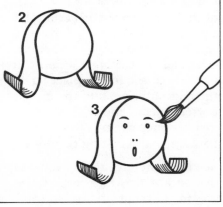

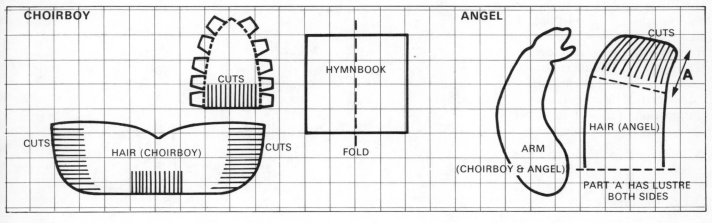

The candlestick

Transfer the pattern to a piece of paper ruled in 1-inch squares. Trace the pattern on cardboard and cut out three of the large pieces all the same size. Join the edges of two together with masking or Scotch tape. Cut the small triangular piece out of cardboard also. This piece helps to form the shape of the candlestick and also stops the candle from disappearing right down inside. Place the triangle in position on the inside of one of the pieces; this should be when the edge of the triangle just reaches from side to side of the upright. Tape it into position, top and bottom. Fold the other side around to meet the triangle and tape as before (Diagram 1). The third part of the candlestick can be added in the same way, securing it firmly with tape along the edges.

Now for the decoration. There are several ways of doing this. Here thin string was stuck on the cardboard with all-purpose adhesive and a few "leaves" cut from cardboard were added. (Diagram 2). The method of using real leaves, pasted on cardboard, is described earlier in this section, and is another way of decorating the candlestick.

Whichever decoration you use, proceed in this way. Cut a piece of foil slightly larger than one face of the candlestick and glue it on the reverse side. Place this on the decorated face and press it into position. Now with a clothesbrush or something similar, gently tap the foil (Diagram 3). Gradually it will take on the shape of the decoration underneath. The slight patterning made by the bristles will add to the effect and make it look like "beaten silver."

Fold the spare foil around the other sides and paste it down. The overlap at the top and bottom should be tucked inside and pasted

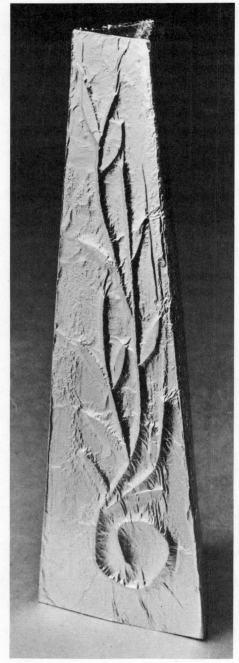

down. Cover the other two faces of the candlestick with crumpled up foil. (Take care, as the foil will tear very easily as you flatten it out prior to sticking.) When you have stuck the foil in place, trim the edges to size, fold the top and bottom pieces and stick them inside. Once again colored foils could give interesting results.

See how effective the woven place mat and "Christmas rose" flowers are, in the color photograph.

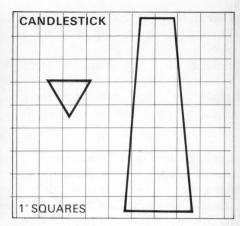

CANDLESTICK

1" SQUARES

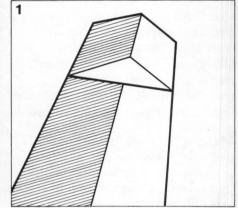

1

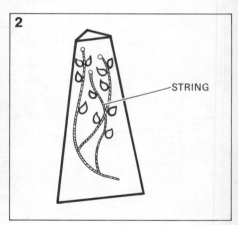

2

STRING

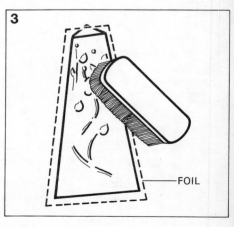

3

FOIL

Christmas Gifts

The eye-catching sparkle of foil makes Christmas packages piled under the tree or on the dining table more irresistible than ever. Here are a few simple ideas to copy. Of course, there are many more you can adapt from the other ways of using foil already described.

Initials   This is a highly personal way of identifying gifts in a decorative manner. Find a suitable sized letter in a newspaper or magazine, cut out roughly around it and place it on a piece of foil paper. With pencil, draw lightly all around the letter. Cover a box with crumpled foil and stick the letter on one side. Finally, add a decorative "bow" made with loops of foil paper. Cut strips of paper of different lengths, fold each strip over and stick to form a loop. You need at least six for a good effect. Push the two smallest loops onto a pin first, then follow with four larger ones. Push the pin into position on the box and arrange the loops to form a rosette.

Snowflake   The different colors of this package give an interesting result. Cover the box with foil and take a different colored foil large enough to wrap around the same box. Fold this foil as shown in Diagram 1 and cut out a pattern (Diagram 2). Unwrap it a little if you want to know how the pattern is progressing. When you are satisfied with your cutting out, unfold the foil, smooth it out and paste it carefully over the box.

Weaving   Everyone will wonder how this is done. Here's the secret. In a piece of foil large enough to cover the gift, cut a series of slits. There is no hard and fast rule about the position of the slits, but bear in mind that you will be threading strips of different colored foil through them so they will need to be equally spaced and there must be an even number of

slits. The pieces to thread through should be the same thickness as the spaces between the slits. Start at one end and begin threading in and out. As you work your way along, stick the ends of the strips down on the underside. When you have completed the weaving use the paper for wrapping in the usual way.

Adding patterns   Perhaps the simplest way of livening up a package is to add seasonal motifs

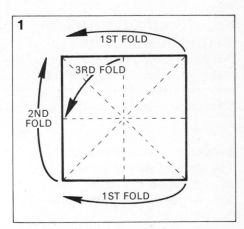

cut from a contrasting color foil. There is no shortage of designs in magazine articles and advertisements. Trace these and transfer them to foil. Cut out and paste in position on the parcel.

This three-sided design can be used as a candlestick or as a vase for dried materials, with a few twigs echoing the design.

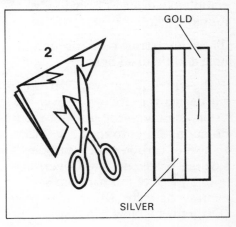

Foil Pendants and Brooches

Pendants made from various materials covered with foil can be most effective. No one would guess how cheaply and easily they are made.

Zodiac and other pendants

The signs of the zodiac were chosen as one way of demonstrating the possibilities of this type of jewelry. They would make ideal birthday presents for teenagers, or "take-home" gifts, as a reminder of their own birthday, for the guests at a children's party.

The base can be of any suitable material—thick cardboard or even illustration board would be ideal. Thick cardboard was used here, and thinner cardboard for the zodiac designs. Copy the "star" sign of your choice on graph paper, transfer it to cardboard, and cut out. Cover the design with crumpled foil, working it carefully around all the edges and turning it over the back. Paste the edges securely on the reverse side. Pierce a hole near the edge of the pendant shape. Cover the shape with foil too, and paste the design firmly to it with all-purpose glue. Pierce through the hole again. You can leave the pendant just as it is, then you will have an interesting, three-dimensional effect, or paint over the design and then rub off the paint before it has completely dried. This will give a muted effect.

Thread a narrow cord through the hole and tie in a knot.

A slightly different way of treating the design is as follows. Cover the "star" sign with foil as before, but do not fold it onto the back. Place a sheet of carbon paper, carbon side up, on the design. Cover this with a piece of foil paper in a contrasting color, shiny side up (Diagram 1). Now rub gently over

the top. After a time the shape of the design will be transferred by the carbon onto the reverse of the paper. Cut out the outline with an X-acto knife (Diagram 2), leaving the shape stenciled out of the foil paper. Paste the original foil-covered design onto the pendant base, line up the foil paper over the design and paste down carefully. Complete the pendant as described. This technique can, of course, be successfully used with other designs.

Molded pendants

Another type of pendant is made by making a base in a compound such as spackle or plaster of Paris. Impress a design into the compound using a fork or the cap of a ball-point pen. When the pendant is dry, stick a piece of crumpled foil over the shape and tap it gently with the bristles of a brush to bring out the pattern. Paste the excess foil on the back.

The larger pendant, like an old coin, was made in the same way, but in this case the design was carefully cut into the compound (Diagram 3) before the foil was added. Copy a design from a history book to make your pendant look authentic.

Finish these pendants as described above.

Identification of Signs of Zodiac

Sagittarius	Taurus	Aries
Scorpio	Cancer	Capricorn
Leo	Virgo	Gemini
Libra	Aquarius	Pisces

The two center pendants on the opposite page are decorated with signs of the zodiac; the others incised with pointed tools.

Friends will think you've just dug up an old coin if you "engrave" a pendant like the one shown above.

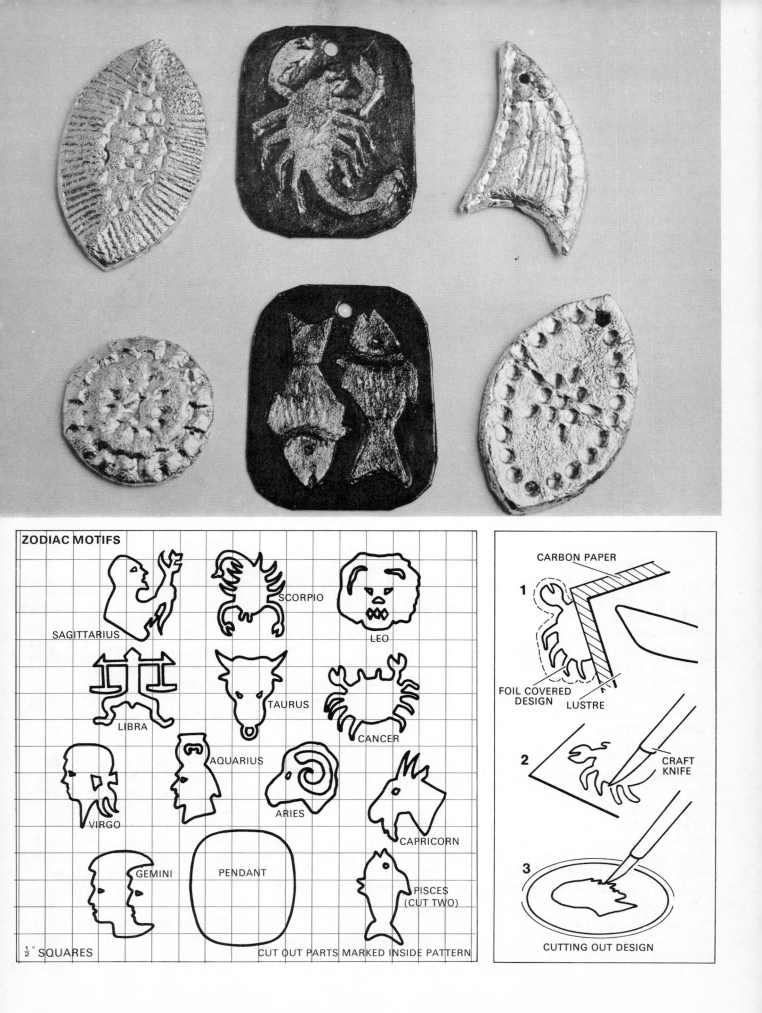

ZODIAC MOTIFS

SAGITTARIUS

SCORPIO

LEO

LIBRA

TAURUS

CANCER

VIRGO

AQUARIUS

ARIES

CAPRICORN

GEMINI

PENDANT

PISCES
(CUT TWO)

½" SQUARES

CUT OUT PARTS MARKED INSIDE PATTERN

CARBON PAPER

1

FOIL COVERED
DESIGN

LUSTRE

2

CRAFT
KNIFE

3

CUTTING OUT DESIGN

Working with Thicker Foil

The materials used in the designs up to now have been household foil paper. Thicker foil (available at artist supply stores) will introduce you to new methods and more varied possibilities for permanent objects. Some thick foil sheets are available with gold on one side and silver on the other.

Begin by experimenting with a piece of this material to discover its potential and properties. Collect various items, such as spoons, ball-point pen, knitting needles and so on, that might make interesting patterns when pushed into the foil and see whether in fact they do. The best way of doing this is with the foil on a pad of newspaper; this will allow the impression to be made fairly easily. A firm pressure is needed, but take care that you don't push right through the foil. Working on the reverse of the sheet, gold or silver side, whichever you prefer, will give interesting designs on the other side.

If you wish to make the impressions permanent, and this will be necessary if you are producing some of the items shown later, the depressions must be filled in some way. There are several ways of doing this (Diagram 1); you can use plaster of Paris, spackle compound or Plasticine, although the latter is less permanent than the others. Make up the material according to the manufacturer's instructions, spread it on the reverse side of the indented foil. Smooth it over with a palette knife so that all the depressions are filled, and scrape off any excess. When the sheets are pasted onto a base they will stand much greater wear if treated in this way.

Covering books Notebooks, albums and books are improved if you add jackets (made specially

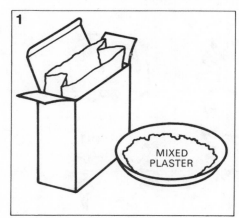

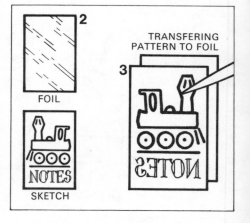

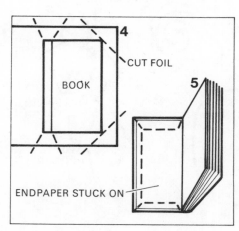

for an occasion), and make ideal presents. It is advisable to draw your designs roughly on paper first before starting with the foil. Decide on the particular pattern or motif you think appropriate and make a rough sketch the same size as the finished cover (Diagram 2). This sketch can then be placed on the foil and traced over with a ball-point pen (Diagram 3). This will give a basic outline and once the paper has been removed you can complete the design. Don't forget, however, that designs will be reversed, so decide which way you want them to be before starting.

Lettering should present no problem at all. Find a typeface you like in a newspaper headline or magazine ad and trace out the word or words you need. Transfer this in the same way as the pattern, not forgetting that it will be reversed—this is especially important with lettering! The completed sheet of foil should then be made more permanent by using the plastering techniques detailed earlier. When the plaster has dried the cover is ready to be added to the book.

Stick the cover to the book with a household adhesive, such as Elmer's glue, leaving sufficient foil to be folded onto the inside of the cover. Snip the corner to neaten (Diagram 4). When the overlap has been pasted down, paste an end paper over it to neaten the inside front and back covers (Diagram 5).

Foil-covered boxes The thicker type of foil gives excellent results if it is used to cover boxes. The technique is exactly the same as that described for book covers. Make sure you allow a generous margin of foil as the impressing of the design "shrinks" the overall measurement of the foil slightly. Try to work your design, too, so that you have enough foil to bend right over and finish on the inside of the box (Diagram 1). Foil on the front of the box should overlap the sides by about $\frac{1}{4}$-inch (Diagram 2) and this should be hidden by the side piece which should touch the corner. Edges such as these will need to be stuck down. An all-purpose glue, such as Elmer's is practical, or rubber cement which sometimes gives a more satisfactory bond. Complete the box as in the previous instructions.

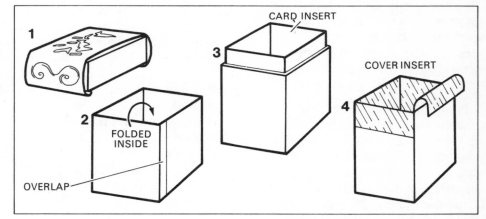

A good way to make the lid fit successfully is to make an insert of medium weight cardboard (Diagram 3) to fit inside the box. The dimension will vary, of course, according to the size of your box. Measure the breadth and width of the box inside and add about $\frac{1}{2}$-inch to the height from the bottom. Join the corners of the pieces of cardboard with masking tape.

For an extra luxurious finish

inside, stick velvet or a similar material on the interior of this board (Diagram 4) bending it over on the outside and running it down about $\frac{3}{4}$-inch. Cover the bottom of the box with a similar material. The insert can now be glued and pushed into position.

For the jewel box, golden thick-grade foil makes a strong covering.

Boxes Just Like Pewter

From boxes covered with extra thick foil to boxes decorated with ordinary household foil, the basic techniques involved are all ones that have been learned earlier in making more simple models. A wooden box forms the base for the decoration. It can be an old cigar box, or possibly one bought from your local arts and crafts store (Diagram 1). The other materials will be at hand if you have made any other foil objects.

A simple method of working
Design and cut out of thin cardboard a series of patterns to cover the box. These may be built up of two or three layers of board to give depth to the finished designs. A few ideas for designs to simulate locks, straps and hinges are given in Diagram 2, but experiment with your own ideas. When you are satisfied with the results, try them out by placing them on the box first. Stick them in position on the box, adding any curls or twisted decoration by drawing the design on the box, gluing along these lines, and pressing string along the glue.

Allow time for all the added decoration to dry before placing the foil on. Tear a piece of foil slightly larger than the lid and crumple it in the usual way, flattening it out carefully afterward. Glue the foil and gently press it down on the lid. You will have discovered earlier that the easiest way of bringing out the patterns is to use a brush, pen top or something similar. When the patterning is complete, fold the sides onto the inside of the lid and make sure they are pasted down securely. Continue this process with the sides of the box and place the finished article on one side to dry.

The painting and finishing of the box is important as it will make

your work all the more effective if done well. Spray or brush the paint over the box, not forgetting inside the lid and the sides where the foil is folded over. When the paint is almost dry, rub it off gently with a cloth. Experience will have shown when you have rubbed off enough. The color should serve to accentuate the patterning. Finally, "seal" the finished box with two coats of polyurethane lacquer. The inside of the box can be lined if necessary.

A treasure chest for jewels. Who would guess this box was just plain cardboard underneath?

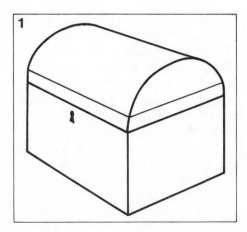

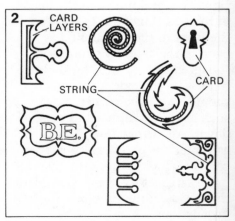

TAKE A PIECE OF PAPER

Just a piece of paper; of all the many and varied craft materials, paper is, without doubt, the most versatile and the most taken for granted – probably because it is so readily available.

Techniques with Paper

The basic techniques of cutting and folding, which we all do at home for one reason or another practically every day, are followed by the more exciting effects to be achieved by scoring, bending and curling. The variations and combinations possible once these simple techniques have been mastered are limitless.

The tools and materials needed for paper work are few, and most households will have them on hand.

Cutting

Heading your list of tools is scissors; any household type will do, provided they are sharp. The more intricate cutting work demands smaller scissors with pointed ends for satisfactory results. An X-acto knife of some kind will be useful for long, straight cuts and any parts you may find difficult with scissors. The ones with disposable blades assure a keen edge at all times; any knife with a permanent blade will need a fine sharpening stone to keep it in good condition. Use a metal straightedge with an X-acto knife, and on no account a wooden ruler, as you will find that you are gently paring away the edges of the ruler and your straight lines will be anything but straight. A ruler is, of course, essential for measuring most of the designs shown in this section.

Drawing circles

Another item of equipment that will be useful is a compass; however, don't despair if you don't have one. Sometimes you can find a plate or an egg cup that is just the right size to draw around (though to achieve a perfect circle you must be sure to hold your pencil at the same angle all the way around). If not, you can improvise by using a strip of cardboard. Stick a pin in one end to make a center pivot and push the point of your pencil through the cardboard at the required distance from the pin. Anchor the pin, holding the cardboard flat down on the paper, and move the pencil around. It hardly seems necessary to add a pencil to this list of essential equipment: use a fairly soft one, say B or 2B, as it will make erasing easier.

Coloring

Coloring your models is important. The best paints to use are poster paints. However, ordinary watercolors are quite satisfactory provided that they are used thick, and you could use colored pencils or felt-tip pens.

Pasting

Adhesives come in many forms. Most of the models in this section were made with a children's glue which has the advantage of being completely removable by washing. Whatever glue you buy, find out if it's water soluble, as modern glues are tenacious hangers-on. Scotch tape, gummed paper strip or masking tape give a quick, strong joint, but should only be used on the back of the models where they will not be seen. For extra-firm hold, use a stapler where the staples will not be seen.

The paper itself

Now for the paper. Sheets of newspaper are very useful for preparing patterns and should be used for "trying out" before better quality materials are used. Throughout the section, the instructions will tell you the best type of paper to use for each item.

Paper can be obtained in many colors and thicknesses. The colored sheets are usually more expensive than the white, but for some work have the great benefit of a satisfying depth and evenness of color.

In case the various thicknesses present problems, indicated below are the main types of papers and cardboard suggested for this chapter so that you can easily match the lines against available stock.

——— **Composition paper**
——— **Lightweight cardboard (1 ply Strathmore)**
——— **Mediumweight cardboard (2 ply Strathmore)**
——— **Illustration board**

It is worth bearing in mind, too, that modern packaging will provide more than adequate materials if you take a careful and critical look at them. Some boxes or wrappings are worth more than the contents! If you are using scrap materials, check first that they will take paint. Some are super-absorbent while others will be too shiny to allow paint to penetrate the surface. It would be a pity to spend time making a beautiful model, only to find you cannot paint it.

The patterns in this section are on a reduced scale. To enlarge them to the appropriate size, square off a piece of paper in inches (graph paper is rather expensive to use for the larger items) then, with a pencil, mark the lines to correspond with those in the reduced pattern, following every outline carefully. When you have the pattern complete, trace it off and then, using carbon paper, transfer it to the appropriate paper for your design; or, if you want to experiment first, to newspaper or strong wrapping paper.

Whenever you are adapting a pattern—perhaps you may be adding features or altering the size—work on scraps of paper first, cutting or adding on until you are satisfied with the result. Transfer this "mock-up" pattern to another sheet of paper when you are ready to produce the finished article.

The drawings and photographs show you how to go about each step in your work. Read them all the way through before starting. It is advisable to work through the chapter, so that you master the basic techniques before passing on to the more difficult projects.

Finally, remember the old blacksmith's golden rule: "Measure twice and cut once." Then you can start drawing,

cutting, tearing, bending and folding and, building from the ideas here, produce some exciting designs from "just a piece of paper."

Cutting and Tearing

Begin with simple paper cutting. For this you will need only a small pair of scissors. Use papers of varying thickness and weight to see the different effects you can get. Try not to use a pencil to sketch out your idea, but if you need to, keep the drawing as just a rough guide to the finished shape of the work. Your scissors should be creating the detail.

Of course, cutting in this way produces a sharp edge which is unsuitable for some effects. For a more subtle, rougher edge try tearing the paper, gradually, a little at the time. Include some colored paper in your experiments, too.

The only drawing needed in the

paper collage illustrated was the circle of the moon. Everything else was cut and torn without recourse to any pencil lines. See how the different textures of paper used create the very effect that was wanted—of a full, moonlit night with only watchful owl on duty.

If your cutting and tearing experiments produce pieces you wish to keep—and we hope they will—stick them onto a piece of cardboard and frame them as described later in this chapter.

Folding and cutting

Cut and folded patterns are easily done, and children, particularly, find them fascinating. But instead of crumpling the designs, throwing them away and starting another one, such projects become infinitely more worthwhile when these admittedly fragile fragments of paper are mounted and put to a practical use, such as for table mats as is the case here.

1

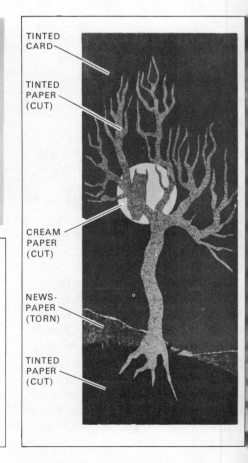

TINTED CARD

TINTED PAPER (CUT)

CREAM PAPER (CUT)

NEWS-PAPER (TORN)

TINTED PAPER (CUT)

The technique of folding, bending, cutting, glueing, stencilling and painting combine to make a regal-looking paper sculpture which could form the start of a collection

Any kind of colored paper would be suitable for cutting the pattern (the mats shown here were made with patterns cut from drawing paper) and suitable shapes are squares, rectangles or circles.

Buy plain cork table mats in a five-and-ten, or you can use cork tiles or tagboard. Check that the material you choose is heat resistant. The small mats illustrated were made of 6-inch squares of tagboard, the medium sized ones for larger dishes, 6 by 12 inches, and the large one, 12 by 15 inches.

Cut the paper into a square, rectangle or circle that will fit within the outline of the mats—or, in the case of the one with the "reversed pattern" within half of the outline.

Fold the paper in half, then in quarters, and then from corner to corner. If you are making a circular pattern, fold in half, then in quarters, then again from the center, into eighths.

To produce rectangular patterns, fold them in half and in half again, as with squares, then fold along the diagonal. Cut out pieces from this diagonal first. Then open the paper out to the quarter-folded stage and complete your cutting.

Now let your imagination run free and cut (Diagram 1 page 206). Take a peek occasionally by unfolding the paper a little, but take care not to tear it, and fold it back in exactly the same way.

Open up when you have finished and see what effect you have produced. If you are satisfied with the result, glue it onto a mat. When it is dry, brush over the mat with two coats of a wallpaper protective such as polyurethane lacquer. Then you can wipe over the mat without destroying your pattern.

To produce the "positive/negative"

effect of the snowflake design, fold and cut a square of paper. Keep all the pieces you cut out and arrange them on the mat next to the original design. Simple patterns are the most effective with this "counterchange" method.

Try using your paper cut-out as a stencil, too. Place it on a mat or other surface and spray through the holes with aerosol paint. When the paint has dried, lift the paper off and you will have an attractive "negative" outline.

To Make Stars

Here we explore the three-dimensional properties of paper. Copy the star patterns on stiff white paper or lightweight cardboard from the squared plan. The introduction to this section tells you how to do this. Enlarge the patterns to any size you like. Alternatively, you can draw stars by using a compass to make a circle, then dividing the circle into

six equal parts, using the same radius. When these six points are joined they form a hexagon. This is the basis of the stars, and the details can be copied from the patterns.

After cutting out, score all the lines on the reverse side of the stars. To do this, place a straight edge along the line to be scored, and run along it with the blade of your scissors. Experience will soon tell you whether you are pressing too hard or not enough.

The pattern shows how these scorings should be folded on the six-pointed star, A: dashes are folded down and dotted lines up. Gently push the sides together (Diagram 1 overleaf) and the star becomes three-dimensional. To preserve this effect, put a dab of glue on the back of each point and press the star onto a piece of thin cardboard, trimming excess from the edge.

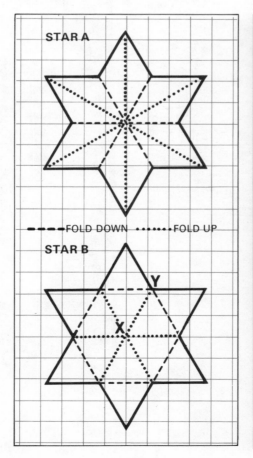

All from paper and cardboard a theater with two backdrops of scenery, all the glitter of a first-class performance and two actors holding the audience enthralled

The other star, B, is made in a similar way, the only difference being that the line X–Y is cut and one point is folded and stuck on another to complete it (Diagram 2).

These stars make effective Christmas decorations when sprayed with gold or silver paint, and are pretty if two are pinned or pasted back-to-back, on top of the tree.

Making and Framing

Silhouettes, popular before the invention of photography, can be entertaining to make, and can provide a permanent record of the family likeness.

To make your silhouette

Victorian silhouette artists could cut out portraits of their clients without preliminary drawing, but you may find this difficult at first.

There are two other ways of making the profile. Look at your sitter and sketch his or her profile on a piece of paper, drawing it the size you want the portrait to be. Paint in the entire shape in black.

Ask your subject to sit in front of a large piece of squared paper pinned to a wall, and move a light so that the profile casts a shadow on the paper (see Diagram 1).

Draw around the profile, then

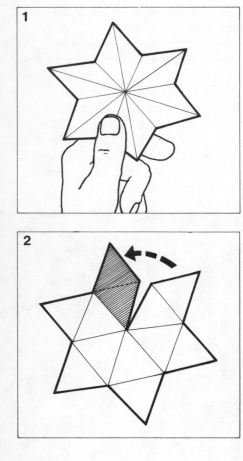

reduce it in size by copying it on a piece of squared paper (Diagram 2). As before, paint the profile in solid black.

To give an "ancestor" look to your portrait, add a few period details, copying the ideas sketched in Diagram 3. This way, with a collection of wigged, bonneted and beribboned profiles, you can build up a gallery of instant forebears!

To frame your silhouette, transfer the pattern, the size you want it to be (this one measures 7½ by 5½ inches), on to medium weight cardboard. Cut out the pattern and then score all the broken lines. Fold each edge of the frame over and stick the lower part to the inside of the frame (Diagram 4).

When the four sides have been completed, cut out the four

decorative corner pieces, making a template first in newspaper, and then cutting it from cardboard. Score the corner pieces across the middle and paste them to the frame (Diagram 5).

The completed frame can then be painted or sprayed gold. Cut a piece of stiff cardboard, smaller than the frame, in a dark color and, from this, cut out an oval, following the squared-up pattern. Paste the "mount" and the cut-out

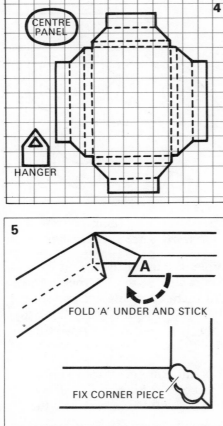

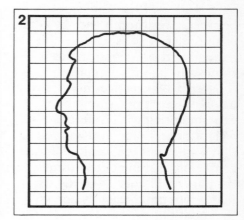

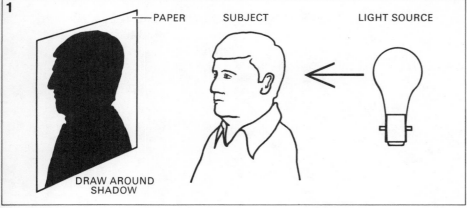

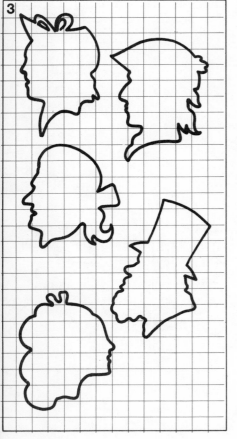

portrait onto the background, as shown.

Finally, paste the hanger on the back. And, for an authentic touch, write out the details of the member of family. Something like "Samuel Joseph, Baker, Ipswich, Massachusetts, Born 21st January 1937" will be of great interest when the silhouette is handed down as a family heirloom in years to come!

Paper Curling: A Panel to Make

Curled paper can give exciting effects by itself or combined with other techniques. It may look difficult at first, but the thing to bear in mind is that the greater the pressure you put on the paper during curling, the tighter the curl will be.

Start curling by taking a strip of smooth medium weight paper and a ruler, or use the cutting edge of your scissors. Place the paper between your thumb and the edge of the ruler or scissors. Pull the paper down and along and as it comes through it will curl (Diagram 1). Practice this exercise using different pressure (and experimenting with different weight papers) and you will see that sometimes you achieve just a gentle curve, and at other times the paper will curl up so tightly that it will practically fly across the room.

To make the decorative panel

Line a piece of paper into squares, and copy the outline for the panel frame. The one shown measures 9 by 4 inches. If you want to make a larger or smaller one, simply use a different scale. Transfer the pattern to medium weight cardboard. Score along the dotted lines and fold up the sides. Diagram 2 shows you the way recommended for scoring long, straight lines, using the point of a scissor blade.

Reinforce the corners with Scotch tape.

Cut strips of paper in different lengths for curling, but all the same width as the depth of the frame—in this case, $\frac{1}{2}$-inch.

Curl the strips as described, using light and heavy pressure to make as much variety in the shapes as possible. As you make the shapes, drop them into the tray and arrange them in any form you find

agreeable, or let them fall into a haphazard pattern (Diagram 3).

When the tray is filled, lift the pieces and paste underneath them. Put them back in place and weight them down with a heavy book to hold them in position until the glue dries.

It is quite unnecessary to paint a panel of this kind. You will see that the patterns created by the light and shade are as interesting

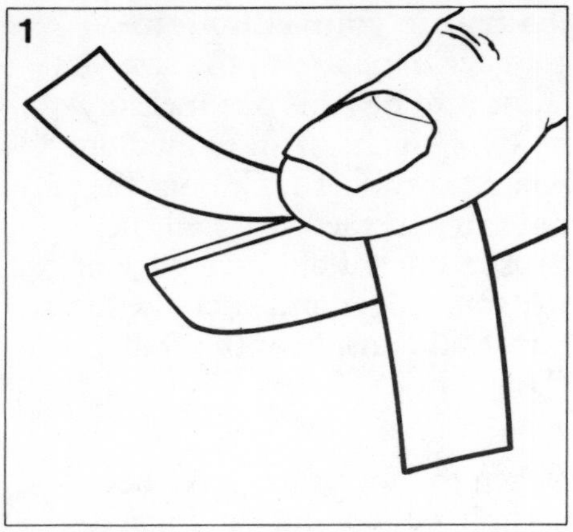

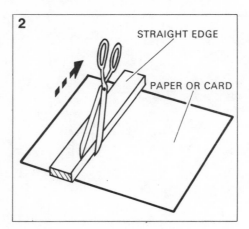

Diagram 1: Holding a strip of paper between thumb and scissor blade and exerting pressure.

STRAIGHT EDGE

PAPER OR CARD

Diagram 2: Scoring along a straight line of thin cardboard, using a straightedge, before bending.

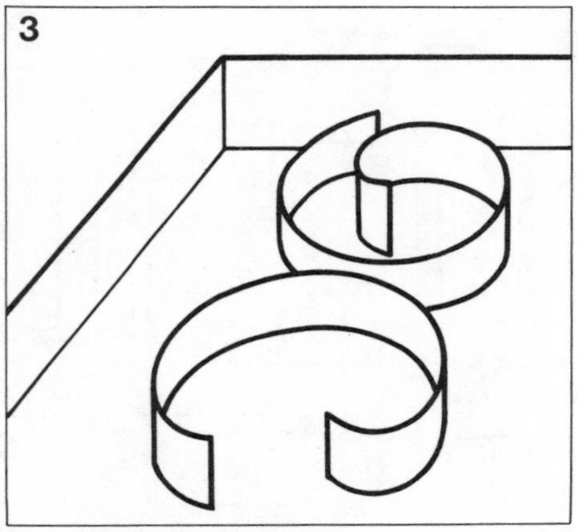

Diagram 3: Curls of paper strips dropped into the panel frame.

as a picture. However, you can spray the finished work—metallic finishes look most effective.

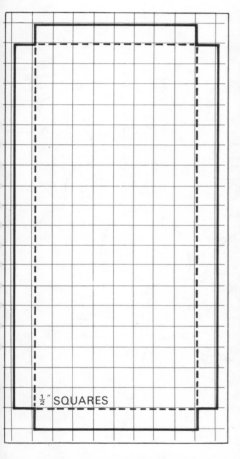

$\frac{1}{2}''$ SQUARES

Above: the shape of the panel for
the curling pattern. Draw the
shape on squared paper, so that
the inside measurement is 9 by 4
inches. Score along the broken
lines and fold upward.

Paper-Bending Experiments

Cylinders   Paper and pliable cardboard can be bent around curves—opening up new horizons for the material! At its simplest, the bending forms a cylinder. Tape along the seam, and you have a versatile shape to experiment with.

There are many types of lamp shades on the market, and most of them expensive, which are based on cylindrical forms with cutting and folding.

Experiment with any scraps of paper and you will see that cuts through the sides (Diagram 1 shows the paper marked out for cutting) give exciting light and shade effects; these, with folding, give a three-dimensional quality to the shape. Diagrams 2 and 3 show some of the many possible variations.

Still a simple cylinder (Diagram 4) but imagination makes it a mask. Cuts top and bottom, which are then curled, give effects of hair and beard. Slits cut and curled make peep-holes and dramatic eyelashes, and small additions, stuck on and bent outward, make ears.

Cones   Cones are the starting point for another type of paper-work. Most often cones are produced by drawing a circle, cutting out a pie shaped wedge and placing the cut ends together – see Diagram 5. Pieces can be cut out or added to the basic shape to make all kinds of things—even a mouse. For this one, the top part of the cone was opened up and bent over. Ears, whiskers, tail and feet were all cut separately and stuck on. It sounds too simple to be true, but there it is.

Bending a Flat Sheet

Another property of paper is that it will bend from a flat sheet. This needs practice, but can usefully be applied to many aspects of

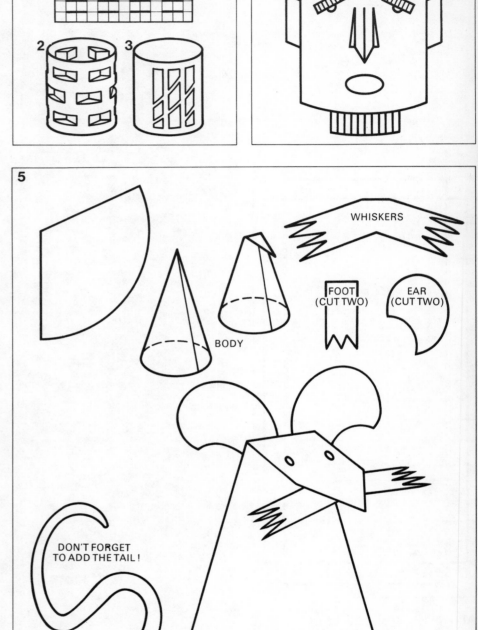

WHISKERS

BODY

FOOT (CUT TWO)

EAR (CUT TWO)

DON'T FORGET TO ADD THE TAIL!

paperwork. The main thing to remember is that patterns must be drawn wider than they will appear in the completed work, as bending narrows the material considerably. Curves are possible, but must be drawn wide to avoid overlapping.

To make the lizard

Transfer the pattern on to your chosen paper in the usual way. This model, before bending, measured 9½ by 5¼ inches. Score

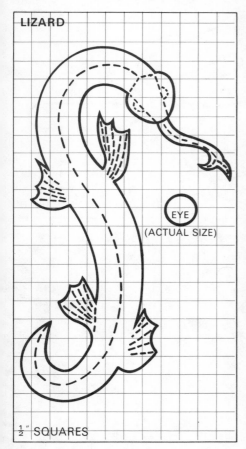

LIZARD

EYE
(ACTUAL SIZE)

½" SQUARES

along all the broken lines. To bend, hold the two sides and push gently together. Move your fingers along the paper slowly and carefully to continue the process.

Trace two pieces for the eye, which is shown here actual size, and stick them in position where the dotted lines indicate.

When you have achieved the three-dimensional shape, paste the lizard onto a piece of cardboard and paint.

To make a mask

The animal mask shown here uses a combination of the techniques mentioned so far. It can be easily made and is very effective. The basic pattern can be adapted to make many different animals. Simply lengthen the ears and you will be surprised how many variations become possible.

Begin by enlarging the squared-up pattern to the appropriate size. You will see that you have to cut the pattern double: only one side is given. The mask shown, before folding, measured 16½ by 8½ inches approximately. It fits over the top of a child's head, leaving the lower part of the face open for any grotesque or comic expressions!

Transfer the outline to stiff paper (or thin cardboard) and score all lines indicated by a broken line on the pattern.

Bend the scored lines on the center (Diagram 1) to form the shape of the top of the head and nose. Bend nose in. Fold in the pasting tags on the top of the side pieces, and ease them around to meet the nose (Diagram 2). Paste the center part to the tags on the side pieces. Fold the nose in and paste the tags inside the side pieces (Diagram 3). Fold the ears out.

Fold the last section of the center part down and ease the ends of the side pieces around so that they overlap slightly. Paste these in position and staple them if necessary for extra firmness (Diagram 4). Before pasting the nose pieces down, push small strips of paper through slits made in them. Paste these on the reverse. Once the nose pieces are pasted down, the whiskers can be curled.

Paint the mask to complete it, giving it any character you please. (Opinions differ about the one here – they vary from a cow on a cloudy day, to a teething boar!) Poster paint will be found most satisfactory for this.

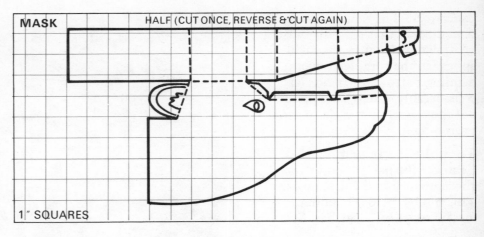

MASK   HALF (CUT ONCE, REVERSE & CUT AGAIN)

1″ SQUARES

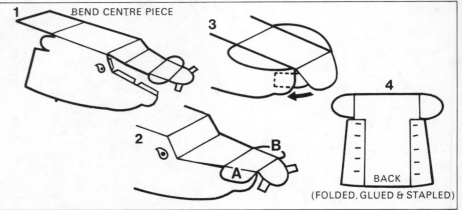

1   BEND CENTRE PIECE

2

3

4

A

B

BACK

(FOLDED, GLUED & STAPLED)

Paper Sculpture

Once you have mastered the bending, folding and curving techniques of papercraft, you can begin to use it as a medium for sculpture. The decorative flower panel shows how the natural colors of the paper, combined with the effects of light and shade, result in an artistic creation without the need for further embellishment.

Materials: A piece of thick cardboard (or illustration board) 8 by 15 inches; a piece of colored cardboard (the one used here is orange) 11 by $5\frac{3}{4}$ inches; paper for the flowers); clear adhesive.

Begin by transferring the pattern for the frame and for the top frame to thick cardboard, scoring and bending where indicated by the broken lines. Paste the under frame pieces to form a panel and secure the corners on the back with masking tape.

Using the same scale—the frame shown measured $12\frac{7}{8}$ by $7\frac{7}{8}$ inches —transfer the shapes for the flowers and leaves to stiff paper or composition paper.

Flower A, the red flower, is made by lightly scoring the petals as marked by the broken lines and squeezing them gently in. The star shape is then pasted to the center. Make two of these flowers.

The buttercup, flower B, has its petals gently curled. The center part of the flower is snipped all around and these edges folded upward; complete the flower by pasting the center in. Make four of these flowers.

Leaves C, D and E are all scored and gently folded. Make one of each size of the leaves marked C, two D and three E.

The plant stems F, G and H are all scored and folded.

Arrange the flowers, leaves and

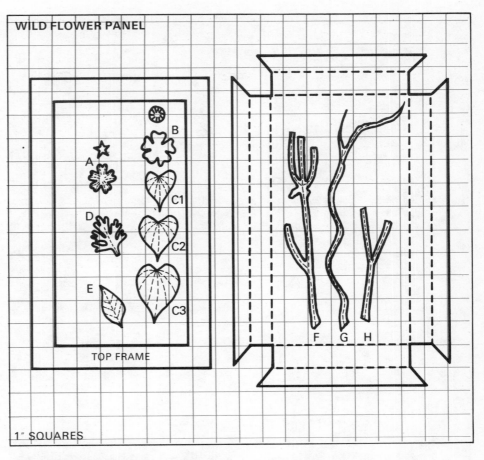

stems on a piece of colored cardboard the same size as the panel, following the photograph. When you are satisfied with the grouping, glue them down carefully, trying not to lose any of the three-dimensional quality, and glue the colored cardboard inside the panel.

Stick the top frame over the lower frame to complete your panel. You can, if you wish, insert a sheet of clear plastic between the two.

To make the medieval king

It is now time to make the colorful medieval figure shown in the color photograph. Although he looks as if he had been sculpted, he is, in fact, made entirely from white paper.

Begin, as usual, by enlarging the pattern pieces on squared-up paper and transferring them to the paper to be modeled. The pattern as shown makes a figure which stands 9½ inches tall. Cut out all the pieces.

Fold in the sticking tags on the lower body section and paste them to each other inside the cone produced. These tags are made in this way so that they can be stapled, out of sight, for extra firmness if necessary.

Bend and paste the upper body section, using the tag in the normal way. Don't forget to cut the two slits marked in each arm position (Diagram 1).

Glue the bottom of the upper body section and push it gently into the lower section. Check that it is upright before allowing the paste to dry. Gently bend the top part of each arm around and bend "A" under the hand, pasting it to the shaded part shown on the pattern (Diagram 2). The arms can then be put into the arm positions, pushing them gently into the slits made and gluing them down by folding the tags back inside (Diagram 3).

To complete the body section, the belt is glued around the figure's waist with the buckle at the front.

The cape is bent over to fit on the top of the body. Roll and paste the neck together to form a cylinder, push this through the hole in the cape and paste the tags down on the underside (Diagram 4).

The figure has been designed with a nearly cylindrical head—easier in cardboard than a spherical shape!

Roll the head piece in a similar way to the neck, and paste the top with the tag inside. Hair is bent around the head and pasted on (Diagram 5). The completed head is stuck to the neck by gluing the back of the neck, putting the head over it and pressing until it has adhered.

Next, add the crown. The completed cape section should be glued back and front and pasted on the main body part.

Now you can add the details to your model. Fur can be made by snipping paper and pasting it down around the edges of clothing (Diagram 6). The ornamental chain and any other pieces should be added before painting.

The heraldic motif was made by cutting a stencil and spraying gold paint through it (Diagram 7).

Poster paints are the best to use for coloring your model. As you can see from the colored photograph, blue was chosen for the main robes, red edged with white for the cape, gold for the crown, chain and buckle, and brown for the belt, hands, beard and mustache. The face and neck are yellow, and all the fur trimming in white.

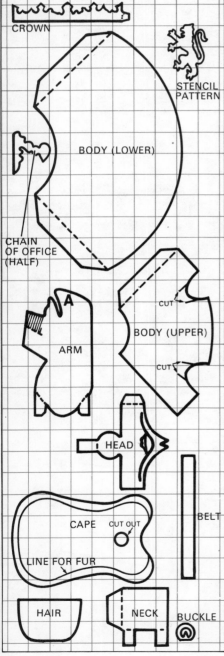

CROWN

STENCIL PATTERN

BODY (LOWER)

CHAIN OF OFFICE (HALF)

A

ARM

CUT

BODY (UPPER)

CUT

HEAD

CAPE   CUT OUT

LINE FOR FUR

BELT

HAIR   NECK   BUCKLE

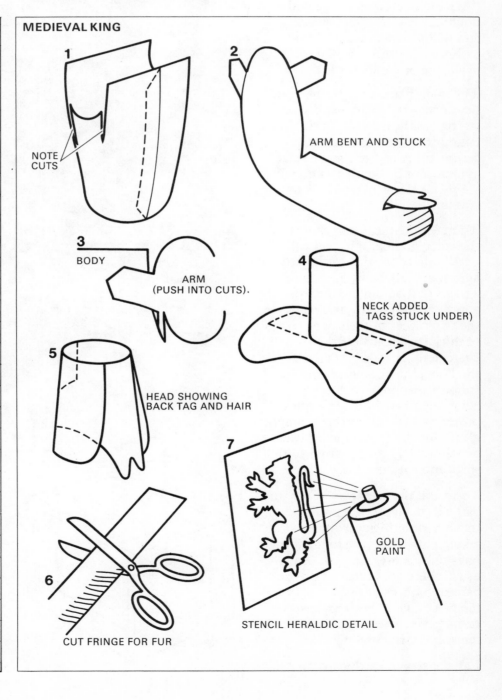

MEDIEVAL KING

1   NOTE CUTS

2   ARM BENT AND STUCK

3   BODY   ARM (PUSH INTO CUTS).

4   NECK ADDED TAGS STUCK UNDER)

5   HEAD SHOWING BACK TAG AND HAIR

6   CUT FRINGE FOR FUR

7   GOLD PAINT   STENCIL HERALDIC DETAIL

Creating Your Own Toy Theater

Toy theaters were immensely popular years ago. Many of the original theaters, plays and characters can be obtained in modern reprints, but the re-creation of your own theater can give great pleasure, as well as providing entertainment for the children. Shown here is the basic form of the theater, with scenery and characters painted for "Aladdin." However, you will no doubt have your own favorites, and will probably want to copy or cut out pictures from a magazine or comic book.

The main part of the theater can be constructed from a suitable, strong cardboard box. In this case, cut out the areas and add a cardboard platform for the stage, as shown in Diagram 1. You will see that a slot is marked for the curtain.

To make the theater as shown in the color photograph, you will need a sheet of thick cardboard approximately 24 by 18 inches; a piece of medium cardboard approximately 14 by 10 inches for the two pieces of the stage; scraps of thick cardboard for the two characters (or more if you wish); small lengths of picture wire to support the figures; clear adhesives; Scotch tape; staples; poster paints and (in this example) glitter for the scenery and poster or watercolors for the front of the stage and the curtains.

To make the theater   Copy the pattern on graph paper and transfer it to thick cardboard taking particular care to mark the lines to be scored and cut. As usual, these are indicated on the pattern by broken lines. Cut out the pieces. Our theater measures 12 inches square, and the area of the scenery is 9½ by 7 inches.

Lay the scored cardboard on a flat

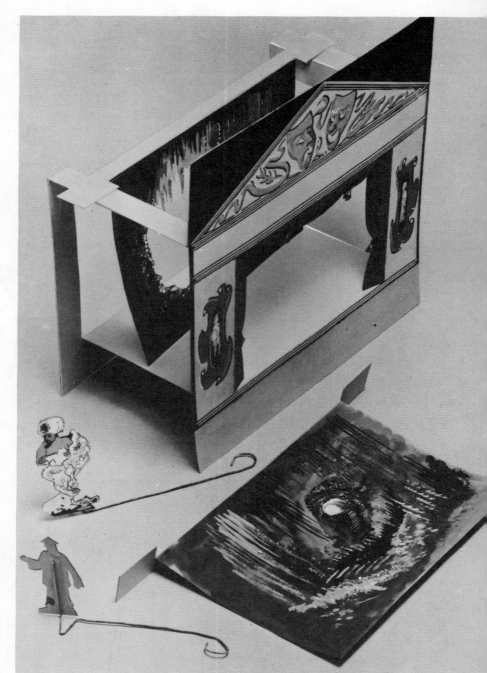

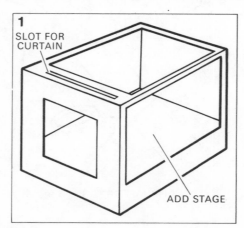

1

SLOT FOR
CURTAIN

ADD STAGE

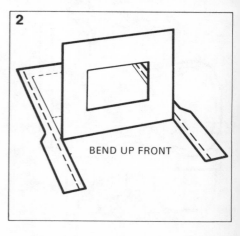

2

BEND UP FRONT

surface, and bend up the front
(Diagram 2). The stage can then
be made by bending it upward.
The rear support of the stage is
folded down (Diagram 3). Before
going any further, glue or staple
the front support to the back of
the theater front. When this is
firm, the strip of cardboard at the
bottom of the rear support should
be bent back to meet the upright
(Diagram 4). Note the position as
indicated by the dotted line. The
small triangle marked "A" is bent
up (Diagram 5). This triangle
tucks down between the two parts
already folded. Bend the top
forward to make a right angle.

The back uprights can now be
glued together or stapled to make a
firmer bond. Finally, the squares
at the other end of the top are bent
out and fastened at the back of the
theater front. The base of the
theater is now complete, and can
be painted.

Bend the side curtains back over
the stage and make your front
curtain. This should be slightly
higher than the theater and ¼-inch
narrower than the width of the
stage. It will then slide up and
down in between the side curtains
and the theater front at the rear.

The holders for the scenery
(Diagram 6, overleaf) are made
from two 1-inch strips, cut
according to the squared-up
pattern. The center part is bent
down, where indicated, so that
the scenery can be pasted on.

From medium weight cardboard,
cut two pieces each 9½ inches wide
and 7 inches deep for the scenery.
From one, cut an irregular shape
so that the audience can see
through to the backdrop. This
gives a three-dimensional effect
to your stage.

Paint the scenery according to
your fancy. The set here glitters
with stalactites and stalagmites,
like a real cave, and has a slightly

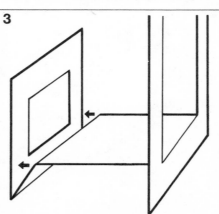

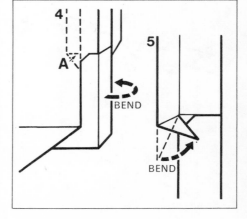

eerie quality. Once you become enthusiastic about your theater, you will probably want to have several sets of scenery and characters, and use them with your stage.

Cut from thick cardboard the two figures given on our squared-up pattern, or some from a magazine. This will give you an idea of the right size to choose. Bend the wire as shown in Diagram 7, so that you have a loop to hold and a V-shape is formed to make the figure stand upright. Stick the wire up the back of the figure as shown. If your figure is cut from cardboard, paint it.

You can see from Diagram 8, and from the two photographs, how your theater will look when it is finished.

Now for the play. Have you decided on one yet? If not, why not try to create a scene from a story you know by heart, or set one to music.

The orchestra starts, the lights are dimmed and, in a darkened room with a flashlight, you are the producer and director of your own entertainment.

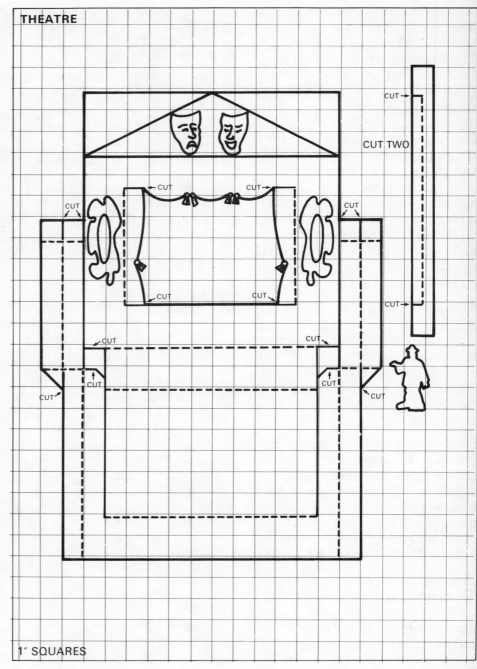

THEATRE

CUT TWO

1″ SQUARES

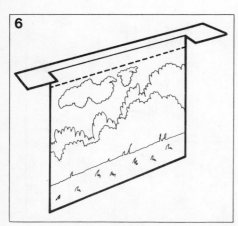

6

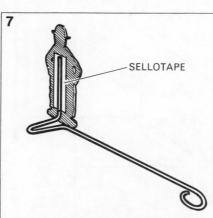

7

SELLOTAPE

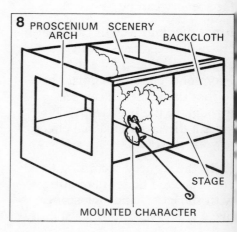

8 PROSCENIUM SCENERY
ARCH
BACKCLOTH

STAGE

MOUNTED CHARACTER

TAKE A FEW BITS AND PIECES

This section is for squirrels . . . natural hoarders who can't bear to throw anything away, "in case it comes in handy." Looking through these pages, they will be in their element, discovering first one design and then another that calls for nothing more than a few scraps of felt, some pieces of braid and trimmings, a couple of curtain rings, some snaps and all the other things that come tumbling out of the rag-bag every time they go there to look for a tape measure.

Paula Critchley's designs, which range from soft toys to traditional patchwork, and button collage to a neat little sewing kit, are the perfect answer to the cry of, "What shall we do?" on a wet Sunday afternoon. It doesn't matter if the stores are closed; you won't need to go out and buy anything. Indeed, Paula made several of the items herself one Sunday, so she couldn't cheat!

The limitations imposed by having to use what you have on hand increase inventiveness," she states. And, as you will see from the designs that follow, this is certainly true in her case.

If your rag-bag doesn't quite measure up to all the designs, or you don't have enough variety of colors and textures, here are some ideas for supplementing it, without spending much.

First, before you spend any money on anything at all, look through your belongings to see if there is anything ready to be discarded, useless in its present form, but made of good or interesting material. If so, open the seams, wash it and cut it up.

If you have a friend who is an able dressmaker, she will probably be only too pleased to get rid of her leftover scraps of fabric.

If you have to spend some money on fabrics, buy remnants or look for bargains. Printed cotton is often very cheap; so is bleached and unbleached muslin. Felt can be bought in 9-inch squares in a huge variety of colors. Some stores sell small bags of cloth and trimmings; the only drawback is that it is like buying a lot at an auction—for every one or two things you want, you get twenty you don't. Second-hand clothes counters offer good hunting grounds. Once you get "bits and pieces" conscious, you'll certainly be buying more than you give away at rummage sales, anyway.

A good selection to have would be: cottons, silks, both plain and patterned; heavy rayons and linens; mattress ticking; tweed, other wool and flannel; net and organdy; velvet and felt—particularly good for beginners, as it is easy to cut and handle. Useful scraps of trimmings are lace, rickrack, eyelet or cut work, crochet work, silk cord, ribbon and upholstery braid.

All kinds of buttons have all kinds of uses: flat, rounded, large, small, with and without buttonholes; any colors, but you should include both black and white.

The essential sewing equipment to have is: a pair of very sharp scissors; a package of needles in assorted sizes, including a few darning needles; a selection of sewing silks and cottons, including black and white; pins, and a tape measure.

Success always depends on doing things properly, and so it is a good idea to remember these points:

Always try to sew in daylight, as it is much more difficult to see stitches and colors clearly in artificial light.

Use very sharp scissors. Children should practice cutting out paper before starting on fabric.

Stitching should be neat and regular, especially where it is meant to show. The exception here is deliberately irregular sewing in fabric pictures.

It is better to start and finish your work with a couple of backstitches, rather than with a knot which might spoil the finished appearance, or become untied.

Tuck under edges of lace and other trimmings to prevent fraying, and sew down.

Beginning with Button[s]

The button box is an essential and integral part of every work basket or rag-bag: where should we be without it? The designs on these two pages show that everyday shirt and overcoat buttons, and even snaps and curtain rings, can be lifted into the realms of artistic creations.

Of course, if button collecting is one of your hobbies, or you have been lucky enough to buy a bag of old buttons, then you can base your designs on those. And even i[f] you decide to buy some, specially to start buttonwork, they will never be wasted. If the cushion wears out, the buttons won't. Cut them off, put them back in your button box, and wait for fresh inspiration.

For the cushion, you need two 13-inch squares of plain dress or furnishing fabric (ours was dark brown); shirt buttons in two sizes a scrap of narrow lace; some bits of rickrack braid and a silk cord.

On a piece of paper the same size as the fabric, arrange your button[s] in a design, following the photograph on the right. Mark in the position of the trimmings. Lightly fix the buttons in place with rubber cement. A dab on the back is enough. Make sure the holes of the buttons all face the same way. When the rubber cement has dried, put a pencil point through all the holes and then peel off the buttons. The rubber cement comes off easily with just a rub of your finger. You now have the pattern.

Diagram 1: Pin the four corners of one piece of your fabric, right side up, to a flat surface. Lay a piece of carbon paper, face down, on top, and place the butto[n] pattern over that. Tape it along all four sides. Pencil in all the dots to transfer the pattern to the fabric.

Buttons are best sewn on with

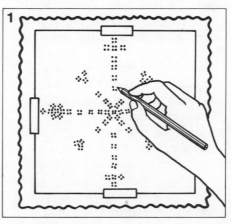

Contrast is important – in the plain and patterned hexagons of the bag and in the size relationship of the triangles and diamonds of th[e] cushion

single thread. If using ones with four holes, such as shirt buttons, always make the direction of the thread the same for each. Sew three or four times in one direction, and repeat in the opposite direction (Diagram 2). Several buttons can be sewn on with one length of thread, but be careful not to pull it too tightly and pucker the fabric.

Lace and rickrack trimmings should be pinned or lightly tacked into position before sewing, and ends neatly sewn under if they are not going over the sides to be seamed. Both sides of these trimmings should be sewn down on the fabric, as shown in Diagrams 3 and 4.

To prevent silk cord from fraying when it is cut, tape it first. Cut through the center of the tape and you will have two controlled edges as shown in Diagram 5.

Button collage   The design right was worked on gray felt, edged with a simple white cardboard mounting, using a basic color scheme of white, gold, pink and purple.

Buttons can be sewn on singly, the right way up or upside down; others can be stuck on— particularly buttons with long shafts. Two or three can be sewn or stuck one on top of the other to gain depth and interest, and they can be stuck on their sides, provided there are two adjacent buttons for support. Large snaps and curtain rings give additional textural interest.

Again, as with all work of this kind, it is advisable to plan your design first, moving the buttons around like pieces on a chess board, until you find the arrangement you like best.

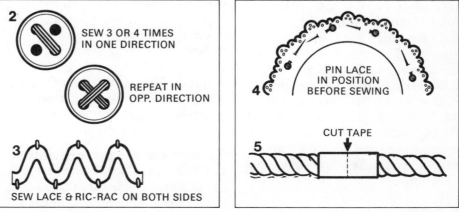

2   SEW 3 OR 4 TIMES IN ONE DIRECTION

REPEAT IN OPP. DIRECTION

3   SEW LACE & RIC-RAC ON BOTH SIDES

4   PIN LACE IN POSITION BEFORE SEWING

5   CUT TAPE

Successful patchwork is an exercise in the careful balancing of light and dark colors, plain and patterned pieces – and of course immaculate needlecraft

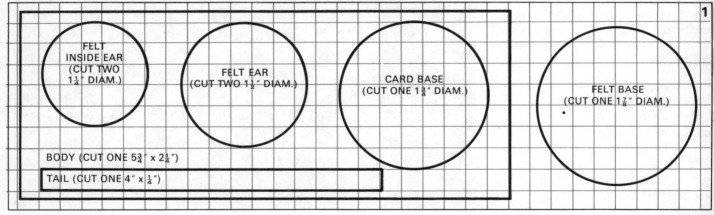

FELT
INSIDE EAR
(CUT TWO
1¼" DIAM.)

FELT EAR
(CUT TWO 1½" DIAM.)

CARD BASE
(CUT ONE 1¾" DIAM.)

FELT BASE
(CUT ONE 1⅞" DIAM.)

BODY (CUT ONE 5¾" x 2¼")

TAIL (CUT ONE 4" x ¼")

Make a Mini Mouse

You can make a variety of soft toys using the basic pattern given opposite. The mouse is photographed, above, actual size: an endearing little shelf ornament or, if you have the heart to stick pins in him, a pincushion. By altering the shape and position of the ears, eyes and nose you can make other animals to form a collection.

For the mouse you will need: A piece of felt, 8 by 5 inches; felt in contrasting color, 3 by 1½ inches; spool of dark thread; sewing needle; a postcard; polyester fiber or absorbent cotton; 2 buttons about ⅜-inch diameter; scraps of felt or other trimmings for collar and tie; picture wire.

To transfer the pattern onto the felt: trace body, tail, base, one ear and one inside ear (Diagram 1) onto a piece of light-weight card-

board. Cut out the shapes and lay the body, tail, base and ear on the larger piece of felt. Draw around them with a pencil, twice for the ears. Cut out the pieces. Cut the inside ears twice, in the same way, from the contrasting piece of felt. Cut out the circle marked "card base" from the cardboard only.

Cut body, tail and felt base once from the larger piece of felt, and the outside ears twice. Cut inside ears twice from contrasting felt.

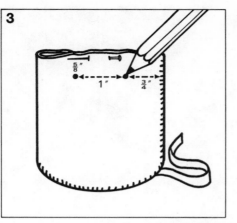

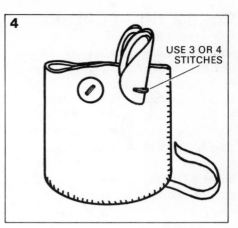

Diagram 2. Keeping the pencil marks inside, sew the long edge of the body to the felt base, using a simple overcasting, as shown. Just a little over $\frac{1}{4}$-inch from the end, insert the end of the tail. With two or three stitches, sew the tail, body and base together.

Diagram 3. Now sew up the back seam and finish off at the top. Pin the top unsewn edges together and, with a pencil, mark the position of the ears on both sides $\frac{3}{4}$-inch from back seam, and the eyes, $1\frac{3}{4}$ inches from back seam.

Diagram 4. Using a tiny dab of glue, stick the inside ears to the center of the outside ears. Pinch the ear at the edge between finger and thumb, and sew about $\frac{3}{8}$-inch from the base of the ear, in the position marked, and finish off. Sew the other ear in the same way. Sew on the buttons for the eyes. If you are using buttons with holes, make sure you get them both sewn in the same direction, otherwise the mouse will have a squint.

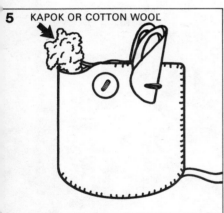

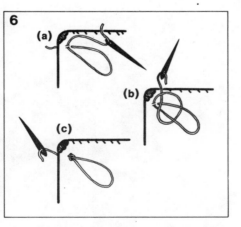

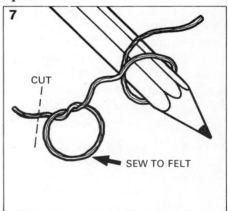

Diagram 5. Now push the cardboard base into the bottom of the body, and stuff tightly, nearly to the top. Sew the top seam until you reach the point level with the eyes. Leave the needle still threaded, finish stuffing the mouse, and then continue sewing the seam to the end. Sew the nose, going over and over the end with long stitches, and finish off.

Diagram 6. To make the whiskers, put the threaded needle in just below the mouse's nose. Pull it through to the opposite side, leaving a length of an inch or so. Make a loop of about 2 inches and hold it as you make a small stitch at the base in the felt. Secure it with a stitch. Repeat several times on each side of the face, and then trim the whiskers with scissors.

Diagram 7. This mouse is dressed formally in a collar and tie, but could be wearing a scarf, a lace collar, bouquet of flowers or an apron. To make the pince-nez, twist a short length of picture wire around a pencil or a pair of scissors to form a small loop through which the wire is passed once. Make a second loop in the same way, leaving a small gap between the two. Cut the ends with pliers and sew on tightly.

Take a Bit of Cotton

It's a comfortable life for this squashy mouse, made from scraps of lightweight cotton and felt. Here again is a pattern which can be adapted by varying the features to take on any personality you choose: or even some personalities that happen by accident. This is the kind of toy which makes an amusing cushion ornament for a child's bed; that is, if he can't commandeer the best armchair all the time.

To make the mouse you will need: ¾-yard of lightweight cotton; 3–4 oz. polyester fiber stuffing; tiny bits of felt for the eyes and nose; sewing thread and needle. For the waistcoat, a remnant of felt or any lightweight woolen material; bias tape, ribbon or braid for the trimming; 2 buttons. For the bow tie, a length of lightweight cotton or ribbon.

To make the pattern: Draw one-inch squares on a large piece of paper or use graph paper, and copy the pattern shapes onto it. They are drawn exactly to scale in Diagram 1. Cut out all the pattern pieces and pin them firmly to the fabric. Cut around the pattern pieces, leaving about ¼-inch, as shown by the broken line.

Hand sew or machine stitch all seams on the wrong side of the material. Double over lengthwise the tail, arms and legs. Sew the seams together, leaving the tops unsewn. Turn them inside out. Iron the tail flat. Lightly stuff arms and legs and sew up the top seams. Sew the seams of the two sides of the face marked A to the corresponding seams on the *front*, marked A. Sew the seams of the two sides of the face marked B to the sides of the *back* marked B. Where the four seams join in the front, sew or paste on the nose, sew in the mouth and, using overstitch, sew on the outsides of the eyes, then the pupils.

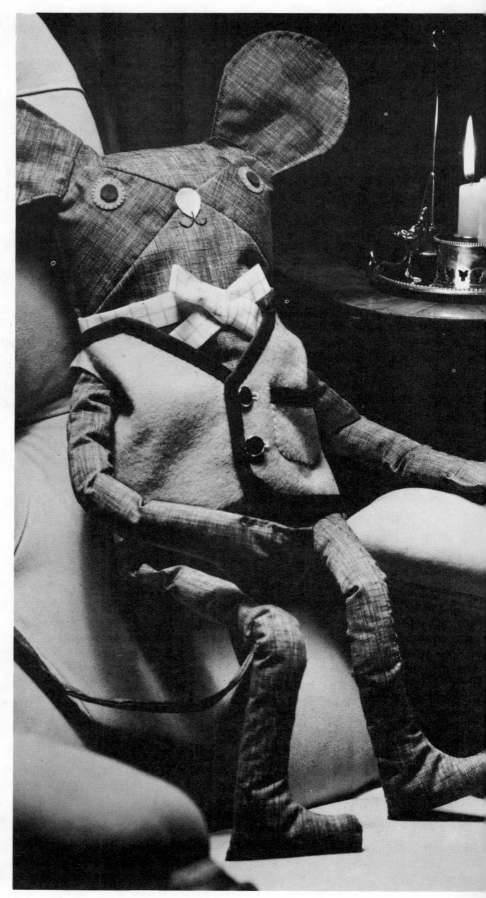

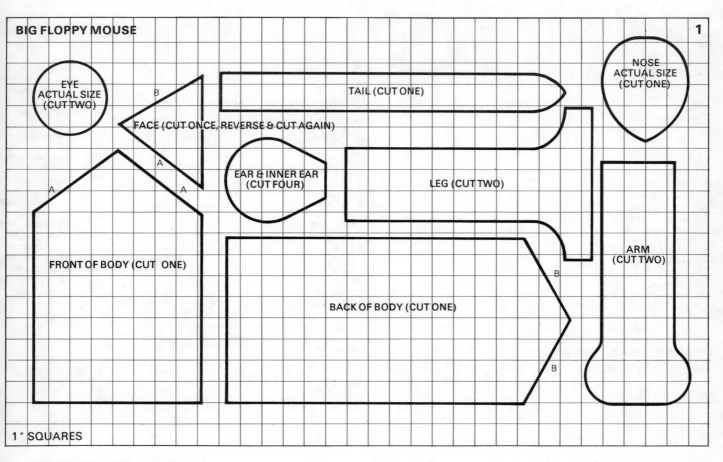

BIG FLOPPY MOUSE   1

EYE
ACTUAL SIZE
(CUT TWO)

B

FACE (CUT ONCE, REVERSE & CUT AGAIN)

A

A

A

A

TAIL (CUT ONE)

NOSE
ACTUAL SIZE
(CUT ONE)

EAR & INNER EAR
(CUT FOUR)

LEG (CUT TWO)

ARM
(CUT TWO)

FRONT OF BODY (CUT ONE)

B

BACK OF BODY (CUT ONE)

B

1" SQUARES

Sew together side seams of back
and front, leaving a gap for the
arms. Turn on to right side and
sew in the arms. The mouse will
now look like Diagram 2. Stuff the
body at the base, loosely.

Tack in the edges of the base of
the body about ½-inch and pin the
legs at the corners and the tail in
the middle (Diagram 3). Sew up
the base.

Sew the inner and outer ear
pieces together, and
turn them inside out. Press them
flat and sew a seam around the
edges. Turn under the bottom
edge (Diagram 4).

Push in the pointed corners of the
head (Diagram 5), and sew in the
ears to the back and front of the
mouse.

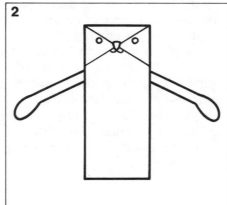

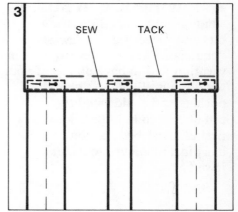

SEW   TACK

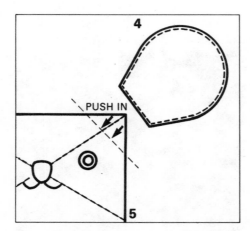

PUSH IN

4

5

A Sewing Kit to Make

Made from bits and pieces, to keep bits and pieces tidy, a new-style "chatelaine" that's ideal to take on vacation and to have on top of your sewing box. By adjusting the pockets and braids slightly, you can alter it to hold handkerchiefs, tissues, absorbent cotton, hairpins, manicure tools, or jewelry.

To make the sewing case you will need: A piece of cotton gingham 7 by 13 inches; two pieces of felt in contrasting colors, each 6 inches square; 3 scraps of white felt for the pockets; rickrack braid in light and dark colors; scraps of ball fringe, daisy and scalloped trimmings (Diagram 1); a tiny pearl button; sewing thread and needle.

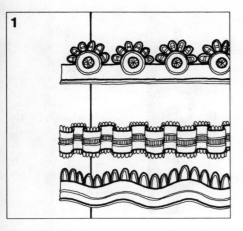

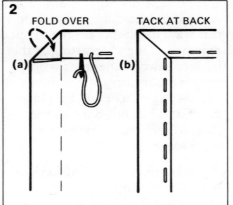

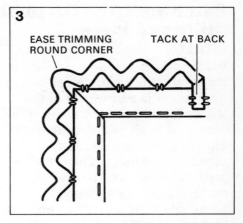

Photograph left: Each pocket is 4 inches square. Left: cut rosettes from lace and sew on individually. Trim with braid as shown. Right: pin trimmings in position on felt, leaving turnings. Pin both pockets in position on gingham and sew, turning in braid neatly. Sew button in middle of right-hand pocket. Sew the two central bands of dark-colored rickrack down the centre of the gingham, leaving short ends to tuck under.

Diagram 2. Turn in $\frac{1}{4}$-inch hem on wrong side all around gingham, and turn under again, making a double hem. Tack all around. When tacking the corners, fold the edges under to form a neat point, as shown in the diagrams above.

Diagram 3. Sew the trimming around the outside of the gingham, easing it carefully around corners so that it does not pucker the fabric. Catch the braid with two stitches only at the curve of the scallops. Stitch down the end of the trimming onto the turned-over edge.

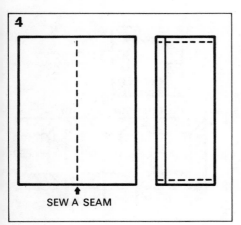

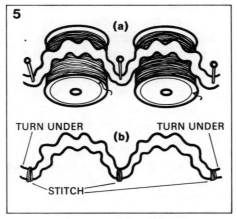

Diagram 4. Cut the two 6-inch squares of contrasting felt and pin to hemmed gingham to check correct size. Unpin them. Cut a piece of white felt $3\frac{1}{4}$ by $4\frac{1}{2}$ inches, place on the light-colored felt square as shown and seam through to the backing felt. Fold over and sew side seams down on to backing felt. Overcast the two felt squares together and cover seam with a length of rickrack. Pin them again to the gingham, sewing the felt to the wrong side of the fabric.

Diagram 5. Measure the rickrack to hold thread spools. Pin one end, allowing a small turning, on to the top edge of the felt. Pass it over three thread spools, and pin it down, taut, between each one. Remove the spools and sew down at pins. Make a braid holder for elastic, thimble, etc., on the other side in the same way. Roll up the sewing kit and make a thread loop to match the button.

Patchwork, the Original "Bits and Pieces" Craft

Patchwork, as we know it today, is the result of the initiative shown by amateur needlewomen in the late eighteenth and the nineteenth centuries. Quilts were made out of bits from the rag-bag as an economic necessity. Then, as they grew in popularity, they were made in practically every household. The oldest pattern known is the "Crazy Quilt"—like crazy paving—described and illustrated later in this section.

The piecing method of patchwork, sewing patches of cloth together by means of a seam, is the method most popular today. There are several basic shapes from which to work a complete design, and innumerable different ways of using each shape, as you will see. Great accuracy is necessary, particularly when sewing the seams together, as they must correspond exactly (except in crazy patchwork). Cottons, silks and velvets of all kinds are the best materials to use; synthetic fabrics usually stretch and fray badly. Use materials of equal weight and strength together. Simple color schemes, using varied tones of two or three colors, are more effective than the complete rainbow. Different tones of one color can look lovely, especially when backed up by a single plain one. Stripes, spots and checks can be used in interesting ways, and cottons with tiny prints in light and dark shades look good.

If you have a few years to spare, by all means try your hand at making a quilt. Otherwise, we recommend opting for smaller items, like cushions, bags, short curtains and fashion trimmings.

For the piecing method of patchwork, a "template" or pattern is cut for each piece, and the fabric cut slightly larger and tacked around it firmly on all sides. When enough patches have been made in this way, the seams are then joined together, using overcasting at the back or sewn at the front with a simple embroidery stitch. None of the basting-stitches or templates must be taken out until all the sides of each patch have been sewn together.

Squares are the simplest form of geometrical shape to use in patchwork. Decide the size you want your finished work to be and calculate how many squares to make—for instance, if you wanted to make the front of a cushion cover 12 inches square, you could decide to make patches in 2 or 3-inch squares. Draw a template on the cardboard accurately, using a ruler, preferably a steel one, a T square and a triangle (Diagram 1). Then cut the others from it, separately for the greatest accuracy, either on paper or cardboard.

Place the template on the fabric, centering the pattern if there is one, and cut the material $\frac{3}{8}$-inch larger than the card (Diagram 2).

Turn the surplus material over the cardboard on the wrong side and baste down over the "paper," turning in the corners neatly, (Diagram 3).

Make as many squares as you need in the same way. Sew the seams together from the back, using overcasting (Diagram 4), leaving the "papers" in place until all the seams have been sewn. Where it is an advantage to have the added "body" and firmness, the "papers" may be left in place, but of course this would affect the washability of the article.

The photograph on the right shows a sample piece of patchwork made with a "cross" of five squares and four "bricks" made with templates cut from half-squares. Notice the striking color balance

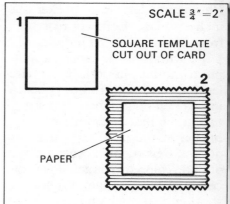

SCALE $\frac{3}{4}'' = 2''$

SQUARE TEMPLATE CUT OUT OF CARD

PAPER

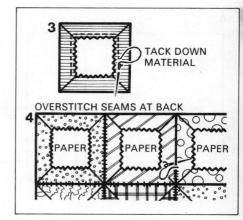

TACK DOWN MATERIAL

OVERSTITCH SEAMS AT BACK

PAPER   PAPER   PAPER

achieved by the use of stripes and florals offset by a plain square.

To make triangles from squares

Using a metal ruler and T square, draw a square template. Then bisect it across one diagonal, or draw in both diagonals, according to the size of triangle you want.

Calculate the number of triangles you need by multiplying the number of squares by two or four.

Two ways of using hexagons

The photograph above shows the "circular" effect created when alternating rows of dark and light colors are used. The contrast of one large-scale and one small-scale floral design is another interesting feature. In the photograph below, a detail taken from a cot quilt worked in shades of lemon, cream and brown; only plain fabrics and those with a single, bold stripe or a cross are used.

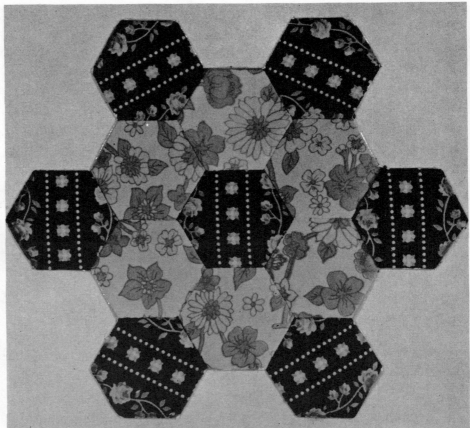

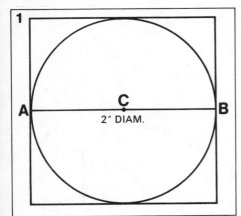

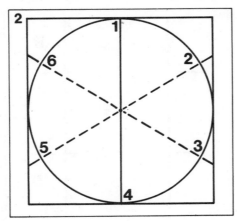

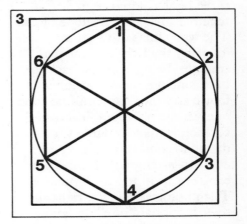

To make templates for hexagons, diamonds and half-diamonds

Diagram 1. Draw a circle with a diameter the length you want your hexagon to be, from point to point; say 2 inches. Draw in the diameter, the line A-B.

Diagram 2. Use a protractor and mark off your circle into segments of 60° each. Join the opposite points.

Diagram 3. To make the six-sided shape, join the points marked 1-6 together, as shown. The result is a hexagon, with three diamonds and, of course, six half-diamonds.

To make long hexagons

This is a variation of the hexagon, described before. To make the template, rule a line, say $2\frac{1}{2}$ inches long. Draw 2 horizontal lines across it at equal distances from each end (Diagram 1). In this instance the distance was $\frac{5}{8}$-inch in each case, and the horizontal lines 1 inch across. Join all the outside lines together all around the hexagon (Diagram 2). Sides A, B, C and D must all be of equal length. Sides E and F must be equal to each other but will, of course, vary in length according to the distance between the horizontals.

You can achieve limitless variations in effect according to how you use light and dark colors, plain and patterned fabrics. In Diagram 3, diamond shapes are simply alternated light and dark, making an eight-pointed star. In Diagram 4, the cross effect is built up of triangles. Notice how one dark and three light-colored triangles together give an "envelope" look. The wavy lines of Diagram 5 are made by the light and the dark triangles being in pairs, back to back, one double row using a dark fabric and the next a middle-tone one. In the photograph above, the cushion is made of large velvet diamonds and smaller ones, eight-to-a-template, in silk; you can see this in the color picture. The photograph lower right shows the traditional "box" design of ascending stairs, an effect achieved with diamonds in two fabrics.

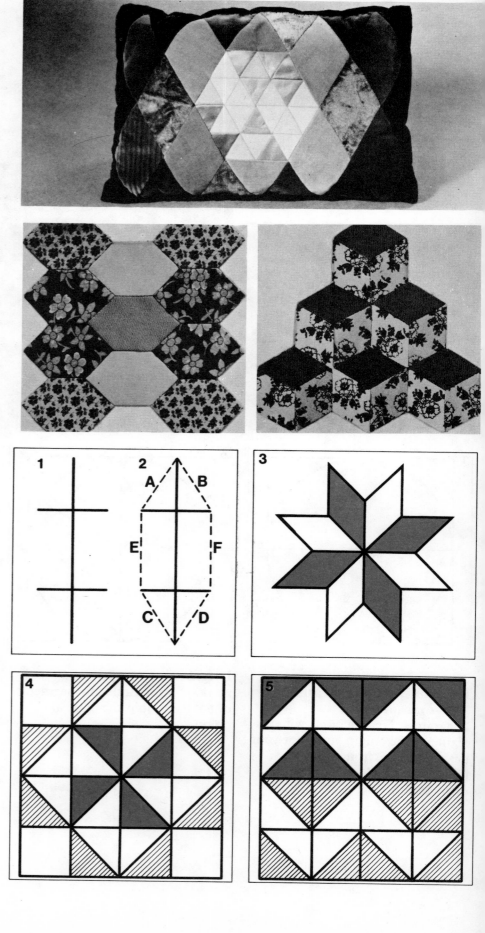

Crazy Patchwork

This looks less orderly than piecing patchwork, yet needs care. Collect together your scraps of material, iron them first and trim the edges neatly. Use a piece of firm cotton or linen as the background and, working from one edge, pin one patch in place, and then another, the edges slightly overlapping (Diagram 1). Sew the patches down with running stitch, going right through the patches and the background material. Carry on in this way until the entire background material is covered.

In order to hide the seams, sew over them with a thick silk thread (black is effective) using feather or chain stitch, or herringbone stitch, as shown in the photograph on the right.

Cut the patches in roughly geometrical shapes, without getting too intricate—you are not creating a jigsaw puzzle!

Giving your patchwork a professional finish

Diagram 2. To finish the borders of your patchwork, use *triangles* made from squares, *half-diamonds* or *squares*. For patchwork in hexagons and long hexagons, make (a) *triangles* based on their shapes, and (b) *half-hexagons*.

Diagram 3. When cutting patches, take care to have one edge of the material cut exactly in the direction of the weave. If it is cut crookedly, the patches may not lie flat.

For extra guidance, a template with a "window" can be made the same size as the template in use, adding a margin of $\frac{3}{8}$-inch. This will enable you to see how the patch will look when using patterned fabrics. You can move the window template around until you have the pattern, or one of the most interesting features, centered.

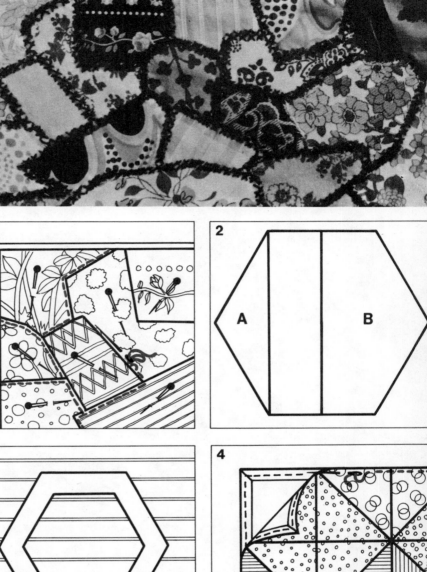

Diagram 4. Patchwork should be lined. Use silk or rayon or velveteen, which come in different colors, for silk and velvet patchwork, and cotton (gingham, poplin, lawn, etc.) for cotton fabrics. Treat the patchwork as an ordinary strip of fabric and line in the normal way.

Fabric Collage
The equipment you will need

1. Background material, which must be strong and not easily pulled out of shape. Suitable fabrics are felt, strong cotton, linen, rayon, canvas, mattress ticking and tweed. The fabric can be plain, providing an unobtrusive backdrop for the picture which is to be superimposed on it, or can be patterned and become part of the picture.

2. Fabrics to use as your "paints": absolutely anything is suitable, from fine nets (which are useful for toning down strong colors, and making "shadows") and lace of all kinds, to silks and felts. Scraps of fabric can be pulled and frayed, even just a few threads used.

3. Any trimmings, including pieces of crochet work, string, knitting or rug wool, braid, cord, ribbon, buttons, beads and sequins.

4. Sharp scissors.

5. Drawing and tracing paper.

6. Pencil, ruler and T square.

7. Rubber cement for sticking down fabrics and a heavier white glue for things like buttons.

8. Pushpins.

9. A package of needles and a selection of sewing threads in a variety of colors and textures.

Method No special frame is necessary for collage, although if you have an old picture frame, it would be useful. Pin the top of the background fabric to a flat wooden surface with pushpins, leaving a 1-inch border all around. Make sure that the grain of the fabric runs straight from side to side of the picture area.

Beginners can start by copying a greeting card or a photograph and soon may surprise themselves by thinking up their own ideas and designs.

At first, it helps to trace outlines, pin them to the fabric, and cut around them. Move the cut-out shapes around on the background until you are satisfied with your arrangement. Use the rubber cement very sparingly, in dabs, and not too near the edges as it will ooze out when pressed down in position. A matchstick is useful for this.

Felt is the simplest material for children to use for collage. It is easy to handle and cut, cheap to buy and available in paint-box colors. Pieces can be stuck on top of each other to create a feeling of dimension and shadow, as shown in Diagram 1. Use dark and neutral colors to offset the bright ones.

Pieces of fabric that are to be sewn onto the background should be pasted or pinned in position first,

before stitching. Put a few stitches here and there (Diagram 2), or use backstitch or simple embroidery stitches. If you want the stitches to be part of the design, to give emphasis to an outline, use a contrasting thread.

Frayed edges can be left as they are: they give a softer outline which is attractive in many designs. To camouflage them, use blanket stitch.

A child's house-tree-sun-dog-and-flowers design, shown in the photograph on the left, is worked in felt pasted to muslin, buckram or interlining.

To mount the finished picture: measure the picture area, leaving a border of 1 inch all around. With a sharp knife cut a white cardboard base to the size required. If it is to be framed, cut the cardboard slightly longer than the picture, but still allowing for a border to be turned back over the board.

Diagram 3. Using very strong cotton or tailor's thread, tightly sew the top border to the bottom border, over the cardboard.

Sew a short piece of thread at the four corners of the picture to mark where the fabric is to be turned back over the cardboard.

Diagram 4. Now fold the corners of the two remaining borders over from (a) to (b). They will look like (c). Then fold the whole border over the cardboard (d). A stitch at each fold will keep them in position.

Place the picture face down on a flat surface and lay the cardboard in position on top of it. The pieces of thread sewn at the corners will correspond to the corners of the cardboard.

Diagram 5. Sew the two remaining sides in the same way as the first two.

This method is more satisfactory

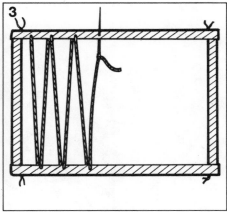

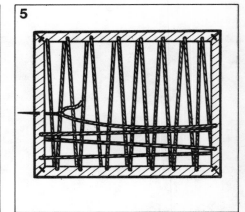

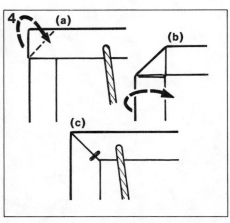

than gluing the material to the back of the cardboard because tight sewing will increase the rigidity of the picture.

"Tiger in the Jungle"
Collage by Eugenie Alexander

The beautiful fabric collage shown below was made by Eugenie Alexander. She is a specialist in this art form, and this high quality could be achieved only after practice and experience. But her work has been included in this section as an encouragement to beginners, because her methods are not complicated. There are no difficult embroidery stitches; here she uses only featherstitching, hemming, running and backstitches.

The background was made of blue and green silks for the sky and ground. Red silk and net were used for the sun, and the tiger has stripes of black and orange felt. Depth and contour are given to his body by the use of net. His whiskers are made of fine string, and the mane of the lion's head, peering through the undergrowth, is bouclé wool.

Felts, frayed cottons and rayon in various shades of green were sewn and pasted on to represent leaves. Nearly all the flowers and fruit are cut out of felt and pasted down.

Eugenie Alexander also designed the collage of which a detail is shown on the right.

The use of net creates the misty appearance, and gives the plants and seed crowns their texture. Creamy-white sequins here and there represent the seeds. Layers of orange, pink and red fabrics, with net, show how much more realistically the "ball of fire" effect for the sun can be created with a variety of tones, rather than the use of a single color.

Footnote   The embroidery stitches referred to throughout this section are fully described in the following section, "Take a needle and thread."

TAKE A NEEDLE AND THREAD

Take a needle and thread and pretend you have a sketchbook and pencil. That's what Mary Kehoe did when she was designing this section. Embroidery is needlework for pleasure and adornment, not for thrift or necessity, and these designs are planned with that in mind. All the shapes and compositions are inspired by Nature—birds, leaves, trees, flowers, eggs, a piece of coral, a feather, even a pile of vegetables in a produce store, and a cactus on a window sill. Not only is beauty in the eye of the beholder—so are the endless possibilities for decoration.

All these designs can be used decoratively in a number of ways—worked as pictures and framed either singly or as a set, with similar motifs in different colors or on varying backgrounds; as borders for plain curtains, tablecloths or sheets and pillowcases; to give individuality to a set of place mats and table napkins, to trim lamp shades, skirts, cuffs and collars—anything, in fact, that presents an uncluttered background and is prepared to let the embroidery steal the limelight.

The designs draw for their main effects on a limited number of stitches, so that the beginner has very little homework to do before she reaches the satisfying stage of being able to execute a finished design.

Starting with the feather, experiment with different types of thread in varying weights to obtain a number of effects. The soft, floating quality of a feather is achieved, in our example, by the use of long stitches in a single strand of thread. It could equally well be arrived at by the use of mohair or fine yarn.

Outlines in embroidery can vary as much as in art—the stitch you use can have the effect of a light or a heavy pencil stroke. Practice couching narrow threads or wool, metallic yarns or textured cotton threads, and then thickening them with a second row or with a row of stem stitch, chain stitch or running stitch.

Some of the designs in this section are meant to be purely inspirational—there is no blueprint for a feather, nor even for a group of cacti.

Where there are diagrams to scale up and copy, you can transfer them to your fabric in a number of different ways. One of the simplest is to use the special non-smudge type of dressmaker's carbon paper. Choose the dark blue one for light fabrics; look for the yellow type if you are working on a dark background. Trace around the outline with a tracing wheel or a sharp pencil.

Alternatively, you can trace the design onto tissue paper, tack the paper in position over your fabric, and then baste around the outline, through the tissue, so that you have a line of stitches on your material when you tear off the paper. This method is particularly suitable where very lightweight fabrics are being used.

Another way is to prick holes close together through the tissue paper, all around the outline, and then paunce a chalky powder over the paper, so that the substance penetrates the holes and leaves a dotted outline.

To draw freehand designs onto medium or heavier weight fabrics, you can simply use tailor's chalk.

Collect together a variety of types of needles, a handful of embroidery threads and other threads, a good, sharp pair of scissors, and you have all the ingredients of an embroiderer's sketchbook.

Throughout this section where the diagrams are intended to be scaled up and copied, they have been given a squared background. One square = one inch.
Copy the design, following the outlines of the diagram, onto paper ruled into 1-inch squares. Graph paper can be used.

Diagram 1: Fly stitch This is a loose, horizontal stitch, caught and held down by a short vertical stitch. Bring the needle out at (1) and insert it at (2), but do not pull the thread tightly. Bring the needle out at (3) and insert it at (4), catching the thread to form a V shape. From (4), bring the needle out where you want to start the next stitch. To make a "Y" stitch, which is very similar, make a longer stitch (3) to (4).

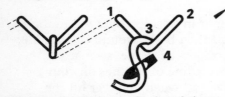

Diagram 2: Long stitch A long stitch is simply a straight stitch. Insert the needle at (1) and bring it out at (2). If there is to be no tension in the work, such as in a picture, a long stitch can be virtually any length. Where, however, there will be "pull," it can be couched (see Diagram 3) in place.

Diagram 3: Couching Where a long, continuous outline is wanted, a thread can be laid against the work and couched with short stitches, either in matching thread or in a contrasting yarn. Bring the needle through the cloth, beside the laid thread (2), over the top of the thread, and back through the cloth (2) as close as possible. It is important not to pull the traveling thread too tightly, and to keep the stitches evenly spaced.

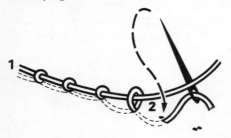

Diagram 4: Curved couching There are a number of examples in the designs that follow where a thread is laid in a curve for a special effect, and then couched. The method is exactly as for couching a straight laid thread. Where a very long thread is being used, or the shape is all-important, it is possible to tack the thread temporarily in place before working the couching stitch.

Diagram 5: French knots This stitch gives textural interest to the work in a number of ways and is often used for the centers of flowers, for seeds and other special effects. To work it, insert the needle in the cloth, wrap the thread twice around the needle, bring the needle out and make a tiny stitch to secure the "knot" in position.

Diagram 6: Seed stitches These are tiny stitches, worked either singly or in pairs, at random to give a light shading effect. Later in the section, you will find these stitches used to represent the texture of a sliced pepper.

Diagram 7: Chain stitch To work a row of chain stitch, bring the needle up through the fabric. Insert the needle next to where it came through, and bring the point of the needle up again through the fabric (1). Do not bring the needle through. Make a loop with the free thread (2) and put it under the point of the needle. Draw the needle out of the fabric (3). Pull the loop and repeat, always inserting the needle inside the stitch already formed.

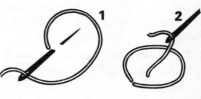

Diagram 8: Stem stitch This gives a corded effect, with each stitch slightly overlapping the previous one, slantwise along the line. The needle is inserted into the fabric for the completion of the former stitch and out of the fabric for the beginning of the next one, with the needle always parallel to the direction of the stitches.

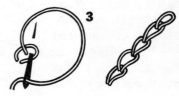

Diagram 9: Cross-stitch If a row of cross-stitches is to be worked, the stitches can be made all in one direction and then worked over with the stitches taking the other diagonal, to form a cross. Alternatively, each stitch can be worked individually, first in one direction and then in the

Top, white threads and yarns of all kinds carry out a natural coral theme in the embroidered collage. The bird in a tree picture, below, has a Jacobean influence with important use of black

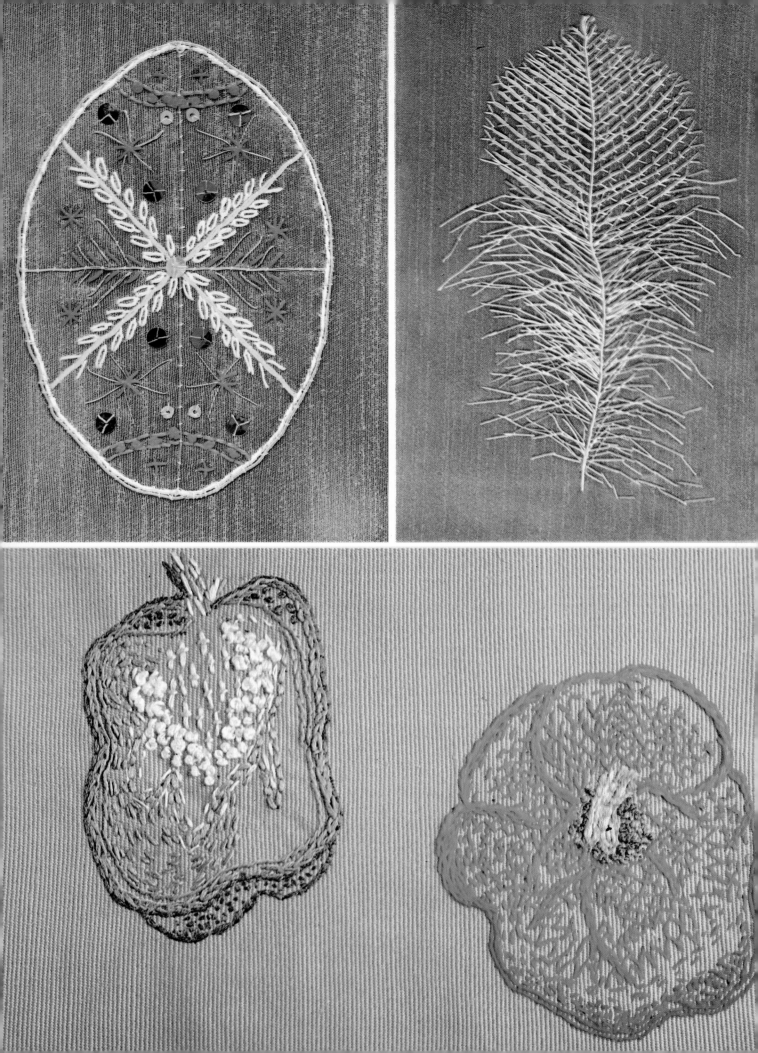

other. It is important, for an even appearance, to keep all the top stitches going in the same direction, that is, not work some from left to right and some from right to left.

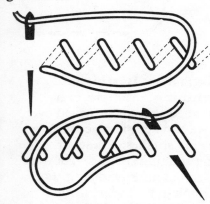

Diagram 10: **Running stitch**
Where a broken outline is wanted in embroidery, take small, even stitches, leaving equal spaces between them.

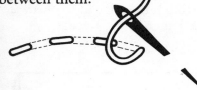

Diagram 11: **Cretan stitch**
Cretan stitch can be worked solid or open, and gives a featherlike appearance. It is worked alternately from the left and from the right, with a small stitch being taken, the point of the needle always over the thread.

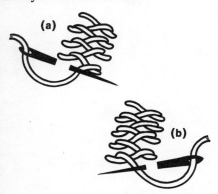

Diagram 12: **Star stitch**   These are like double cross-stitches, and can be worked all in one color, or with each pair of stitches in contrasting color. As with cross-stitch, it is important to

work the stitches in the same direction in the same order. It is important, too, to make each stitch of the star the same length, so that if a circle were drawn around the star stitch, all the points would touch it.

Diagram 13: **Blanket or buttonhole stitch**   Blanket stitch (where the stitches are more widely spaced) and buttonhole stitch can be used, as the names imply, for edgings. They have a decorative use, too—for instance, in the fish design that follows later in this section. To make a stitch, the needle is inserted in the work and brought out in a straight line below, with the thread being carried along underneath the needle.

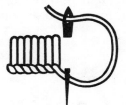

Diagram 14: **Herringbone stitch**
This stitch can be used to apply patches to a background, as in crazy patchwork. Make one diagonal stitch, from left to right (1), take a small stitch under the fabric and make a diagonal stitch in the opposite direction (2). It is important to space the stitches evenly and to ensure that they are all parallel (3).

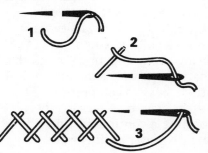

Diagram 15: **Satin stitch**   This is used where areas such as leaves or petals are to be filled in to give the appearance of a close fabric. It is a number of straight stitches worked side by side. The length of the stitches will depend on the outline to be filled—for example, if a pointed oval shape is being worked, the stitches will start very small, will gradually become longer until the widest part is reached, and will then diminish in size again. All the stitches must be worked close together and parallel.

Diagram 16: **Lazy daisy stitch**
Chain stitches are worked in a circle, when five or more represent the petals of a flower. To make the loop, the needle is inserted in the center of the imaginary circle and brought out at the circumference (1), with the thread held under the needle. A small stitch is taken to secure the loop (2).

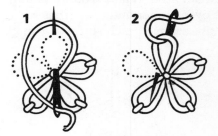

Diagram 17: **Covering with buttonhole stitch**   This stitch can be used to cover a button loop, or a curtain ring (as in the case of the "coral" collage in this section). To make a button loop, start with two backstitches on the fabric to stop the thread from coming out. Make three or four loops from right to left, the correct size to fit the button (1). Make a loop with the thread and take the needle under the sewn loops and

Top right, a delicate feather design in couching and long stitch; below, red and green peppers in French knots, chain and cross stitches, and, top left, a Fabergé-inspired egg design in couched metallic thread over the thread loop (2). Pull tightly and repeat all the way around. To cover a ring, secure the thread by tying and work as described above, keeping the stitches close together all the way around. Finish off with a few stitches to secure the end and darn in the original end of the thread.

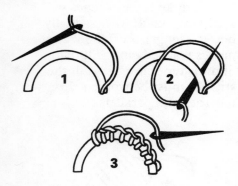

Diagram 18: **Spiderweb**

This special effect is used in the "coral" collage later in this section. To copy it, you can take four lengths of narrow cord and cross them to form an 8-pointed star. Secure them at the center with a few stitches. Thread a needle with crochet thread or the yarn of your choice, secure the end with a few stitches to one of the "spokes" and start weaving the needle and thread around and around, taking it over, under and over (that is, right around) each spoke as you go.

Diagram 19: **Featherstitch**

Insert the needle up through the fabric at A, down through the fabric at B and up again through the fabric at C, as illustrated in part (1) of this diagram. Pull the

thread (2) and repeat on the opposite side (3). Continue, from left to right (4).

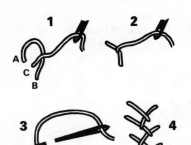

Diagram 20: **Overcasting**

Overcasting is usually used for sewing two pieces of material together at their edges; you will find reference to it in the "Bits and Pieces" section. It is a very useful stitch to use with felt, where the stitching is part of the decorative finish and, because the fabric does not fray, no hemming is needed. The stitches, whether upright or slightly slanting, must be regular in size and direction.

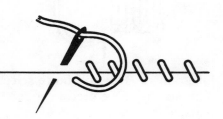

Diagram 21: **Backstitch**

Backstitch looks like a running stitch, but a stitch taken back each time greatly strengthens the sewing. It should be used for sewing seams together. Stitches should be no longer than those illustrated. Insert the needle up through the fabric (1), bring it out and take a little stitch back (2). Bring the needle up through the material just over the distance of a stitch away (3) and repeat. The stitches can be close together, forming a continuous line, or slightly apart as illustrated.

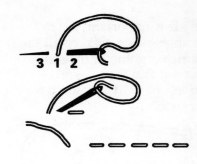

Diagram 22: **Basting and hemming**   Material to be hemmed should be turned over twice and kept in place with basting stitches. These are long running stitches. They are taken out after hemming. For hemming, take a small stitch through the edge of the turned-over hem.

Immediately underneath, on the single fabric, take a tiny stitch toward the left. Bring the needle up through the edge of the hem about $\frac{1}{4}$-inch away. Repeat.

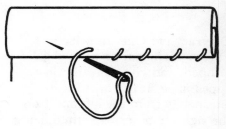

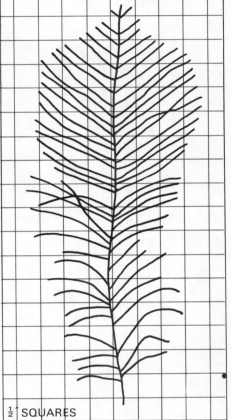

½ SQUARES

Feather Design

Feather design in couching and long stitch (shown in the color picture).

This type of design, drawn from real life yet almost an abstraction, could form the basis of a picture, with two or three large feathers grouped with some smaller ones. Or the same stitches and treatment could be worked more formally to make flowing, curving fleur-de-lis feathers.

The background is a dark Chinese green silk, with the feather worked mainly in shades of pink. The top part has long stitches of four strands of embroidery thread, first deep pink, then salmon, then pale pink, all "couched" with fly stitch in matching thread. The fly stitches point in the same direction, with the open "V" outward. Between these, to vary the texture, a few long stitches are worked in single thread, and caught with fly stitches.

The center vein, of five strands of the palest shade of pink, is couched all along with matching thread, and fanned out at the top to soften the outline.

Random long stitches compose the lower half of the feather. They are worked in pale, medium and deep pink, and in pale blue. Some of the longest stitches are couched. Where a number of stitches overlap, an almost solid block of color is formed.

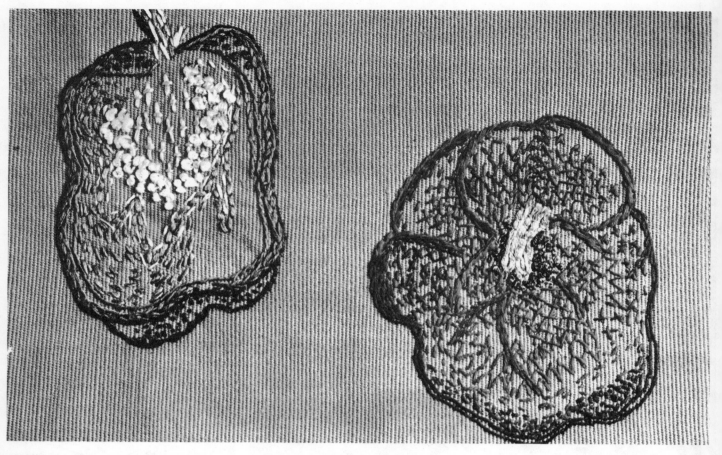

Red and Green Peppers

Red and green peppers in French knots, chain and cross-stitches (shown in the color picture).

The produce store is a treasure chest of ideas for embroidery. The color, shape and texture of so many vegetables and fruits lend themselves perfectly to the sketchbook embroidery treatment. Designs such as this composition of peppers are suitable for a set of place mats, with one motif on each, or for a tablecloth, with a "sketch" worked in each corner. Look carefully at eggplants, mushrooms, the purple kohlrabi, cauliflower and so on, make a rough pencil sketch and then copy the technique shown here.

When the green pepper was cut in half, lengthwise, the texture seemed to call for French knots and seed stitches (not for the seeds, but for filling in).

The outline is worked in dark green embroidery thread, closely couched, with an inner row of chain stitches and then of stem stitch.

The seeds are worked in large French knots, in two shades of pale lemon embroidery thread, and the texture is provided by groups of seed stitches and long stitches couched once across the center.

The red pepper is a view from the top, looking into the cut stem, so that the irregular curving shape is emphasized. Again, the outline is a row of couched stitches thickened with rows of stem stitch.

The dimension is shown with the curving lines of stem and chain stitch and the filling in provided by seed, cross-stitches and fly stitches.

For the stalk, multiple strands of pale green and pale blue

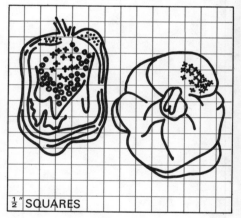

embroidery thread are couched, and surrounded by clusters of seed stitch and French knots.

The background is a deep golden piqué.

See page 241 for copying instructions.

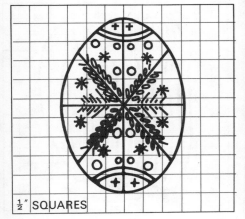

½" SQUARES

Decorated Easter Egg

Decorated Easter egg using metallic thread (shown in the color picture).

This is a bright, flamboyant design, the kind of thing that could be used for a set of pictures, with one egg motif worked on each of, say, four different colored backgrounds. Or the same technique could be used for other shapes—a bell, or a star, for instance—shapes that somehow suggest a festive occasion.

The background is again deep green Chinese silk, on which the egg is outlined in golden metallic thread, couched with yellow stranded embroidery thread. An inner ring of white wool is couched with golden thread.

Two rows of couched, narrow golden metallic thread cross at the longest and shortest points of the egg, and a star shape is formed by bright yellow couched embroidery thread outlined in lemon chain stitch.

Red running-stitch arcs are filled in with rows of red French knots, giving the illusion of a three-dimensional curve.

Long stitches in metallic thread and long and cross-stitches in red are scattered like snowflakes. Sequins in two sizes are an eye-catching, glittering finishing touch.

Cacti

Cacti in Cretan and cross-stitch.

Who ever heard of embroidering a cactus? Mary Kehoe found that a window sill collection of plants gave her inspiration for an exaggerated flurry of stitches, which she worked on buff-colored linen.

For the right-hand section, teased mohair wool in pale silvery gray suggests the long white hairs. This is worked over a trellis of pale and dark green open Cretan stitch. Long stitches in brown stranded embroidery thread are worked over the edge of the design, realistically random.

In the center, dark green threads in vertical rows are first couched and then covered at intervals with silvery-gray French knots. Between these, long stitches are worked in deep rust brown.

On the left-hand section,

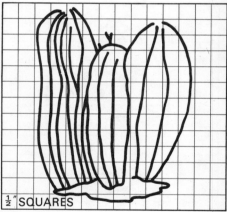

cross-stitches and star stitches are worked in daffodil yellow and pale lemon, with seed stitches in green. This provides a complete contrast to the techniques and colors used earlier, and entirely alters the "mood" of the piece.

Barren, sandy soil is represented by blocks of satin stitch and long-stitches in brown-gray with French knots (for the stones) in pale eucalyptus green.

A Glittering Fish

A glittering fish in metallic thread.

The shimmering metallic threads used for this design give an illusion of movement through the water and are so effective that the work can—and should—be kept simple.

The outline is defined by long stitches of black wool twisted with a blue metallic thread, invisibly couched at intervals. Inside this, a thick row of chain stitch emphasizes the shape.

For the scales on the lower part of the body, black wool with a green metallic thread is worked in large, slightly uneven open buttonhole stitch; above that there are four rows of graded herringbone stitch in the same yarn.

For the fins, black and blue metallic yarn is couched with blue embroidery thread, with a row of

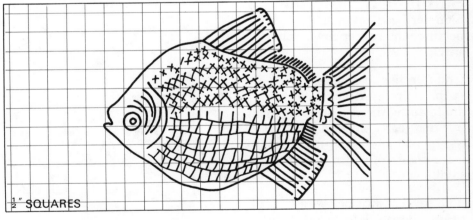

buttonhole stitch in turquoise thread at the end.

The tail is a spread-out fan of long stitches in all the threads used in the design.

The eye is a turquoise-colored sequin, and there are rows of couching in black and silver thread around the gills.

Textured blue linen has been used for the background, the nubby texture being most appropriate to the theme.

See page 241 for copying instructions.

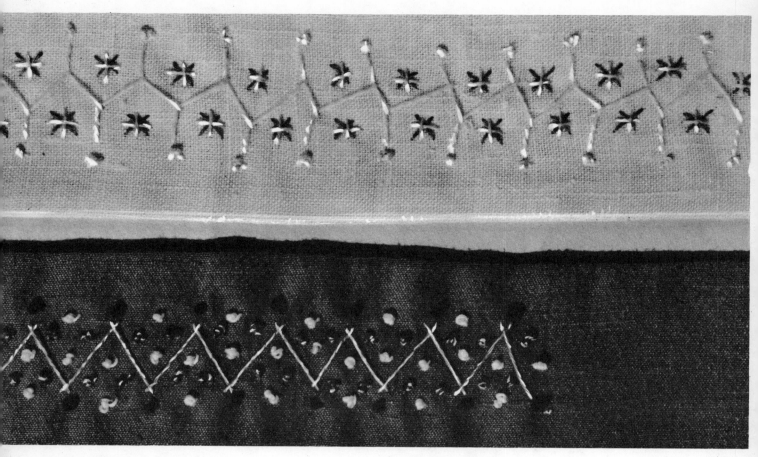

Sampler Headbands

Sampler headbands in herringbone and open Cretan stitch.

Children like to make sample strips of embroidery when they are learning the stitches. Let them put their early work to practical use by making headbands. (Simply leave plenty of width to turn a small hem.)

The band shown below, a strip of bright green silk from the rag-bag, is worked in red herringbone stitch. For a pleasing effect, it is important to keep the distance between the stitches, and the length of each stitch, even.

The herringbone "V" patterns are filled in with French knots in black, lemon yellow and purple—children like to experiment with bright colors, and a variety of shades gives them more interest in the early stages.

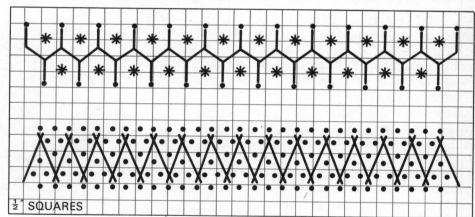

½" SQUARES

For the other band, a pale pink linenlike cloth is worked with an open Cretan stitch in pale blue, with a French knot in the same color at the end of every "spine." Each stitch is filled in with a star stitch in deep cyclamen pink and deep purple—and the whole effect is harmonious and pleasing.

Borders of this kind can be worked on skirts, collars and cuffs, or to edge sheets, pillowcases or place mats.

Flower Spray

Flower spray in stem and chain stitches and French knots.

Flowers are perhaps the most versatile of all "raw materials" for needlework compositions. You can arrange any number of flower heads, leaves and stems into the most pleasing pattern, taking a little embroiderer's license as you go. Or you can compose a design of just flower heads, arranged in a formal or a random pattern. Choose a background material that complements the flowers in both color and texture—this one is textured blue linen.

The flower heads are worked in simple stitches filled in with a nosegay of French knots in different colors.

The petals are worked in chain stitch in deep pink stranded embroidery thread, and filled in with long and short stitches in a

" SQUARES

paler shade. Notice that the petals are of slightly different sizes, and not quite equally spaced: even flowers are not always perfect! The stamens are worked in French knots in white, medium pink, pale lemon and green.

Stem stitch is used in two rows for the stems, to outline the leaves, and for the central veins, with long stitches for the small veins.

See page 241 for copying instructions.

Collage Embroidery

Take a piece of coral and copy it in white on a tan-colored background. With a variety of stitches and plenty of imagination, you can easily create something that has the feeling of Mary Kehoe's collage (shown in color), even though you might not follow it exactly.

So that you can get an idea of the effect, sketch your design roughly in white crayon or white paint on colored paper. (If you do it in pencil or ink on white paper, it will be very difficult to visualize it in "negative" form.)

Collect a handful of materials from your piece bag, with as much variety of texture as possible. You will need threads of different thickness, smooth wool and some with a bouclé texture—this is the most realistic of all—white beads, scraps of veiling, net and patterned lace, buttons, curtain rings and trimmings.

When you have decided on the size and scale of your design, break it down into separate areas which you can work one at a time. For a beginner, this is much more encouraging than to try to put in a little work here and there without seeing any particular shape emerge.

This picture was started in the center, with a block of long stitches made in 2-ply knitting wool. The vertical stitches were worked first, then crossed with a single diagonal thread, and then with stripes of horizontal stitches in the same yarn. Radiating from this block of stitches, work long stitches diagonally, toward the right-hand corner of the picture, also in the same yarn.

Taking a nubby yarn, work long stitches upward. To get a natural, curved effect, lay the threads on the background in the shape you want, and then couch them with white thread.

With a thick crochet yarn, work long stitches radiating to the left. Again, where a straight stitch is wanted, you can leave it unsupported (there will be no strain on it in a picture). When you want to introduce some shape to it, lay it against the work and couch it in place.

Fill in between these rays of long stitches with French knots in thick clusters. You will be surprised how like the real thing—the coral you are copying—they look.

Scatter some white dress buttons—or pearl shirt buttons would do—around the central block of long stitches, and when you are satisfied with the balance you have created, sew them in place. Arrange a piece of veiling or dress net, and a twist of white trimming braid if you have it, and tack it in place so that the stitches do not show.

Cover about six curtain rings with buttonhole stitch in a smooth fine wool (see Diagram 17 page 245). Push stitches close together so that none of the ring shows through. A glimpse of brass would spoil the pure whiteness of your design.

To make the "spiderweb," take four lengths of narrow cord (such as thin piping cord) and cross them to form a star. Tack them at the center to secure. Using a crochet cotton or 2-ply knitting wool threaded in a blunt needle, and starting at the center, weave around each "spoke," taking the thread under, over and under the spoke, as shown in Diagram 18. Work the stitches close together so that a solid effect is achieved.

Taking a nubby yarn again, couch long stitches to form the random piece of coral at the top right of the picture.

Sew the six covered curtain rings

and the spiderweb in place. Surround them with long stitches and a cluster of small beads as shown.

Wind spirals of the nubby yarn, leaving ends trailing, and sew these in place.

Pad pieces of net, and cross them with long stitches in wool, to make the "shells" shown beneath the central block of long stitches and work a bed of cross-stitches below them.

To the left of this section, sew a curve of white beads, surround them by a hoop of satin stitches in wool and then by random rays of long stitches. Overlay this with an oval cut from veiling.

For the lower left corner of the picture, make two "fossils" from veiling sewn with clusters of tiny beads and crisscross long stitches.

Scatter more tiny beads, clusters of French knots and trails of running stitches to give balance to your picture.

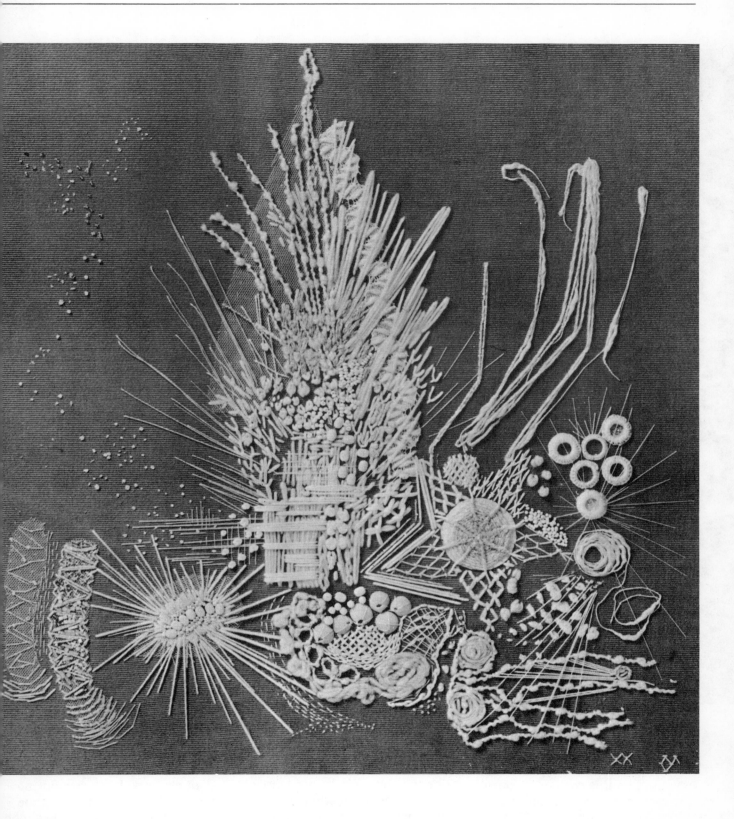

½" SQUARES

Cushion Cover
Cushion cover in stem stitch.

A small circular motif, such as the one used on this cushion, is one of the most adaptable shapes of all. Here, Mary Kehoe's theme of "inspiration from nature" has been carried out only lightly—the leaves are simplified and stylized.

The cushion has an overall measurement of only 12 inches square. You can scale the design up or down according to the size of your cushion, picture or place mat.

The two inner circles are worked in turquoise chain stitch and the third circle in pale pink chain stitch. In the center, four long stitches in pale pink are caught with a cross-stitch and surrounded by long and cross-stitches.

Between the circles, there are rows of cross-stitches in lime green, deep pink and pale pink.

All the leaves are outlined in stem stitch, alternately in lime green and dark green with the contrasting color in long stitch forming the stem. French knots in pale lemon yellow add textural interest to the leaves, and in rust brown give the impression of falling autumn leaves.

See page 241 for copying instructions.

Tulip Place Mat

A tulip place mat in satin stitch and French knots.

It is easy to see that this design, running across a fringed linen place mat, could be readily adapted for a border, maybe on a tablecloth, skirt or wide hem of a sheet. To make the design fit your particular purpose, take a piece of paper the size you require, draw into 1-inch squares, and copy the flower and leaf pattern. To extend the pattern, omit the two leaf designs on the right-hand side and draw in some more flowers and leaves, finishing with the little treelike shapes at the end of your intended border.

The tulip flowers are worked in satin stitch in a pale yellow color, with a little deep golden shading. The satin stitch gives the shine one expects to see on these petals. In each case, one petal is not filled in completely, but is speckled with French knots: some tulips, the designer says, *are* speckled!

All the leaves, except those trailing below the main part of the design, are marked in satin stitch, in bright, sharp green shaded with a slightly darker color. The trailing stems are worked in stem stitch and their leaves in lazy daisy stitch.

It goes without saying that the evenness of stitch is all-important for a satisfactory finish in a design of this kind. If you are new to a filled-in satin stitch pattern, it is as well to practice it on a spare piece of fabric before beginning work.

You can see how well this type of design, which is really a modern, free-style adaptation of botanical shapes, fits in with a traditional setting.

See page 241 for copying instructions. You can, of course, extend it or omit part of the design.

½" SQUARES

Bird-in-a-Tree Picture

Bird-in-a-tree picture in chain stitch (shown in color).

Inspired by the song "I had a little nut tree," this picture is worked in a mixture of brilliant colors. The outlines of the tree, fruit and bird are defined in fine black wool worked in chain stitch. This contrasts well with the unbleached muslin background and insures a crisp appearance.

The fruit is filled in with chain stitch, using only three or four strands of embroidery thread together so that the work is flat. The color blending is subtle and important. Just inside the black outline of the fruit on the right of the picture, two lines of deep golden chain stitch, then two lines of dark green, then blue, yellow, pale pink, pale green, deep pink and more deep blue. The fruit on the left of the picture is slightly less ripe, so the pink is omitted

and more green and blue substituted.

The tree trunk is two arcs of chain stitch in coffee and milk chocolate browns, looking for all the world like a ribbed pattern in bark.

The bird is as exuberantly colored as can be—with wing in black and white buttonhole stitch worked in wool, which cleverly emphasizes the brilliance of the other colors. His beak is filled in with bright yellow satin stitch. The top of his body is in stripes of chain stitch, alternating light and dark blue, and these are crisscrossed with long running stitches of gold metallic thread, glistening like raindrops on his back. His underside is in blocks of scarlet, coral and bright yellow, and the area under his chin is filled in with light and dark turquoise.

Cretan stitches and open Cretan stitches, long stitches, stem stitches

and satin stitches are used to give variety and interest to the leaves. As you can see from the color photograph, these are not all filled in.

See page 241 for copying instructions.

You can alter the scale by ruling the paper into smaller or larger squares and copying the shapes as usual.

TAKE A BALL OF CLAY

Natural Clay

Clay is basically composed of particles of rock ground down by the wind and weather over thousands of years to a fine powder. This has generally been moved from its place of origin by the action of running water and deposited in shallow stream or river beds where it builds up into layers and becomes mixed with other materials, such as sand and iron oxide, which give its variable color and texture. Clay can be found almost anywhere; you may even have some in your garden which you could use, though usually it requires some preparation.

The other ingredient present in workable clays is water, which gives it its "plastic" quality, making it possible to mold, press and form it into an infinite variety of shapes. Most of the water present in clay will evaporate if it is left exposed to air for any length of time, so it is important to take care of your unfinished work, covering it with plastic bags or damp cloth and storing in an airtight can or plastic container.

Since most people do not have access to facilities for firing and glazing their work, no more than a brief outline of these processes will be given here. But it is helpful to understand the changes which occur when clay is fired and glazed.

Dry, unfired clay

will quickly revert to its original plastic state when in contact with water; it does not become "pottery" until it has been heated to a very high temperature, somewhere in the region of 1652°F., in a kiln, when the nature of the clay is changed. It is then no longer posible to convert it to its original state by adding water.

Once-fired articles

(biscuit pottery), while durable, are porous—pottery flower pots are a good example in everyday use. To overcome this porosity man discovered long ago how to apply a layer of fine glasslike substance to wares intended for holding liquids or simply as decoration. The glaze is applied as a powder, mixed with water to make it adhere more readily to the biscuit pottery. The article is usually dipped in this mixture, allowed to dry and then refired in the kiln at temperatures ranging from 1830–2372°F. The heat acts upon the glaze ingredients, melting and fusing them into a thin film over the surface of the fired articles.

The form and decoration of your designs can be a problem when you begin working with clay. But a study of natural objects such as flowers, leaves, seed pods, pebbles, and shells, can be most rewarding. Keep a sketchbook at hand and make drawings of anything you see which could prove useful, or borrow a book from a library— there are a number on the subject of designs from nature.

Try to keep your pots simple in outline. Models of animals are easier to make and less likely to be accidentally broken if rounded, simple forms are chosen, without spiky pieces or slender legs.

Other Modeling Materials

For the beginner in clay work, there are several excellent modeling materials available in craft stores which do not require firing and glazing. All the work shown here is modeled from self-hardening clay; none of it has been fired.

Articles made from self-hardening clay will harden into a durable state and can be painted with ordinary poster paint and varnished. However, they should not be immersed in water, but only wiped with a damp cloth as, being basically composed of clay, they will soften if they become wet. However, you can also work these designs in ordinary clay and fire and glaze the articles for greater permanence.

A readily obtainable material which can be bought at most arts and crafts stores or educational suppliers is art utility moist clay— a gray clay used in schools that does not need to be fired. Self-hardening clay is manufactured under various trade names. Check your local art or craft supply store and follow the manufacturer's recommendations. For potters with no kiln, self-hardening clay is a real breakthrough. It is best used for small articles—models, tiles, jewelry, but, for the most part, is less suited for modeling large pieces.

A substance has been added to the clay, strengthening it and rendering it far less likely to crack and warp as the work dries out. Once dry, it is much stronger than ordinary unfired clay and may in some cases be further hardened by following the instructions on the package.

Modeling tools   Very few tools will be required, all of which can be easily improvised. These are the basic needs:

A board—wood or laminated
  plastic
Small kitchen knife or X-acto
  knife
Nail file, ice-cream sticks and
  cocktail stirrers for modeling
Sponge for dampening work,
  cleaning board, etc.
A variety of brushes for
  painting models and glazing
Wooden rolling pin or a bottle
Plastic bags, for covering
  unfinished work, storing damp
  clay
Tin box or plastic container for
  storing unfinished work
Broken hacksaw blade or
  similar for scraping and
  texturing clay
A piece of lath or old ruler for
  beating clay into shape.

Working with Clay
As the moisture in the clay evaporates, four stages of dryness make various treatments and decoration techniques possible.

Damp Plastic Clay
Parts of a model or pot may be joined together by squeezing, smearing or "stitching" across with a modeling tool.

Clay may be "impressed" by pressing in a design with tools or fingers.

Cheese-hard (soft)
Clay has begun to harden but is still soft enough to shape by pressing and beating.

Parts of models or pots may still be joined, but surfaces to be joined must be roughened and dampened before pressing together.

Clay may be textured by scraping or pressing in a rough-edged tool, "stamped" and impressed with nails, shells, etc. "Applied" clay may be added in the form of coils, medallions and so on.

Leather-hard (hard)
Incised lines and patterns can be added, clay may be carved with a sharp tool.

With ordinary clay, color can be added by painting with oxides: resist decoration can be used—painting over patterns cut from paper or leaves.

Dry clay
Self-hardening clays may be painted. It is advisable to mix your poster paint with diluted polyvinyl acetate or other water-insoluble resin. Paint mixed in this way is less likely to smear when a final protective coating is applied as a "glaze." Ordinary household emulsion paint is also effective over these clays (stain with poster paint).

Experimenting with Shape
Your tools assembled, begin by experimenting with shape. Take a small handful of self-hardening clay and slap and squeeze it between the palms of your hands until it takes on a rounded shape.

Now try changing the shape by squeezing with your fingers or banging with your hand. Try rolling a piece of clay with the palms of your hands in various different ways. Bang it gently against a board so that its sides are flattened in places or beat it with a knife handle or ruler edge so that its shape is changed (Diagram 1).

You will find that the wood leaves marks on the clay, making an

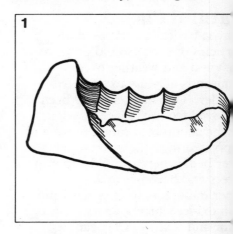

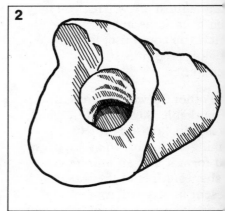

interesting pattern. You will notice, too, that the form the shapes take varies according to the different surfaces that come in contact with the clay.

Now try shaping a lump of clay by squeezing or pressing with your fingers. Press a finger deep into or through a lump of clay and gently squeeze the clay around the edges into a flaring shape (Diagram 2). The clay now takes on a shell-like form.

A child's nursery lamp, formed from a thin sheet of rolled clay, has the added interest of a mouse family inside the cosy living room

If any of the shapes you have made please you, keep them to dry out and paint them later. They can make attractive paperweights. Otherwise, slightly dampen each piece and bang them back into a larger ball, storing carefully in a strong plastic bag or airtight container to use another time.

Experimenting with Pattern

Make a collection of odds and ends with a textured surface, small pieces of rock, old brick, cinder block, wood, sea shells and so on.

With the palm of your hand, flatten a piece of clay on a wooden board. Place a piece of burlap on the board if it sticks.

Now use different items you have collected and press them into the clay to make a textured surface. Try out various patterns and keep any object which gives a really interesting finish: you may need it later.

An assortment of pointed objects will make different patterns on your clay. Try nails, screws, cocktail stirrers and old ball-point pen cases. Again, keep anything which makes an attractive design.

Candleholder

A useful candleholder can easily be made from a lump of clay. Simply shape the clay in the palm of your hand until it is about $1\frac{1}{4}$ inches thick and a pleasant shape. Flatten the base by pressing onto the board. Press a candle into the clay about $\frac{3}{4}$–1-inch deep. Slightly enlarge the hole by twisting the candle, to allow for shrinkage of the clay. Now make a pattern or texture on the clay with something from your collection of objects. The texture here was created with a broken piece of brick. Remove the candle and allow the clay to dry, checking when leather-dry that the candle still fits into the hole. Finish by painting and "glazing" or spray with gold or silver paint.

The different techniques using clay – the articles are made from rolled slabs or modeled into simple, basic shapes

Tiles and Mosaics

Take a lump of clay and flatten it on the board with the palm of your hand. If it sticks, you may find it easier to work with a piece of burlap over your board; sacking is ideal. Roll out the clay with a rolling pin, just like rolling out pastry, until it is about $\frac{1}{4}$-inch thick. To help you get your tiles an even thickness, place pieces of $\frac{1}{4}$-inch thick wooden lath on each side of the clay as you roll out your slab (Diagram 1). If you wish to make larger tiles, increase the thickness of your slab.

When your slab of clay is ready, carefully mark out the tile against the edge of an old ruler, remembering to check that the corners are right angles. Cut out the tile with a sharp knife, keeping the blade steady and pressed firmly against the edge of the ruler.

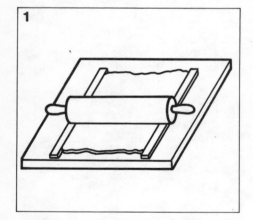

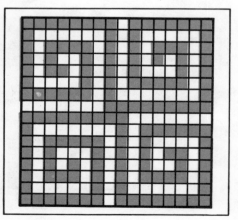

½" SQUARES

Firebird tile (measures 6 inches square)   For this tile you need to cut a square of clay 6 inches by $\frac{1}{4}$-inch thick. While the clay is still damp, mark out your design. Draw this on 1-inch squared paper from the pattern given. Transfer the design to the tile by placing the paper over the tile and carefully drawing around the lines with a sharp pencil, pressing down gently to leave an impression on the clay. Leave until the clay is cheese-hard, then dry out carefully by placing between clean paper, covering with thick layers of newspaper and weighting with a heavy book (a telephone directory is ideal for this). When it is leather-dry paint on your design. The one here is painted in shades of yellow, orange, red and brown on a bright yellow background. When paint is dry, replace it under the book until clay is completely dry, then glaze with a wallpaper protective or regular gloss varnish.

Paper-resist design (4 inches square)   This tile, 4 inches square by $\frac{1}{4}$-inch thick when damp, is painted in dark green and ocher. For this effect, cut out a piece of paper the same size as your tile when leather-hard, fold it in half and draw on the design, copied from the squared-up pattern. Keep it simple enough to cut out in one piece, as you will need the cutaway piece for the other half of your tile, but as a safeguard cut out half at a time (Diagram 2),

marking the design on the second half once it is cut out (Diagram 3).

Paint the tile with the lighter color and leave to dry, then take the cutout pattern and place firmly on half the tile. A strip of paper fixed over the other half, exactly to the center, will help you to paint the center line neatly (Diagram 4). Fix at the back of the tile with Scotch tape.

Now stipple the uncovered area of the tile with the darker color.

When dry, remove the paper and pattern from left-hand side and using the paper from which you cut the original design, paint the "negative" half of the design, reversing the pattern (Diagram 5). When the paint is dry, coat with protective gloss finish—clear lacquer, varnish or shellac.

Mosaic Tile   For the mosaic tile you will need a 6-inch square of masonite. Self-hardening clay is particularly suited to this technique. The clay is cut into tiny squares (tessera). The ones here were treated with hardener, then painted with an emulsion paint stained with poster paint and finally varnished. You could use polyurethane for a completely heat-resistant finish; it would then make an effective table mat.

First mark out the pattern on squared paper (16 tessera = approximately 6 inches). Roll out the clay, using two ordinary

wooden rulers as a guide to obtain an even thickness. Mark the clay into $\frac{3}{8}$-inch squares, then cut carefully with a sharp knife against a ruler edge, taking care not to drag the clay and distort the squares. When the tessera are dry, treat with hardener and paint in your chosen colors. The tile here is painted in shades of coffee, caramel and white.

When dry, carefully cut and trim the tessera as you need them with a pair of scissors, arranging them, according to the pattern given here, on the masonite square, and sticking down firmly with all-purpose adhesive. You will probably find it easier to work across a line at a time. When complete, coat with varnish.

Wall hanging   To make a wall hanging like the one in the photograph, you will need an assortment of objects to mark the clay (Diagram 1). Nails, screws, knitting needles, will all prove useful.

Some of the patterns on this wall hanging were based on traditional Viking designs and incised with linoleum-cutting tools, but you could get the same effect by scoring out the pattern with a small, sharp-pointed knife or nail file.

Roll out the clay to a thickness of about $\frac{1}{4}$-inch for the medium-sized shapes. Larger ones can be thicker, smaller ones slightly thinner than this.

Each piece is cut out separately, using a sharp knife. Here a tin lid made an excellent template for cutting the smaller pointed oval shapes (Diagram 2). The size and number is up to you. The largest shape on our wall hanging measures 4 inches across, the smallest $\frac{3}{4}$-inch, but larger hangings are extremely effective against a plain wall.

Assemble your shapes as you cut them out (Diagram 3), arranging them into a pleasant pattern. Number them on the back to make it easier to reassemble and so that you will know where to make the holes for joining them.

To make the patterns, press the "objects" into the clay while it is still damp. If you decide to incise parts of your hanging, mark out the pattern lightly on the damp clay and leave until leather-hard before incising.

The holes for joining must be made while the clay is still soft. Mark positions about $\frac{1}{4}$–$\frac{1}{2}$-inch from the edge and then gently press a knitting needle through from front to back, smoothing the back afterward.

Our hanging was painted when dry with dark brown poster paint, working it well into the hollows, then stippled with lighter brown, before coating with a diluted mixture of protective clear shellac.

When completely dry, join pieces with wire loops bent to shape with pliers, or tie with cord, knotting neatly at the back.

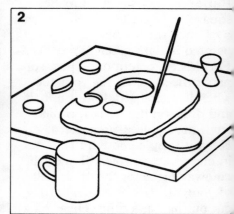

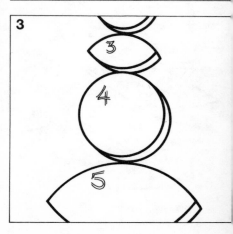

Models from Slabs of Clay

Human and animal figures can be made from slabs of clay. The figure of the choirboy (unfinished) in the color photograph, shows the simplest method. Skirted figures are made from a slab of clay with slightly rounded edges as shown (Diagram 1). Simply wrap one short edge over the other (Diagram 2) and add arms, head and any other details you

wish. Texturing the skirt, either before or after wrapping into position, gives a suitable decorative effect. The frill is formed before adding the head, by bending over the top edge of the skirt.

To make the frog: Roll out a $\frac{1}{4}$-inch slab of clay and cut the pattern, following the squared-up shapes. Let it harden slightly, turning once. Copy the dotted lines on the pattern by lightly marking them on the clay. When cheese-hard, gently bend into position, lapping A–A under B–B to the points X–X, to form the rear. Points C–C are similarly bent under D–D to form upper mouth. Fix the round flap into position, dampening and scoring where pieces join, to form lower jaw and chest. Bend under on dotted lines, cutting at points shown and rejoining to form fronts of legs. Add pea-sized pieces of clay at points Y–Y for eyes and mark eyes with the end of an old

ball-point pen case. Cut out claws and leave model to dry (Diagram 3). Then paint in "froggy" colors of yellowish greens. Give a coat of varnish when completely dry.

Leaf-Shaped Dishes

These designs make attractive dishes for candies or nuts, or ash trays; remember though, that unfired clay must not be immersed in water, and can only be cleaned by wiping with a damp cloth. Choose flat leaves of good shape,

preferably with an interesting network of veins. Roll out the clay about $\frac{3}{4}$-inch thick, depending on the size of your leaves. Press each leaf onto the clay, vein side down, and cut neatly around the edge.

When the clay is cheese-hard, remove the leaf and carefully bend up the sides to form a dish shape, supporting the sides on crumpled newspaper (Diagram 4). When dry, paint the "leaves," using poster paint mixed with diluted

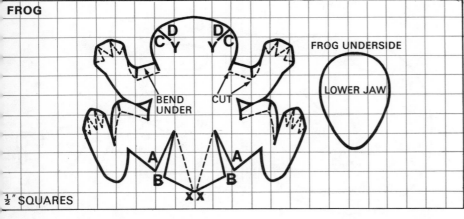

FROG

FROG UNDERSIDE

LOWER JAW

C D D C
Y Y

BEND UNDER   CUT

A A
B B
X X

$\frac{1}{2}$" SQUARES

protective varnish. "Glaze" with a heat-resistant polyurethane or varnish.

Modeling with Clay

Small, sturdy figures can be modeled very simply. Choose a chunky-shaped animal, or model animals and humans in a sitting or lying-down position to avoid putting strain on the clay and the designer! Work from suitable pictures or photographs if you find it easier. The simplest way to start is using a "carrot" of clay, the thickness depending on what type of animal you are modeling.

To make the otter:
The baby otter is made from a long, tapering "carrot." The head is shaped by squeezing in with the fingers at the neck (Diagram 1). Two forelegs and two hind legs, modeled to shape, are joined firmly to the body as shown (Diagram 2), merging the clay with a finger and smoothing the join. Model claw details with a small, sharp tool, and bend the tail into position (Diagram 3). The ears are tiny pieces of clay firmly added to the head, and details of eyes, nose, and mouth are modeled with a cocktail stirrer (Diagram 4). When completely dry, paint and varnish.

To make the dog:
The dog is modeled from a fat, blunt-ended carrot, bent and squeezed to shape as shown, to form the head and neck (Diagram 5). When adding the hind legs (Diagram 6) you may need to carve off a slice of the "carrot" where upper hind leg joins on each side (Diagram 7). Bend sausages of clay for the forelegs (Diagram 8) and join firmly. Ears are thin flaps of clay bent over and joined firmly at the upper end. Add a tail and model details of eyes, nose, etc. (Diagram 9). Scoop out clay on underside (Diagram 10) so that the model is hollow. This greatly helps drying. Paint and varnish when dry.

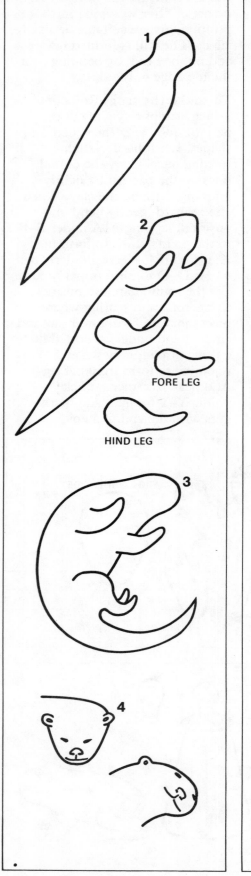

FORE LEG

HIND LEG

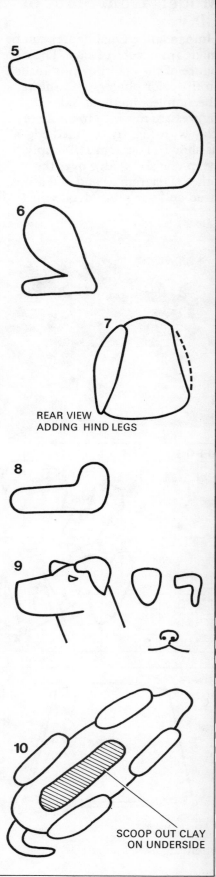

REAR VIEW
ADDING HIND LEGS

SCOOP OUT CLAY
ON UNDERSIDE

Jewelry

Attractive jewelry can be quickly and simply made in much the same way as the pieces for the wall-hanging.

The incised and impressed brooches shown in the photograph were made from modeling clay rolled out to an even thickness of $\frac{1}{4}$-inch, and cut into round and pointed-oval shapes. Smaller items could be thinner, say $\frac{1}{8}$-inch.

While the clay is still damp, mark the patterns, using a variety of textured objects, and, in the case of pendants, pierce a hole with a knitting needle, about $\frac{1}{4}$-inch from the edge, to take a cord or leather thong. Incise patterns when the clay is leather-hard.

You can buy brooch-pins from most arts and crafts stores; stick them on the back of the clay shape, when dry, with all-purpose glue.

Paint the jewelry, using poster paint mixed with diluted varnish. Give a final coat of gloss varnish or, for a gilt finish, spray with gold paint. (Keep the nozzle to one side so that the spray does not penetrate the hollows.)

If you prefer, you can make abstract shapes, or use some of the work you did at the experimenting stage, and finish them, either for use as brooches or pendants, as described above. The two pendants in the photograph were decorated with swirls of diluted poster paint.

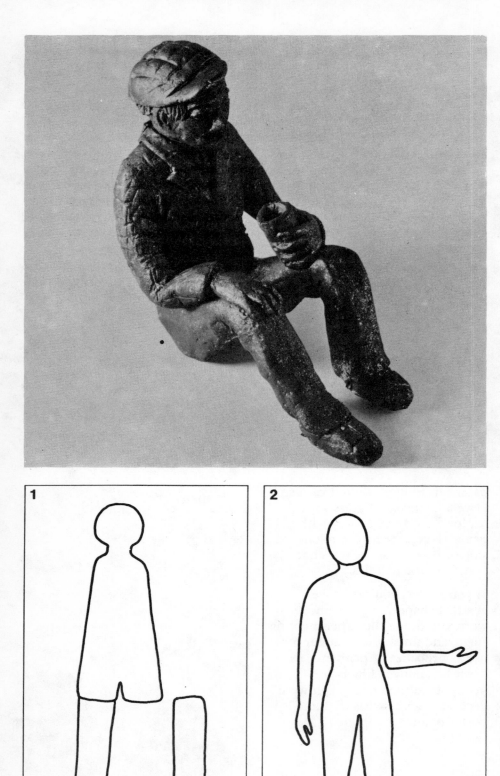

Human models

Avoid single standing figures, as they are extremely difficult to make without support and are easily broken. Seated, kneeling or reclining figures are much simpler. Sometimes wire supports can be used in the clay, but even with support, groups of figures are generally best; a single standing figure is very tall in relation to its base.

As with animal models, start with a "carrot" of clay, squeezing in the thinner end for the neck. Divide lower, fat end of carrot for upper part of thighs and join in sausages of clay for legs, from above the knee to ankles (Diagram 1). Bend your figure into position. Now add arms formed from clay sausages, joining them firmly onto the body. Try to get the proportions right (see Diagram 2). You may find you need to add extra pieces of clay to build out shoulders. Bend arms into position and flatten ends to form hands, by squeezing between finger and thumb. Add an oval piece of clay to the head to build out the chin and face (Diagram 3) and model on a nose shaped from a scrap of clay. Press in the end of a thick crochet hook or blunt twig for eye sockets and model eye, nose and mouth details. Add the feet and model details of hands (Diagram 4), gently separating thumb with a knife point.

When adding clay, remember that it should be of the same degree of dampness as the figure, as far as possible. Some self-drying clays are more versatile, allowing the addition of dryer pieces. It is always best to check manufacturers' instructions and experiment with caution.

Hair, clothing, buttons and other details can be added, as you wish (Diagram 5). If the figure appears to be drying out too quickly as you work on it, dampen the surface slightly with a wrung-out sponge and cover securely with a plastic bag leaving for a short while before continuing, so that the moisture content of the clay can even out.

The model here was lightly sprayed with gold paint, then finished with dark green poster paint mixed with wallpaper protective which gives a bronzelike finish.

To Make "Pinch-Pots"

Take a handful of clay and slap it into a round shape between your hands. Hold it on your hand and with the thumb and fingers of the other hand positioned as shown, press down centrally into the ball (Diagram 1). With the hands in this position, press and squeeze down into the clay, rotating the ball as you work. Work rhythmically, gently squeezing the clay into an even thickness, working from the base upward. Try not to open out the top of the little pot until all the rest of the clay is worked to an even thickness of $\frac{1}{4}$-inch (Diagram 2). Success depends on regular, gentle movements, with your hands rotating the pot as you work.

Keep your hands cool and damp, and don't put your pot down on its base until you have finished—put it rim-down if you need to leave it. Once it is finished, gently tap the base on to the board to flatten, and if necessary, trim the rim as shown (Diagram 3).

Typical pinch-pot shapes are shown in Diagram 4. If you leave a part-finished pot until it is cheese- or leather-hard, you can improve the shape and smooth the surface by gently beating with a piece of lath or the back of an old wooden spoon.

Try decorating one of your pots with impressed decoration, or texture it by scraping or pressing in a pointed tool.

When you can successfully manage a regularly shaped pinch-pot, try making two pots with top openings the same size, score and dampen the joining edges (Diagram 5 overleaf) and join to make a hollow egg shape (Diagram 6). Make a small hole in the bottom with a knitting needle, so that the air pressure evens out as the clay dries and shrinks, otherwise your pot will crack.

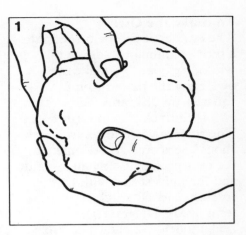

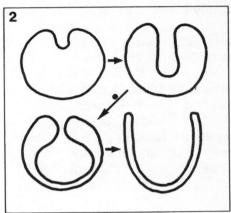

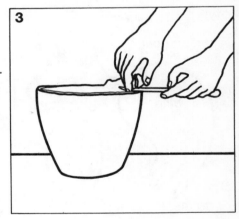

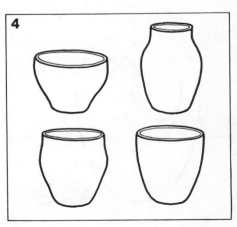

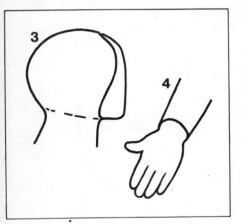

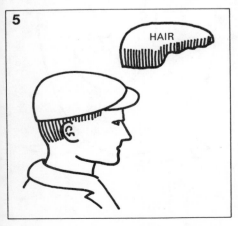

To make the Owl:

The egg shape can be turned into a bird or animal by adding tail, wings, legs, etc. To make the owl, copy the patterns on the squared-up diagrams, add ovals of $\frac{1}{8}$-inch thick clay to form eyes. The surface where eyes are joined should be scored and dampened, the eyes pressed firmly all around, and the joins sealed with tiny scoring marks ("stitched" is the term used—Diagram 7). Add a beak modeled as shown and fixed firmly between lower half of eyes. Wings are cut from thin slabs of clay and joined as for eyes, but don't "score" around lower end (Diagram 8). Bend feather-tips outward slightly. Add modeled tail and claws (Diagram 9). Texture while still damp dry, paint and varnish. To turn your model into a money-bank, cut a slit in the top when leather-hard.

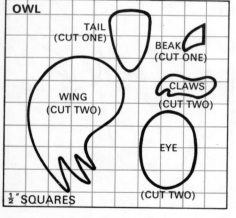

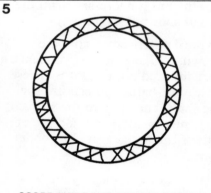

SCORE AND DAMP JOINING EDGES

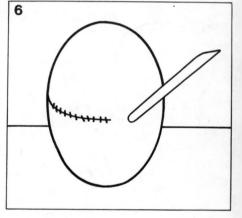

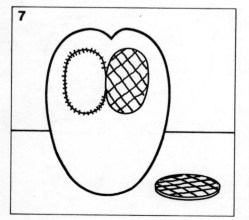

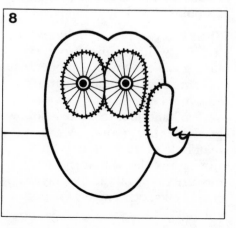

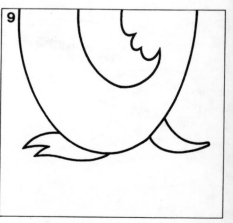

To Make Slab Pots

Small, cylindrical-shaped pots and lidded jars can be simply made from slabs of clay. To make a lidded jar like the one shown, roll out enough clay about ¼-inch thick, to cut two circles, one 3 inches across and one 3½ inches across.

Using the 3-inch circle as the base, cut a rectangular piece 2½ inches wide and long enough to fit around the circle, plus about ¾-inch. Roll the rectangle around the base, carefully marking length required, and make diagonal cuts at each end, as shown in Diagram 1, so that edges join neatly.

Roll out more clay to about ⅛-inch thick and cut another circle about 2½ inches across to form inner part of lid. Join this circle to the center of the 3½-inch circle, scoring ("stitching") and dampening joining surfaces. Model knob as shown in Diagram 2 and join to center of lid (Diagram 3).

When the rectangle is firm enough to handle, join sides of pot to the base, scoring and dampening all joining edges (Diagram 4) and then scoring across seam with a modeling tool. Smooth all seams and check lid for fit, cutting away inner circle if necessary so it fits neatly in the top of the cylinder.

Decorate with impressed pattern, taking care to support the inside as you press into the outer surface; or, when the jar is dry, decorate with a leaf-resist pattern like the one shown. First paint with light color. When dry, hold small leaves firmly in place and stipple darker color over the leaves and the rest of the jar. When leaves are removed, paint details of veins etc., with a fine brush. Give the jar a final coat of varnish when the paint is quite dry.

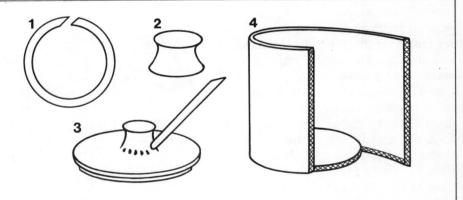

Hollow-Tree Nursery Lamp

For the "mouse house" you will need a sheet of 1-inch squared paper; self-hardening clay; a chipboard or wood base approximately 9½ by 7 inches; poster and emulsion paints and "glaze"; masking tape; a small piece of masonite for holding the house in position on the base and a screw-in bulb holder with flexible neck attached. The switch should be the external type, as opposed to pull-chain. Use a small 25- or 40-watt bulb or a candle-type bulb sold for wall fittings.

Carefully enlarge patterns onto squared paper, marking dotted lines which are cut out later. Cut out patterns.

Roll out a large piece of clay to a good ¼-inch thickness, placing a piece of burlap or several layers of newspaper on the working surface for ease of handling. Mark on the pattern with a pointed tool, then carefully cut out, using a sharp-pointed knife and cutting down vertically through the clay to make a clean edge. Do not cut out dotted-line windows until parts are joined. If you cannot manage to roll out a large enough piece for the main part, cut pattern at X–X and add ¼-inch to the length of the smaller piece at X–X to allow for an extra join. Roll another slab of clay for the roof and cut out in the same way.

Leave the slabs to dry until cheese-hard for a few minutes for ease of handling, turning over once and marking position of windows on other side.

Carefully lift main piece and bend into position, supporting main part with rolls of newspaper secured with adhesive tape as shown in Diagram 1. Roll newspaper around a central taller roll of newspaper to make it easier to remove.

Rolling around newspaper support (adjust thickness as necessary) match windows and small doorway. Dampen and score clay where it joins and press firmly together. Remove the newspaper when model seems firm enough to stand without support.

Now bend the second flap of clay (Diagram 2) to form top half of a figure 8 (Diagram 3) with flattened center. Join very firmly, "stitching" clay across and smoothing joint. The top, smaller loop of the figure 8 is where the lamp is positioned.

If the structure seems firm, carefully cut out remaining windows.

Take the roof and cut away dotted piece which forms the roof support. Fix this firmly in position, scoring and dampening surfaces to be joined, above arched windows.

Score top edges of house and place

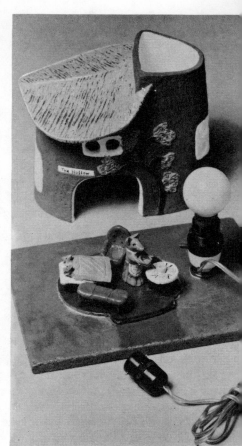

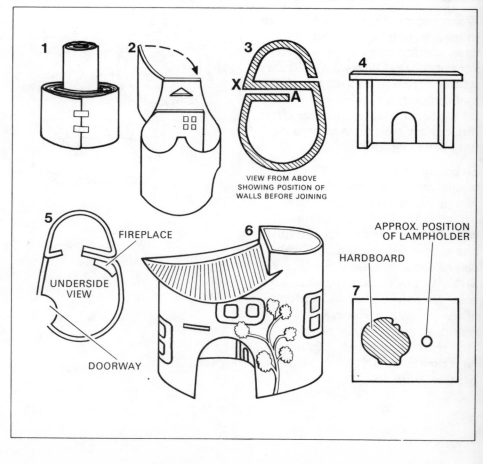

roof in position. Mark underside of roof, at the top of walls and remove the roof. Score and dampen underside of the roof $\frac{3}{4}$-inch inside line and fix roof firmly in place, trimming if necessary.

While still damp, stick roses around door, forming stems from thin coils of clay, leaves from tiny pieces of clay pressed into thin slabs. Attach fireplace (Diagram 4) to inside wall where shown on pattern (Diagram 5). Cut a small channel for flexible neck attachment on the back of lamp side of house. Mark position of name plate and window frame. Texture walls and roof (Diagram 6).

Make tiny models of furniture and mice from small pieces of clay, joining parts firmly. If any parts break away later they should be stuck firmly together with household glue. Dry out house and models slowly, watching for any

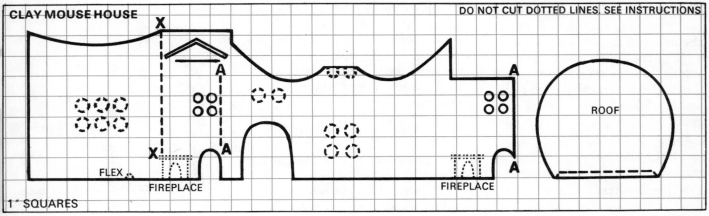

cracks; dampen and score together any which occur. When completely dry, harden by following the manufacturer's instructions.

Paint in bright colors, using emulsion paint stained with poster paint mixed with diluted wallpaper protective or varnish.

When dry, give a final coat of diluted gloss to all or part of house, model furniture and figures.

Place house on a piece of paper

and carefully draw around inside. Cut out this shape and use as a template for cutting out masonite (Diagram 7). Sand edges of masonite and check for fit before fixing down on base. Sand edges of base and paint as for house. Mark positions for furniture, making sure there is space enough to remove house without damaging models inside. Using undiluted gloss, stick models in place. Screw down lamp holder and join

flexible neck. A 25-watt bulb is sufficient to give a pleasant light, as you can see from the color photograph.

Coiling Clay

Bottle shapes can be made from cylinders of clay with built-on tops, using the coiling method. The cylinder is made with a slab of clay as described for the lidded jar, but using any suitable straight-sided jam jar, plastic bottle or cardboard container, wrapped in corrugated cardboard to form a support (Diagram 1).

Providing you are not going to fire your work, the container may be left inside, since the result will be purely decorative. You must obviously never fire a pot with a glass container built into it, or the result may be disastrous to your pot and other articles in the kiln.

Once you have made a cylinder, joining edges and base carefully, and while the cylinder is still damp, roll out a rope of clay to about ½-inch thick. Use the palms of your hands for the rolling and try to keep the rope (or coil) an even thickness and well rounded. Cut off ends if they have become hollow during rolling-out. Place the first coil in position on the top edge of the cylinder, and using a regular, steady movement, smear down about one-third of the coil on the inside.

Work around the top of the cylinder in this way until you reach the starting point. Break off the coil and smear across the join. Position the next coil above the first, joining ends of coil in a different place, and work in the same way. When 3 or 4 coils have been added, smear joins on the outside, with fingers or a modeling tool (Diagram 2). To narrow the neck of your bottle, position the coil slightly inward as shown (Diagram 3), joining as before. As you reach the narrow point of the neck you will probably find you cannot reach inside to smear down the coil, so smear it on the outside, again merging about a third of the coil down into the lower coil.

Complete the top of the bottle by trimming with a sharp knife, as shown for pinch-pots, if necessary, then smoothing with a wet finger until the top opening has a well-rounded, even edge. Decorate, paint and varnish.

The success of coiling depends upon:

Supporting the wall of your pot with the other hand as you work. Regular, steady movement as you smear down each coil. It helps to place the pot on a turntable (banding wheel) obtainable from pottery suppliers.

Coils being of even thickness and thoroughly joined by smearing downward. Gentle beating with an old wooden spoon when leather-hard will improve shape and joins.

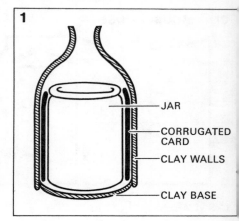

JAR

CORRUGATED CARD

CLAY WALLS

CLAY BASE

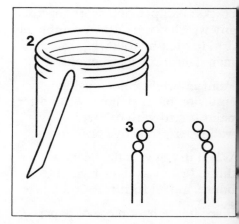

TAKE A BLOCK OF WOOD

The craftsman has always known and appreciated the magical feel and texture of natural wood. He delights in the warmth and tactile qualities of a piece of timber, turning it in his hands and feeling it with the tips of his fingers, he almost caresses the texture and graining on its surface. He studies the living beauty of the grain—so fine and so perfect—and is aware of the subtle smell of timbers like walnut, cedar and humble pine. Experience shows him instantly how he can transform the wood into something beautiful, lasting and real.

But the delights of successful woodworking need not be confined to skilled craftsmen. With scarcely the initial ability to recognize one end of a saw from the other, anyone can quickly learn to create lovely things—making use of one of the oldest and most fascinating materials used by man. Wood is ideally sympathetic to the skills of the human hand. It will cut into literally any shape and yet still manage to retain the qualities of the original timber.

Look at a tree, see its grace and its dignity, standing proudly against the elements, bending but rarely breaking, sympathetic in shape and form, an asset to the face of the earth. All over the world trees are growing, providing not only beauty in our environment and habitat for a host of animals and birds, but

huge reserves of the raw material we need. Cut down a tree and it is dead . . . but the wood that makes up its trunk and branches lives on, ready to be transformed into all manner of decorative, delightful and useful objects.

In this section there are simple— and some not quite so simple— things for you to make in wood for your home, your children and yourself. No matter if you have never tried your hand at anything like this before, you'll be surprised how quickly the designs take shape.

What you will need
There's no need for a special workshop—a garden shed or a workbench in a garage are ideal. And no need for a workbench either—make use of an old kitchen table, even a couple of planks over sawhorses will do for a start.

Obviously you will need a few basic tools before you can make a start on your woodwork, remembering that it is always advisable to buy the best tools you can afford, as poor quality equipment will do nothing to help you with your work. To make the designs in this section, and many more you can create yourself, you will need:
Fine-toothed backsaw—for cutting joints and doing fine sawing;
Small ripsaw—for cutting larger pieces of wood;
Smoothing plane—for cleaning

the wood after sawing and smoothing surfaces;
Firmer (large) chisel—for cleaning up joints, etc.;
Mortising (small) chisel—for cutting mortise joints;
Mallet—for use with chisels and for assembling items;
Brace and bit—for drilling large diameter holes;
Hand drill—for drilling smaller holes for screws;
Carpenter's square—for accurately marking cutting lines, etc.;
Ratchet screwdriver—for rapid screwing;
Jig saw or small compass saw— for cutting curves;
Marking gauge—for marking joints;
C-clamp—for holding joints firmly until glue is hard;
Sandpaper (various grades)—for final hand finishing.

Types of wood
There are literally thousands of different woods, but all broadly fit into the category of either hard- or softwood.

All wood is built up from cells that form a honeycomb type of structure. The size and arrangement of these cells is relatively constant in each species of wood, and they can provide a reliable way of distinguishing one wood from another.

As a tree grows it adds a layer of wood each year, just below the bark, on top of the layer formed in the previous year. The cells formed at the beginning of each year's growth are much larger than those formed later in the season. In this way the wood formed early in the year is lighter in color than that formed later, so distinct boundaries can be seen between each year's growth. Hence the age of a tree can accurately be determined by simply counting the growth rings or boundaries between each year's growth.

Generally speaking, softwoods, or conifers, grow at a faster rate than hardwoods, and hence their annual growth rings are broader. Hard- and softwoods differ from each other in their cellular structure, but there is no need to go into details here. Usually, as the name suggests, hardwoods are harder than softwoods, although there are exceptions. For example, the spongy soft wood of the balsa tree is technically a hardwood.

Softwoods come from conifers, which are most often evergreen. An exception to this is the larch, a deciduous tree, that is cone bearing and yields softwood.

The structure of wood is a fascinating topic, but the beginner need not worry too much about it at this stage. Possibly as your interest in working with wood grows you will want to broaden your knowledge.

On the whole, softwoods are cheaper and easier to work than hardwoods, and for that reason all the items in this chapter are made in softwood.

Softwood   Often different names are used for what is essentially the same wood, the name usually being derived from the source of the particular timber—Australian pine, British Columbian pine, or western yellow pine, for example. Coniferous evergreen trees—those that do not shed their leaves in winter—pine, spruce and fir are all softwoods.

Hardwood   Oak, elm, ash, maple, walnut, sycamore, beech, lime and birch are all hardwoods and are deciduous, that is they shed their leaves each autumn. Also in the hardwood category is mahogany, of which there are hundreds of types, mainly indigenous to Africa and the West Indies.

Plywood   This is made from thin parings cut from the log, arranged one on top of the other and glued under pressure to make large sheets, later to be cut into standard size panels. Plywood is usually made in three-, five-, or seven-ply, arranged with the grain of each layer running at right angles to the next to add strength to the finished plywood sandwich. So reliable are modern adhesives that these days "marine quality" plywood is used to make boats, something undreamed of in the days when plywood was stuck together with animal or fish glues.

Timbers most often used to make plywood are birch—for internal quality—and Douglas fir for exterior rough work. Marine ply is usually made from the mahogany family of timbers.

Plywood is used extensively where large areas of unjointed timber are required, for example, for paneling, doors, play equipment and some furniture. The more expensive sorts of plywood can have a surface veneer of walnut or other figured wood for decorative use.

Veneer   This is the thin layer of figured wood which is used for decorative purposes.

Years ago cabinetmakers would veneer solid wood furniture to make it more attractive. Much fine seventeenth- and eighteenth-century antique furniture is in fact veneered.

Blockboard   This is constructed by sandwiching strips of softwood between two layers of veneer. The strips are arranged side by side with the curve of their grain running in alternate directions. The whole is glued together as with plywood.

Blockboard has the advantage of being lighter than solid timber and being resistant to twisting and warping. It is made up to a greater thickness than is usual for plywood; it is cheaper; it has strength, and it is useful in the construction of furniture, where large pieces of unjointed wood are required.

Joining Wood

Almost inevitably—except for items such as a breadboard, or a cheese board—to make even the simplest item in wood involves joining one piece to another.

Most simply nails, screws or glue can be used to attach one piece to another. Nails are obviously the crudest way of joining wood; the other two methods are the ones used in the construction of the designs throughout this section. Also described are doweling, the loose-tongue joint, the classic mortise-and-tenon joint and the half-lap joint.

The fifth well-known joint—not used in any of the designs in this chapter—is the dovetail. There are, of course, various other joints, each of which has been developed for a specific use.

Doweling   To join two or more pieces of wood in this way, a hole is drilled with a brace fitted with a bit identical in size to the doweling being used. The inside of the hole is coated with wood glue and then a doweling peg is driven through with a mallet.

Loose-tongue joints   This is the method of joining two pieces of wood which are first grooved,

A fleet of boats give the children the reassuring feel of wood at an early age, and Father the satisfaction of having made a fine toy

MORTICE & TENON JOINT

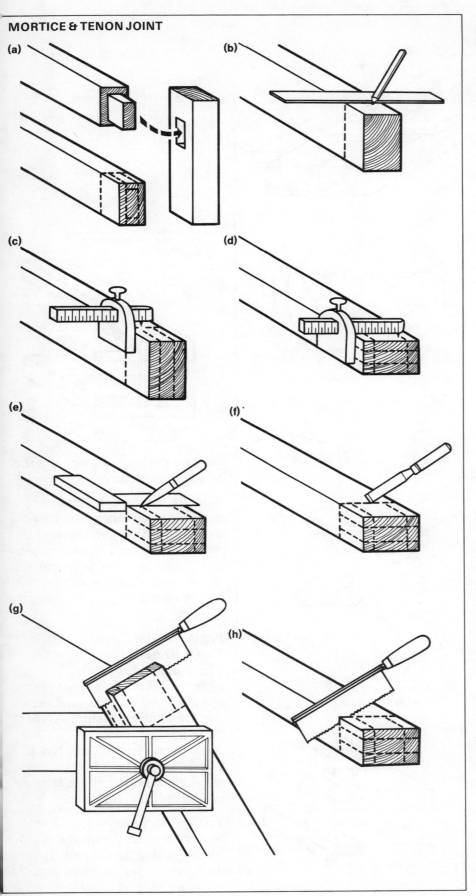

(a)

(b)

(c)

(d)

(e)

(f)

(g)

(h)

HALVED CROSS LAP JOINT

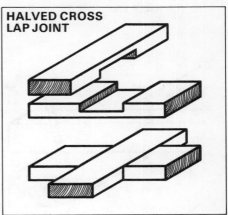

then glued and joined with a spline fitting into the groove in each piece of wood.

Mortise-and-tenon joint   This joint is formed by cutting a tongue on one piece of wood and a slot, or mortise, in another to fit the tongue. The joint is made using a mortise (small) chisel and a mallet. The tongue, or tenon, is slid inside the mortise which has first been coated with glue. The joint is held in position with a C-clamp until the glue is hardened.

Half-lap joints   Two pieces of wood can be joined by paring half the thickness away from each piece, using a mortise saw and then a firmer (large) chisel. The two half joints are then "married" together and glued and clamped until hard.

Dovetail joints   A number of equally spaced dovetail shaped wedges are cut into the end of a piece of wood. Matching slots are

Built-in furniture to your own design – full instructions are given in the chapter for making units ranging from kitchen shelves to a dresser with cupboards

MIDDLE HALF LAP JOINT

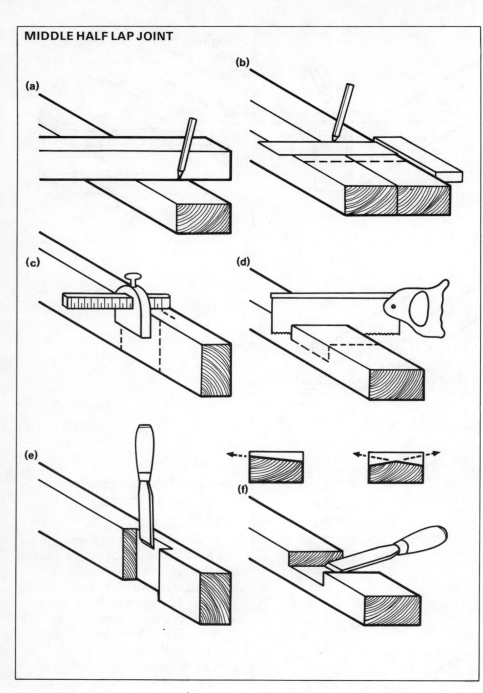

(a)

(b)

(c)

(d)

(e)

(f)

END HALF OR CORNER LAP JOINT

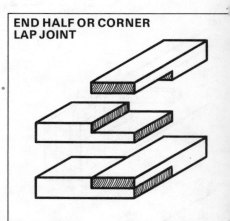

cut into the second piece and the two glued together.

The diagrams on this and the preceding page show you how to make some of the joints described above. Detailed step-by-step instructions to these and other joints appear with the appropriate design throughout the section.

Egg Rack
You will need:
Three pieces of pine 2½ by ½ by 10 inches; four pieces of pine 2½ by ½ by 12½ inches; one brass mirror plate; twelve No. 6 1½-inch-wide countersunk screws; two No. 6 ⅜-inch countersunk brass screws; wood glue; polyurethane lacquer or wax polish.

Tools: Vise; smoothing plane; jig saw or small compass saw; compass; steel knife; pencil; drill; sandpaper; screwdriver; brush for lacquer.

HALF CORNER LAP WITH RABBET JOINT

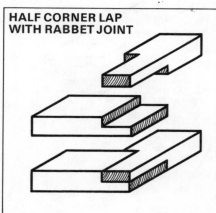

To make the egg rack:

Chamfer both edges of the four 12½-inch pieces, by placing in a vise and using a smoothing plane. Cut curved notches in top and bottom of outside pieces, using a jigsaw or small compass saw (Diagram 1). Cut similar notches in the front edges of each of the 10-inch shelf pieces.

Mark out four circles 1¼ inches in diameter in each shelf piece, making sure that they are equidistant from each other (Diagram 2). Then drill ½-inch-diameter holes anywhere on the *inside* edges of the marked out circles. This makes a starting point for a jigsaw or small compass saw to cut out the 1¼-inch circles. Sand all pieces smooth.

Use a woodworking glue to bind the edges of the upright pieces together. When this has set hard, mark positions of shelves on the back and drill holes and countersink for screws as in Diagram 1. Make four pencil marks on the back edge of each shelf to match holes in back panel. Place each shelf in vise and drill holes for the 1½-inch screws.

Apply wood glue to the back edges of the three shelves and screw through the pre-drilled holes in the back and in shelves, making sure that all shelves are at right angles to the back panel (Diagram 3). Finally, screw on the brass mirror plate centrally at back to hang the egg rack on a wall.

To keep the wood clean apply a coat of clear polyurethane lacquer to all surfaces; alternatively, wax surfaces with a good furniture polish.

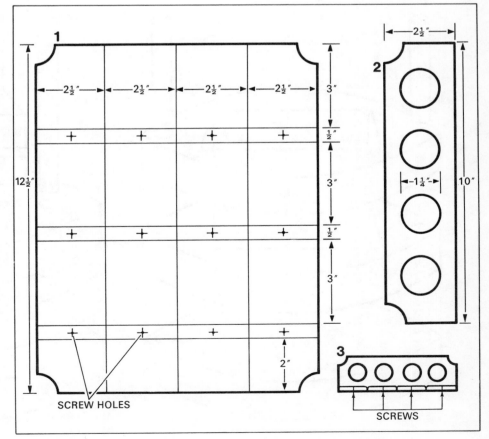

SCREW HOLES

SCREWS

Tug and Barges
(shown in the color photograph).

You will need:
12 pieces of 6 by 1-inch softwood, 12 inches long; one broom handle; one piece of $\frac{1}{2}$-inch dowel, 48 inches long; picture cord or twine; waterproof glue; one can wood sealer; picture wire; curtain hooks and eyes; paper for pattern; cardboard for template; woodworking glue.

Tools: Steel rule; pencil; small compass saw; drill; clamp; mallet; brush for sealer.

To make the toy:
Copy the boat shape onto paper drawn into 1-inch squares. Make standard cardboard template of the shape, using this to mark out the twelve 6-inch by 12-inch hull pieces. Cut outside shape carefully on each piece, using a compass saw. Clamp top two hull pieces of a barge together (see Diagram 1 for construction), drill $\frac{1}{2}$-inch hole through them at one corner of "cargo hold" and cut out with compass saw. Keep the waste pieces. Repeat for other two barges. Clamp three hull sections of one complete barge together and drill right through each end for dowel. Sand inside of cargo hold thoroughly and cut two lengths of dowel so that each shows $\frac{1}{2}$-inch above deck surface.

Glue the three sections together and tape in glued dowels into drilled holes at each end of barge. Keep assembly clamped or under pressure with weights until the glue has set hard. Then sand all surfaces completely smooth and apply one or two coats of clear wood sealer. Repeat shaping and assembly method for the other two barges.

Clamp the three pieces of the tug's hull together (see Diagram 2 for construction), drill four holes right through—one at each side, one at rear for dowel and one at front for mast. Glue and dowel the pieces together as for barges. Cut cabin and bridge from waste pieces cut from barge cargo holds. Cut funnel section from broom handle, sloping top at slight angle. Drill through the bridge and cabin into hull for dowel, and through rear of cabin into hull for funnel. Glue and assemble superstructure. When glue has set, sandpaper tug smooth and seal.

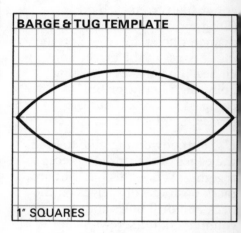

BARGE & TUG TEMPLATE

1" SQUARES

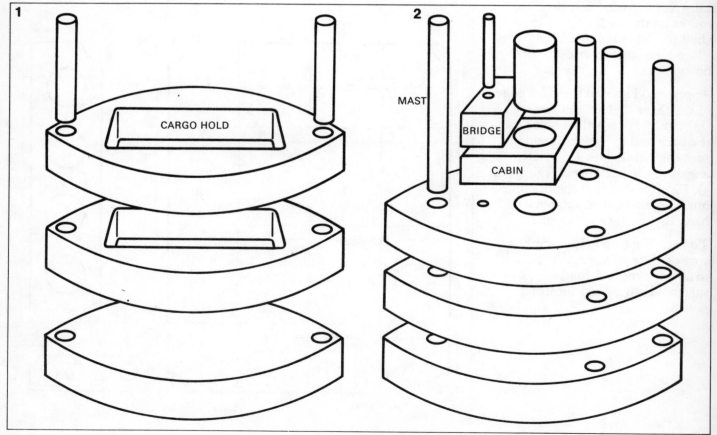

CARGO HOLD

MAST

BRIDGE

CABIN

Cut "cargo" from remainder of broom handle and waste wood cut from barge cargo holds, or make up a cargo of nuts and sweets. Make towing lines from picture cord or twine and join up convoy of tugs and barges, using curtain hooks and eyes.

Toy Box
You will need:
Wood (such as pine or fir)—four pieces 7 by 1 by 30 inches (for front and back)★; four pieces 7 by 1 by 17 inches (sides)★; three pieces 7 by 1 by 32 inches (top)★; two pieces 2 by 1 by 17 inches (sides); two pieces 1 by 1 by 17 inches; two pieces 1 by 1 by 26 inches; one piece ¼-inch plywood, 17 by 28 inches for base; timber for loose tongues—two pieces ¼ by 1 by 32 inches; four pieces ¼ by 1 by 30 inches; two pieces ¼ by 1 by 17 inches; four small casters; 2-inch panel pins; screws; string; pencils; woodworking glue; polyurethane lacquer.

Tools: Rabbet plane (if you do not have a rabbet plane, ask your lumber dealer to groove all the pieces of timber marked with an asterisk). Note that the timber is grooved only along the edges where it is joined (see Diagrams 1 and 2); drill; small compass saw; screwdriver; plane; sandpaper.

To make the toy box:
Sand all the pieces of timber smooth. Chamfer the edges of the 2 by 1-inch timber. Apply glue to the tongued-and-grooved edges of the three 32-inch lengths and join them together, using twisted string and pencils to pull them tight. Glue and screw the two lengths of 2 by 1-inch across the underside of the lid, 12 inches from each end and 2 inches from each edge, as in Diagram 1. When dry, mark out handle for lid, 3 inches from edge and equidistant from each end. Cut handle using 1-inch drill and small compass saw.

Glue and joint the 17-inch-long end pieces. When dry, glue and screw 1 by 1-inch strips along the inside bottom edge, leaving 1 inch at each end. Using the 2-inch panel pins, tack sides to the ends and the plywood floor piece to the 1 by 1-inch strips, then carefully mark and drill for dowels as in Diagram 2. Glue and dowel sides to the ends and glue and screw base to the 1 by 1-inch strips. Sand smooth and sand corners of the top to round them off.

Finally, fit the four small casters to 1 by 1-inch base supports as in Diagram 3a. Fix base as shown in Diagrams 3b and 3c. Finish with a coat of polyurethane lacquer.

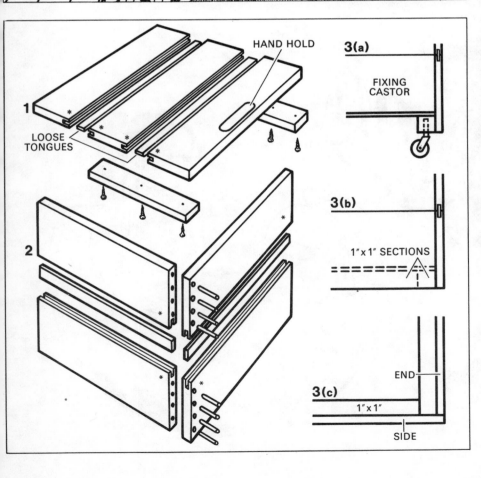

HAND HOLD

1

LOOSE TONGUES

2

3(a)
FIXING CASTOR

3(b)
1″ x 1″ SECTIONS

3(c)
1″ x 1″
END
SIDE

Hobby Horse

You will need:

One piece of softwood $1\frac{1}{4}$ by $1\frac{1}{4}$ by 48 inches; one piece $\frac{3}{8}$-inch plywood 12 by 18 inches; $\frac{1}{4}$-inch dowel rod to use as "pegs"; large sheet of paper (newspaper) for pattern; woodworking glue; lead-free primer, undercoat and white lead-free gloss paint; brown or black vinyl-coated fabric; stud tacks.

Tools: Steel rule; pencil; small compass saw; sandpaper; chisel; mallet; drill; paintbrush; hammer.

To make the hobby horse:

Rule large sheet of paper (newspaper) into 1-inch squares, copy the shape of the horse's head from the diagram, and transfer the pattern to the plywood panel. Cut out with a compass saw. Sand smooth. Chisel out mortise, using a chisel and mallet, in one end of $1\frac{1}{4}$ by $1\frac{1}{4}$-inch wood, $\frac{3}{8}$-inch wide and to a depth of 6 inches. Slot head shape into this mortise and drill right through mortised section and head in three places for dowels, as in the squared-up diagram. Glue and dowel mortised section and head in position and when dry, sand smooth. Prime head with lead-free primer. Allow to dry, paint with undercoat, allow to dry and apply topcoat of lead-free white gloss paint.

Mark eyes, nostrils and mouth, and paint over very carefully, allowing one side to dry before painting the other. Make mane and bridle from strips of black or brown vinyl-coated fabric. The reins can be turned in and glued to make a neat finish and the mane fixed with a row of stud tacks along the top edge of the head.

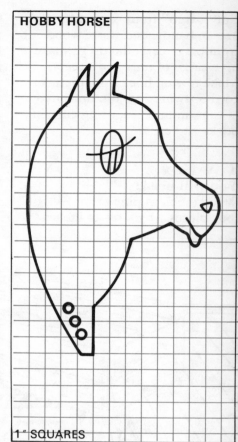

HOBBY HORSE

1" SQUARES

Rocking Duck

You will need:

From a piece of 1-inch blockboard you will need to cut: two pieces 6 by 21 inches; one piece 12 by 4 inches; one piece 12 inches square; one piece 12 by 6 inches; one piece 12 by 10 inches; one piece 12 by 2 inches. You will also need woodworking glue; a length of $\frac{1}{2}$-inch dowel rod to use as "pegs"; 14-inch length of broom handle; large sheet of paper; 2-inch nails; primer, undercoat and lead-free paint.

Tools: Steel rule; pencil; jigsaw or small compass saw; sandpaper; drill; hammer; chisel; mallet.

To make the toy:

Rule a large sheet of paper (newspaper will do) into 1-inch squares. Mark out duck shape from the squared-up diagram and cut out twice in paper. Lay patterns on the sheet of blockboard so that, by interlocking, you waste as little material as possible. Cut out shapes with compass saw or jigsaw and sand very smooth.

Mark position of floor, ends, seat support and rocking handle on inside of shapes, then drill $\frac{1}{2}$-inch-diameter holes for dowel fixings. Using 2-inch nails, tack cross pieces into position on one side, making sure that positions are accurate. Drill into cross pieces about $2\frac{1}{2}$ inches. Dismantle, removing nails, then glue and dowel. Repeat for other side. Cut off any projecting ends of dowels, using wide chisel and mallet. Then sand ends of dowel smooth.

Prime, undercoat and paint in bright colored lead-free paint, leaving each application to dry thoroughly before continuing with the next. When dry, paint waves at base and eyes and beak on sides.

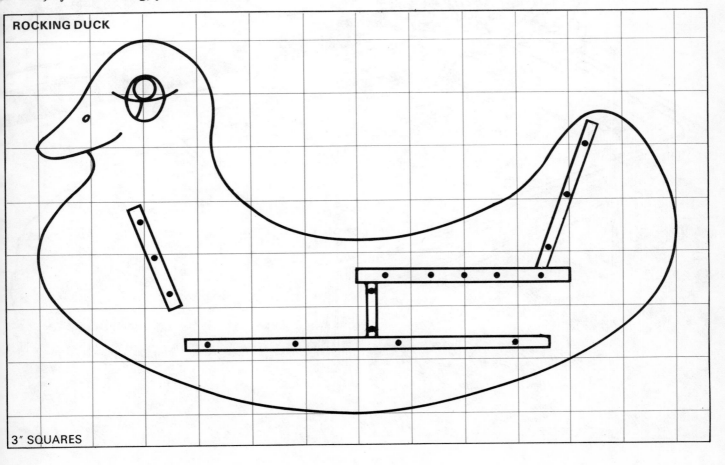

ROCKING DUCK

3″ SQUARES

Glass-Topped Coffee Table

You will need:
One piece $\frac{1}{4}$-inch plate glass, 2 by 3 feet—edges ground and corners rounded; dressed pine—four pieces 3 by 3-inches, 1 foot long; two pieces 3 by $1\frac{1}{2}$-inches, 2 feet 3 inches long; one piece 3 by $1\frac{1}{2}$-inches, 18 inches long; four black rubber washers; woodworking glue; wood filler; linseed oil.

Tools: Steel rule; pencil; chisel; mallet; fine-toothed backsaw; sandpaper; drill.

To make the table:

Check that the four legs are square at each end so that they will stand absolutely level. Mark out mortise area for the mortise-and-tenon joints at the center of each leg that is 5 inches from top and 5 inches from bottom)—Diagram 1. It can be seen from Diagram 2 that the tenon to be cut at each end of the side rails is 3 inches long (the width of the legs), 2 inches high and $\frac{1}{2}$-inch wide. This, then,

is also the area that has to be cut from each leg, using a chisel and a mallet. Use a fine-toothed backsaw to cut accurately the tenon at each end of both side rails (Diagram 3).

Similarly, mark out the joints in the center of each side rail and the two matching tenons on the cross rail as in Diagrams a and b. Chisel out these mortises and loosely assemble the complete leg structure to check that all joints are square. Take apart and sand

all wood smooth—assemble again, this time gluing all joints with woodworking glue.

When this has set hard fill any cracks with wood filler and when filling is dry, sand smooth all joint ends and filler. Polish finished leg base with linseed oil. Drill very shallow recesses for rubber washers in center top of each leg and glue the washers in place, so that they are slightly higher than the top surface of each leg. Finally,

place plate glass squarely on top of the table frame.

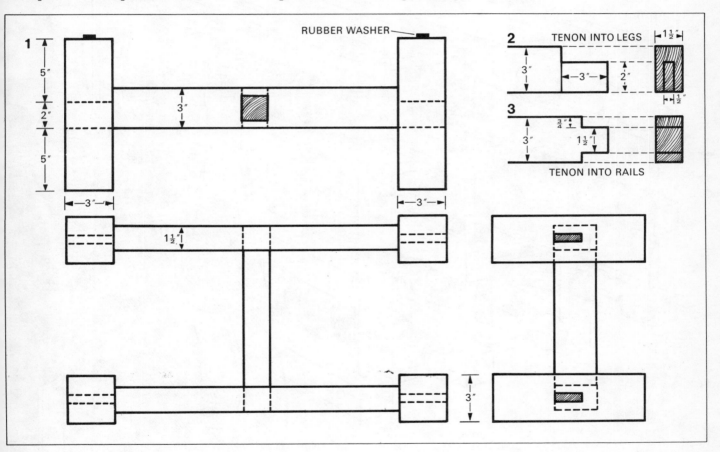

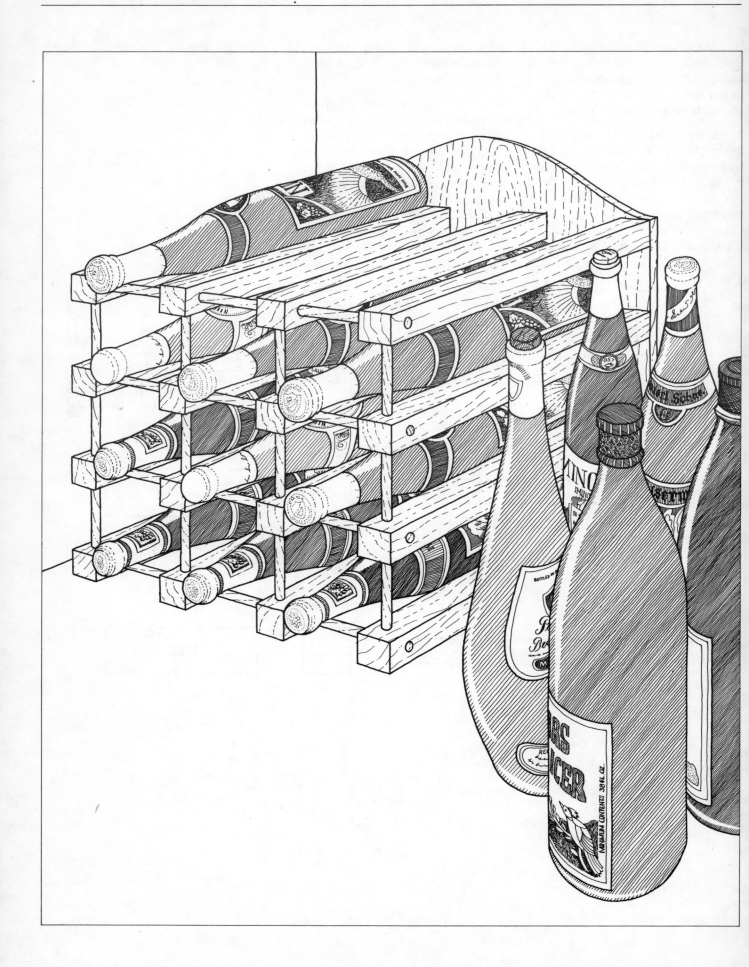

Wine Rack

You will need:

16 lengths of dressed pine $1\frac{1}{4}$ by $1\frac{1}{4}$ by $11\frac{1}{4}$ inches; one piece interior plywood ($\frac{1}{2}$-inch thick), $12\frac{1}{2}$ by 16 inches; $\frac{1}{2}$-inch dowel rod—24 pieces each $3\frac{1}{2}$ inches long; 16 1-inch No. 8 countersunk screws; woodworking glue; matte polyurethane lacquer.

Tools: Small compass saw; steel rule; pencil; sandpaper; screwdriver; drill; smoothing plane.

To make the wine rack:

Mark and cut plywood back panel with a compass saw as in Diagram 1, taking care not to splinter facing veneer. Sand edges smooth. Mark positions of support bars on back of ply panel and mark out centers for screw holes at $3\frac{3}{4}$-inch intervals as indicated in Diagram 1. Drill and countersink these 16 holes.

At one end of each support bar, 1 inch from the end, drill $\frac{1}{2}$-inch hole through at center point.

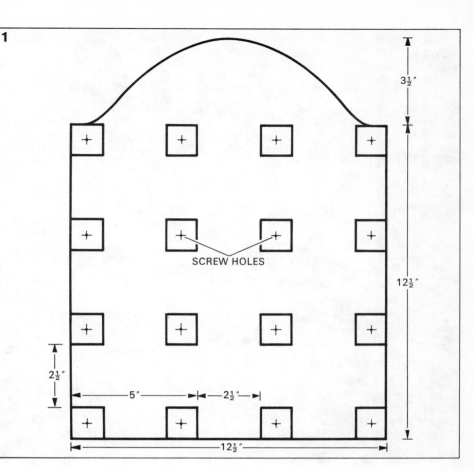

1

SCREW HOLES

$3\frac{1}{2}''$

$12\frac{1}{2}''$

$2\frac{1}{2}''$

5″ $2\frac{1}{2}''$

$12\frac{1}{2}''$

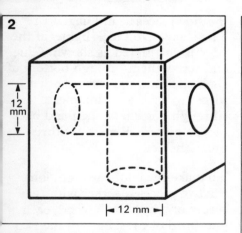

2

12 mm

12 mm

Repeat for other faces as in Diagram 2. Sand all bars smooth and sand off corners at ends drilled for dowels. Chamfer the top inside edge of the right outer support bars and both top edges of the eight inner bars with a smoothing plane along their length.

Sand pieces of dowel rod, slightly chamfering each end. Assemble support bars and dowel rails to check fit, as in Diagram 3. Drill screw holes at center point at the

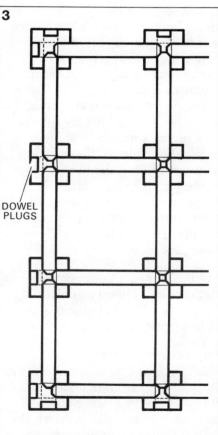

3

DOWEL PLUGS

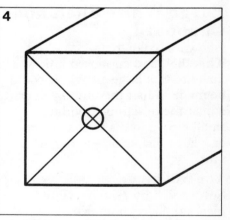

4

end of each support bar (Diagram 2), to prepare for gluing and screwing predrilled back panel to them (see Diagram 1). Glue dowel rods in place, then glue and screw free ends of the 16 support bars to ply back. Plug holes on the outer eight support bars with waste dowel, first applying a little glue in each hole. After glue has set, sand smooth and finish wine rack with a coat of matte polyurethane lacquer.

Large White Shelf and Cupboard

(shown in color.)

This shelf and cupboard unit was made to fit a large alcove. It could be made as half the unit—you can adjust the design by dividing a small alcove into a two-door unit or a large alcove into a four-door unit.

You will need:

Softwood 8 by 1-inch—eight pieces the length of alcove (shelves); two pieces 21 inches long (center, front-to-back, division); 3 by 1 inches—five pieces the length of the alcove, eight pieces 8 inches long and two pieces 16 inches long (for shelf borders); two pieces length of alcove minus 3 inches (to cut for top and bottom rails of doors); eight pieces 21 inches long (side rails for doors). Of 1 by 1 inches, two pieces 10 inches long (shelf supports); 4 by 1 inches—one piece length of alcove (scuff board or kickplate); 5 by 1 inches—two pieces length of alcove less 1-inch (cut for inside cupboard shelves); 2 by 1 inches—two pieces 21 inches long (side frame); eight pieces 14 inches long (side frame and center division and joining pieces for shelf). Of 1 by ½-inch—four pieces 4 inches long (door stops). Four pieces of ¼-inch plywood to fit at the back of door frames, 1 inch wider and 1 inch deeper than inside opening. Eight 2-inch hinges; four cupboard catches; screws; filler; sandpaper; paint and glue.

Tools: Saw; backsaw; chisel; mallet; plane; hand or power drill; screwdriver; carpenter's square; paintbrushes.

To make the unit:

Mark the position of the shelves on the wall and check that each shelf fits; shape with a plane or sandpaper as necessary. Mark the shelf for later identification. Shape the side pieces as in Diagram 1. The shelves will look lighter if the edge is chamfered as shown. Glue and screw them through bottom of shelf and glue and screw back pieces to shelf and side pieces (through bottom of shelf and back of side pieces). Repeat for three other shelves.

To make the cupboard top, join the two pieces together with two pieces of 2 by 1-inch wood, each one-third of the length of the two long pieces, one-third of length in from each end, and flush at the back (Diagram 2). Plug and screw end and back supports and front side members to wall (see Diagram 3).

Glue and screw center division together, noting that joining pieces become shelf supports, and glue and screw center division in the center of the bottom shelf, screwing through the bottom of the shelf.

Screw and glue scuff board to bottom shelf as in Diagram 3.

First screw bottom shelf in place, then screw top shelf in place. Plug and screw four narrow shelves to wall, through back and side rails with—in this case—12 inches, 11 inches, 11 inches, then 8 inches between shelves, the smallest gap at the top. Fit half-depth shelves in cupboards. Fill all countersunk screw holes with filler and smooth. Paint with primer, allow to dry, then sand smooth. Paint with undercoat, allow to dry, and finally gloss or satin finish topcoat.

Check measurements of door openings. Square off each set of four door frame pieces and mark out for mortise-and-tenon joints. Cut and check fit. Glue together, making sure angles are at right angles. When set, glue and screw plywood panels to back of frames (Diagram 4). Fill cracks with matching wood filler. Sandpaper

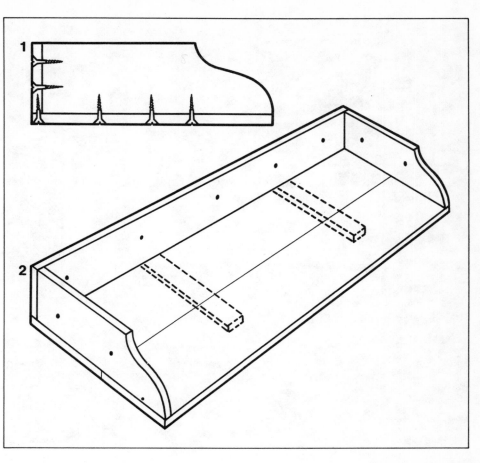

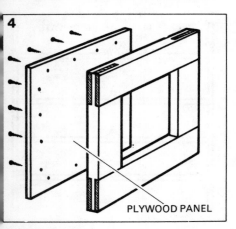

PLYWOOD PANEL

smooth. With a chisel, cut recesses for hinges and apply primer, then undercoat and when that is thoroughly dry, top coat. Screw hinges to doors, then hang doors in openings. Screw in handles. Glue and pin door stops top and bottom. Fit cupboard catches.

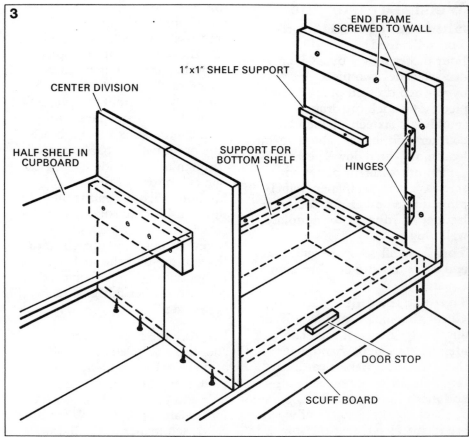

END FRAME
SCREWED TO WALL

1″ x 1″ SHELF SUPPORT

CENTER DIVISION

SUPPORT FOR
BOTTOM SHELF

HALF SHELF IN
CUPBOARD

HINGES

DOOR STOP

SCUFF BOARD

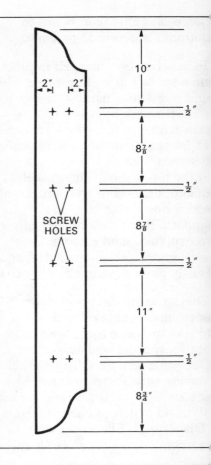

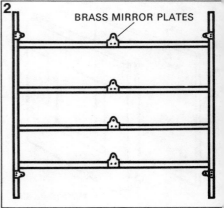

Welsh Dresser and Shelves (shown in color.)

You will need:

Four pieces 6 by $\frac{3}{4}$ by 48-inch dressed pine; two pieces 6 by $\frac{3}{4}$ by 52-inch dressed pine; three pieces of $\frac{1}{2}$-inch quadrant (molding); sixteen $1\frac{1}{2}$-inch No. 8 countersunk screws; about 12-inch length of $\frac{1}{2}$-inch dowel; eight $\frac{3}{4}$-inch brass mirror plates and screws; glue; sandpaper; panel pins; linseed oil or polyurethane lacquer; cardboard for template; wall plug.

Tools: Small compass saw; brace and bit; screwdriver; carpenter's square.

To make the unit:

Check that all 48-inch lengths are absolutely square at each end and identical in length. Sandpaper them smooth. Make a cardboard template for shaping the end pieces and mark the wood as in Diagram 1, checking that lengths of wood are identical and that the shapes

match end-to-end.

Cut shapes carefully with the compass saw, then sandpaper them and the lengths until completely smooth. Mark screw holes as in Diagram 2, using a carpenter's square. Very carefully drill halfway through an outside face with $\frac{1}{2}$-inch countersunk bit and brace (the point will probably just come through to the inside face). Glue one end of one of the shelves, holding it firmly against the upright. Use the square to make sure it is at right angles.

Screw through the upright into the end grain of the shelf; repeat for remaining three shelves, then repeat for other upright. Leave till glue is set.

Measure the depth of each countersunk hole and cut a piece of dowel a fraction longer for each. Put a little glue into the hole and tape dowel in. Repeat for remaining dowels. When glue is set, sandpaper until all dowels

are flush. Cut the quadrant carefully to fit, then sand smooth. Put a little glue along one edge then pin to shelves $1\frac{1}{2}$ inches from front edge with panel pins—about four to each quadrant should be enough.

To finish: Rub in linseed oil liberally or brush with clear polyurethane lacquer. When dry screw the glass plates to back of shelves as shown in Diagram 2. Use a wall plug to fix in place.

Index